Passenger 642

Molly Darcey

Cover Art by Mikey Brooks

ISBN:
ISBN-13: 978-0-9965254-2-8

ACKNOWLEDGMENTS

I know I could never have gotten this book into your hands without the support of my husband, James.

WHITE STAR LINE.

YOUR ATTENTION IS SPECIALLY DIRECTED TO THE CONDITIONS OF TRANSPORTATION IN THE ENCLOSED CONTRACT.

THE COMPANY'S LIABILITY FOR BAGGAGE IS STRICTLY LIMITED, BUT PASSENGERS CAN PROTECT THEMSELVES BY INSURANCE.

Second Class Passenger Ticket per Steamship Titanic

SAILING FROM

10/4 1912

CHAPTER ONE

April 9th, 1912 – Southampton, England

"Grand dining hall painted by the finest artists in all of Europe! Menu fit for a king! Read all about it!" yelled the newsboy on the corner, striving to draw attention in the noisy market clamor.

A man in a business suit brushed past George Corbridge to drop a coin in the newsboy's outstretched hand before snatching a paper from the dwindling stack. A few others stood around the boy scanning the pages of the papers they held, as though the news would be old if they waited to read it until they reached their destination.

Bessie Corbridge looked up at her husband George, whose mop of red hair was a good foot higher than her five foot, brown-haired frame. Her hazel eyes sparkled as excitement surged within her.

"Let's pick up a newspaper!" Bessie said, as her hands gestured in the air. They always tried to say about three times as much as the words she spoke. "You know that we won't get to see the Grand dining hall. Only the first-class passengers will see it."

George gave a soft chuckle as he glanced down into those hazel eyes that he could never refuse, "Of course, my love, though we still have to hurry to Ludvig's shop so that we can retrieve Grand-mama's clock."

"You're too accustomed to telling the children things. She's your mother, and she'd scold you to not make her any older than she already is."

"Of course, you're correct, my love, and there are so many other details to attend to before we sail back to America," George said as he leaned down to kiss her forehead.

George squeezed through the others to toss a coin to the boy, who snatched it mid-air with practiced ease, and pulled his own copy of the paper from the stack.

There was no other topic that filled the steady chatter of the market street. Everywhere they turned people talked of the magnificent ship sitting at the pier, awaiting its maiden voyage. The Unsinkable Titan of the sea, some called it, preparing for the historic journey across the ocean.

George and Bessie hurried through the remainder of their errands, picking up the clock and a few other essentials, before climbing back onto the wagon and returning to George's ancestral home.

Their three oldest children waited inside the door, fidgeting and whispering amongst themselves, as the parents stepped through. The click of the latch signaled the barrage of questions. The three voices overlapped each other leaving no room for answers between questions.

"When are we leaving?" Mary asked.

"How big is the boat?" chimed in David.

"Did you see it? Is the boat here?" Lizzie asked.

Their father laughed as he looked around at the eager faces hungering for any news. The similarity to the people in town wasn't lost on him.

"We are leaving first thing tomorrow. It's actually a ship, not a boat. A boat is something smaller like you saw Old Mr. Herrick fishing in. And no, Lizzie, we didn't make it down to the docks, but wait till you see our cabins. It will be grander than you could ever imagine! Much better than the ones we had on Carpathia coming from America."

A soft thump from the other side of the foyer drew Bessie's attention. Paul paused between sliding down each stair to yawn and rub the sleep in his eyes. He yawned once more as he made his way over to George's leg, wrapping his arms around it to draw attention to himself. Finally, he settled for tugging on the trouser leg.

Paul looked up with a sleepy grin, "Candy? Where's sweets?"

He didn't really even wait for an answer before toddling off to Grand-mama Martha to ask the same thing, only this time it was for a biscuit.

The children were every bit as excited as the adults, if not more so. The friends that lived nearby talked about it just as much as the adults in town, only they had a special interest to know somebody that would actually be on the ship. Nothing could beat the bragging rights of holding tickets aboard the biggest and fastest ship in the world as it sailed off to the fantastic city of New York.

George and Bessie at last managed to divest themselves of coats and packages, and moved to the parlor with the children still spouting more excitement filled questions. George set the clock on the buffet just as a knock sounded at the door. Mary, David and Lizzie raced to the door, as fast as they could to see who it was.

Lizzie beat Mary and David by a tenth of a second, though she stopped to draw a breath before lifting the latch. Mary didn't wait, and pulled the latch first. They both flung the door open.

Bessie gave an exasperated, "Mary, you know better."

Their Uncle Laurence and Aunt Elizabeth stood in the doorway, grinning as the children shouted greetings. Bessie wound her way through the bouncing children to hug her brother and his wife.

"Children, please, let them come in out of the cold. Come in Lawrence. I'm so glad we were able to secure tickets for the both of you to journey back to New York with us."

"Yeah," piped up David. "I hear they serve cakes with every meal!"

"It feels like we just arrived yesterday, don't you think Mary?" Uncle Laurence joked.

"No, Uncle Laurence, we have been here for practically forever. I had a birthday here. You know I'm seven now," Mary said.

"Wait, you're seventy now?" her Aunt Elizabeth joined in the teasing. "You can't be seventy, you were five just yesterday."

"Aunt Elizabeth, Grand-papa Thomas was seventy, not me," Mary said seriously.

The grown-ups laughed with a tinge toward nervousness. Bessie cast a glance toward Martha, who grimaced slightly before returning to her soft smile.

"Go and play with Paul, you three, so that we can finish the final packing. There won't be time for it tomorrow," Bessie said with a light laugh as she shooed them out of the entry way.

Grand-mama Martha came into the room and

hugged Lizzie and David to her side, "Let us be artists, but first you each need to find a bit of paper and a crayon or two. Then meet me at the sofa."

The three older children squealed and scrambled to find the paper she had asked for. Paul looked from Mary to Lizzie to David, and settled for holding on to Grand-mama's leg as the search continued. They all loved these random games that she dreamed up.

Mary pulled the tin of crayons from the old desk drawer as David found a few blank pages in Grand-papa's old desk. Lizzie returned with a few old receipts that still had blank backsides.

"Now why don't you all draw me pictures of what you'll be when you grow up? That way I'll be able to recognize you when you come to visit," Grand-mama Martha said.

"I'm going to be a teacher, I think," Lizzie said.

"Not me. I'm going to be the captain of a big ship. Maybe even the Titanic!" David said.

Mary set about drawing herself surrounded by children. She aspired to be a mum, just like her own, except she was going to give her children more sweets.

Bessie smiled at her mother-in-law and her ability to get all the children engaged without a bit of fuss. The family had come to England when Martha's husband Thomas grew too weak to mind the farm, and now it was time for their return to America. Bessie knew the old house would feel extra empty after their departure and prayed for every bit of comfort Martha could get from the drawings.

"It's a shame that George's brother Stephen is no help at all around here," Bessie muttered, too softly to be heard by anyone.

April 10th, 1912 – Winchester, England

Grand-mama and George stood by and watched the drivers, Mr. Ainsworth and Mr. Hammond, load the motorcars.

She leaned over to whisper to her son, "Are they really going to fit all that on the roof?"

"They assured me that these motorcars are capable of holding a grand piano on the roof. A few odd trunks and wardrobes should be no problem."

David struggled down the front steps, dragging a chest nearly as big as himself. Lizzie came after him and offered to carry the other end of his load as she leaned on it. David shook his head and yanked it out from under his twin. He got the chest halfway to the motorcars before he set it down to catch his breath.

Grand-mama smiled at all the antics of the children. As much time as she spent keeping them busy and such, she would miss them a great deal. The old house would be quiet for the first time since they arrived, and quieter still after the passing of her Thomas.

Two-year-old Paul was so excited that he couldn't stop talking, "Papa, are we going on the ship? Do we get to ride in a motorcar again? Will we get wet if it rains?"

He never stopped long enough to hear an answer, and he didn't seem to mind that no one was answering his every thought. Paul ran over to grab a case bigger than he was.

"This one next, Papa."

George walked over and ruffled his young son's hair, "Yes, yes, and no. I know your mother was busy dressing the girls, so go with your Aunt Elizabeth so that these drivers can finish loading the motorcars. You wouldn't want them to strap you to the roof along with the trunks would you?"

Paul hopped up and down, "Yes! Yes! Strap the roof."

George nudged him toward Bessie's brother Lawrence, "Say, Lawrence, my good chap, would you mind helping him find his Aunt Elizabeth?"

Paul grabbed Uncle Laurence's hand and dragged him off the porch and towards the first motorcar. Just as they rounded the end of the motorcar his Aunt Elizabeth scooped him up, "Ooh, I've got a Paulie. Can you keep me company?"

Elizabeth and Laurence sat in the middle seat of the motorcar with their nephew Paul between them. They took turns guessing which bit of luggage the men would strap onto the motorcar next.

At long last the men tossed the final trunk to the roof of the other motorcar, and cinched the ropes tight. With a word from their mother, the other three children scrambled for seats. George helped settle the debate over seat ownership by taking the seat in the first car, right behind Bessie's brother, Laurence, taking little Lizzie with him.

Bessie scooted the other two children into the second car and took her seat with them. She assured them that everything would be fine, "Both motorcars will get there about the same time. We'll all be on the same ship, so nobody will get to America first."

Martha walked around the vehicles, leaning in to give each of her grandchildren a hug and a kiss on their foreheads. She gave an extra-long hug to George, "Thank you for coming Georgie. I know your father was glad to see you at the last."

"We have room in the motorcar for you, and I know that I can secure you a ticket on the ship. Come to America with us. The house has plenty of space for your garden, too."

His mother stiffened a bit, "Let me think about it Georgie. I don't want to sell the Oust house just yet. It's been my home since… Since your father asked for my hand."

George glanced back at the house with the large rough-shaped bricks and thick shingles. Growing up he'd always thought the best parts of the house were the cone topped turrets at the corner. None of the other houses around were built quite like it.

"I understand Mother; I just don't like the idea of you being here all alone. Stephen is never around to do anything for you. It would be nice to know that you're being taken care of."

Martha put on her motherly smile, "I'll think about it. I promise I will. Now run along. If you don't hurry you'll all miss the boat. The children won't be happy with you then."

At that moment Paul sniffled once before letting out a howling cry.

"What's wrong Paul? Why you crying?" Aunt Elizabeth asked.

"Keykey."

Elizabeth sighed. She glanced at Paul, and then to his grand-mama, "Martha, would you be so kind as to let Bessie know that Paul can't find Keykey, please?"

"I will, my dear. Best not to let him out or you'll not ever get him back in that seat before noon."

Martha walked back to the second motorcar, "Bessie, Keykey is lost. In all the excitement Paul just realized he didn't have it."

"Keykey is missing? Dang that child. Fine, tell George to go ahead without me. Mary, David and I will look for it."

The three of them searched the house frantically for the missing Keykey, Paul's toy monkey, under the worried eyes of Grand-mama Martha. David searched through the second floor where all the bedrooms were. He even checked the little cubby that Paul had discovered on their second day in the house.

Mary tore through the first floor, pretending that it was a race with her brother. Besides, Mary hoped that finding the monkey would get her another hug from Grand-mama, and perhaps a biscuit for the journey. Bessie did her best to follow along behind and double check everywhere. They finally located the missing stuffed monkey lounging in the potato bin. They all hurried back to the motorcar, and the waiting driver, Mr. Hammond, was still waiting with the motor idling. In a moment, he had them rolling along the country roads toward Southampton and the waiting ship.

They hadn't even reached the outskirts of the city when smoke and steam began billowing out of the motorcar's bonnet.

Bessie, already frustrated at the delays, couldn't keep the concern out of her voice, "What's wrong Mr. Hammond?"

"Not to worry yourself, Ma'am. I'll have this figured out in no time, don't you worry none. We won't be late."

By the time their driver had pulled the motorcar to the side of the road, the children were just shy of climbing over the seats to catch a glimpse of what was happening.

“Mother, is the motorcar going to explode?” David asked. “You know Cedric told me he’d seen one go poof into a ball of flame one time.”

“Are we on fire mother?” Mary half shrieked. “My books will burn up!”

Bessie pointed the children back to their seats, giving them the look that told them it was best not to argue the point. She watched over Mr. Hammond’s shoulder as he poked around the machinery tucked under the bonnet. After a moment, he pulled his head out and turned to her. Bessie motioned for him to notice the big black smear along his cheek. With a chuckle, he pulled a cloth from his pocket to wipe it away.

"I'm sorry Ma'am. I'll have it fixed in right short order. It shouldn't be more than some water and a spot of oil, hopefully."

“I can do this Mum, I’ll find a horse for you,” David said.

“David, don’t be silly. A horse couldn’t pull this. Can it Mother?” Mary asked.

“Look. That guy over there has two horses to pull his wagon, and it’s nearly empty. I can go get his horse for you.”

Bessie sighed. She took a deep breath, letting it calm her nerves a bit before she turned back to their driver.

“Mr. Hammond, just do your best. We really don’t want to be late.”

Mr. Hammond had to unstrap one of the trunks to gain access to his tool chest. He whistled as he set about making a few adjustments and adding oil to several spots under the bonnet. At last, he pulled the bonnet closed and buckled the strap. A moment later the tools were all stowed and the chest re-strapped.

Bessie sighed and leaned back. She was excited to go home! It had been so long since she had seen America that it felt like a distant memory. The motorcar traveled another few hundred feet before Mr. Hammond pulled it to a stop once more.

This time it wasn't a mechanical failure that brought their journey to standstill. Mary pointed off to where a small herd of cows had wandered into the roadway. The farmer did his best to move them along, but the cows were in no hurry to ignore the tasty grass along the roadside.

Bessie's moment of relaxation evaporated as the delay stretched on for several minutes. By the time the cows had cleared the road enough for Mr. Hammond to squeeze the motorcar past them, she had been ready to get out and push them herself. It had only taken a matter of minutes, however those minutes felt like an eternity to Bessie.

Bessie did her best to take her mind off the delays as she listened to Mary and David swap stories their friends had shared about the Titanic. Some of the things seemed almost too fantastic to believe, such as wild animal tamers roaming the decks to thrill the passengers with shows. This time her reverie lasted until the motorcar entered the beginnings of Southampton.

It didn't take long for the traffic in the city streets to become a chaotic flow of buggies, wagons, pedestrians, and other motorcars, all trying to wind their way through to various destinations.

"Mother, why are we going so slow?" Mary wanted to know.

The motorcar had slowed, and came to a complete halt when a tram passed along the road. The other wagons and motorcars had to get out of its path. People and horses went every which way to get out of the way, but eventually Mr. Hammond announced that he had brought them as near to the docks as he could get them.

"You run along to your cabin, Ma'am. I'll get a purser to get your cases onboard right away," Mr. Hammond said.

He began to loosen the straps as Bessie shoved her way through the milling crowd, towing Mary and David right behind her. Hand in hand they managed to make it to the first gangway, only to be turned away.

"Dreadfully sorry Ma'am, but this is for the first class passengers only. You'll have to make your way to the second class one. Best hurry too."

"But where?" Bessie asked. Any vestiges of patience evaporated.

"The next embarkation gate is open for the second and third class tickets. If you haven't got ticket in hand then you'll need to see a steward in the offices."

Bessie pulled Mary and David behind her as she hurried to the embarkation station. The closer they made it, the thicker the crowd. Everyone was looking up to wave to the passengers already lining the ship's rails.

The dock was filled with so many people that it was as tightly packed as a roll of shillings, and she could barely push her way through the crowds, let alone run. Twice she felt Mary's hand pulled from hers and turned to keep from losing her children to the crowd.

Mary said something, but the words were lost in the blast from a ship's whistle. The crowd responded with its own cheer to dissuade any thought of conversation. The noise was deafening with the whistle blowing and the buzzing of the excited conversations.

Mary made a face as she got a whiff of the fresh salty sea mixed with the smoke from the ship stacks, motorcar exhausts, and the smell of too many people crowded together. Everyone had come to watch this amazing ship. The Titanic was the queen of the sea, and nothing was going to slow her down. Nothing was a grander spectacle in all of England!

"Hurry, it's going to leave!" Mary had to yell to David at her elbow to be heard.

"You really think the ship will leave without us?" David yelled back.

A piercing whistle reverberated all along the dock, echoing from the nearby buildings. It momentarily drowned out the crowd.

"I don't think it will," Bessie called to her children, trying to keep the calm in her voice, "Though it is set to depart promptly at noon."

"Too bad our motorcar had to be the one to get busted on the way here," Mary said.

"It's all that stupid Keykey's fault. If Paul hadn't left him we could be on board already," David chimed in.

"We need to hurry children! We're almost there. We can still make it!" Bessie shouted just as a third whistle sounded.

They reached the gangway just as the ropes were dropped that held Titanic to the pier. The gangway had been pulled back, and all the connections were now clear.

Bessie tugged at the arm of a uniformed man, "Is there any way…?" she began.

He shook his head, "I'm sorry, Ma'am. It's too late."

Bessie let out a sigh of frustration, and pulled her children close. The three of them watched the massive ship pull farther away with each moment. It was such a beauty, rising from the water like a monster of steel. Smoke billowed from three of the four stacks that towered over everything. To David it looked like three dragons breathing fire and belching smoke.

Seemingly endless rows of windows sparkled in the sunlight. The ship looked as graceful as a ballerina dancing across a stage. Lining the rails of the massive ship stood hundreds of passengers, dressed in their best attire, all waving to the crowds below.

Bessie searched the rows of faces that she could barely make out, hoping she could catch a glimpse of George, or Laurence, or any of her family, in the rows of people lining the rails of the ship.

Bessie gave a half-hearted laugh in frustration. She couldn't let Mary and David see her cry. She imagined George would be just as dismayed as she was, that his wife and two of their children were left behind.

Mary pointed out a group of people near the stern that she insisted must be the rest of the family. Bessie could picture George's face; the disappointed, frustrated look of bewilderment-- what she called the 'help me' face. The rest of her children, Lizzie and Paul, her brother Laurence, and her sister-in-law Elizabeth stood nearby at the ship's rail, waving at them.

All they could do was to wave back. She even saw little Paul, awake and waving as he held Elizabeth's hand. Bessie struggled to keep the avalanche of emotions from crushing her. She looked down into Mary and David's anxious faces as she brushed away tears welling in her eyes.

"It will be fine, children. We'll catch up to them when the ship stops in Ireland."

"Ireland?" they said in unison. "How?"

Bessie took their hands once more, and turned toward the White Star officer standing nearby. She waited patiently as he finished giving instructions to a dock worker, and then tugged at his sleeve.

"I need to get a message to George Corbridge. Please tell him that the rest of his family will catch up to him in Ireland."

"You may arrange for a radio telegraph from the offices. The operator there will help you get your message through."

"Will they be able to sell me a ticket on a ship to reach Ireland in time for the Titanic?" Bessie asked.

"I'm afraid that there isn't coal enough in the whole port to fuel any ship at the moment. It took everything in the area to fill the Titanic's coal bunkers. And with the strike, I doubt anyone could get you to Ireland in less than a week," the officer replied.

"The coal shortage? I completely forgot! I didn't think that it would affect us. I thought it was over a few days ago," Bessie said, shaking her head.

"I'm sorry Ma'am, there is nothing we can do. You can try and catch it in Queenstown, Ireland. You will need to go to Pembroke Dock and take the ferry to Rosslare Dock, then drive as fast as you can to Queenstown. If you hurry, you might just make it, but it's a long shot. A very long shot."

"Yes, yes, we'll do just that. Could you send that message to my husband, Mr. Corbridge, on the ship? Tell him to expect us there," Bessie said.

Bessie led the way, walking as fast as she could, back to the car. Mr. Hammond, their driver, stood beside the huge pile of luggage next to the car. He was holding a lively discussion with one of the White Star porters.

"Lizzie's gonna have all the best stories about the ship before I have a chance to get them first," David complained.

Mary nodded, feeling just as bad as her brother. She was determined to find any word she could on the ship. Bessie looked at the fallen faces of her children. She could tell that David was trying to be brave and not cry as his lip kept on quivering. Mary wasn't in much better shape.

Bessie sighed to gather her thoughts, "No use to us watching it sail further away. We can't exactly swim after it. Come now, we need to hurry so that we can make it to Ireland in time!"

"Well, Mr. Hammond," Bessie said. "How long will it take you to get all of these cases loaded back onto the motorcar?"

The driver blinked at her, and nodded. The porter had taken a single step away when Mr. Hammond grabbed his shoulder.

"You were slow enough getting this stuff off the motorcar that we missed the boat as it were. Now you're going to help me get it all back up there right quick," Mr. Hammond said.

April 10th, 1912 – Southampton, England

George turned to help everyone out of the motorcar, and caught the sleeve of a passing porter. Pressing a crown into the fellow's hand he gave directions for the luggage to be delivered into their cabin. The porter nodded and turned to motion a few longshoremen over. George turned, expecting to see the other motorcar pull up so that he could help Bessie out.

"Where are they? How long does it take to find a simple stuffed monkey?" George muttered under his breath.

"Nothing to worry about old chap, Bessie will be along any minute now," Laurence said, placing a hand on George's shoulder.

"Would you do me the grandest of favors, Laurence? See if you can secure our place in the queue for boarding. I'll tarry a moment."

Laurence and Elizabeth headed off, winding their way through the crowds keeping Lizzie and Paul close. They had barely reached the gangway when the uniformed man asked for the tickets. Laurence ran back to get George.

"You've got all the tickets on you. There's nothing to worry about. Bessie will be right here in a moment, and we'll have the cabins all set when she arrives," Laurence said.

The White Star officer was gently urging everyone in the queue to hurry aboard as they arrived back at the gangway. George attempted to bargain with the man over holding Bessie and the children's tickets for when they arrived, but he just motioned them aboard.

"I'll keep a good eye for them Sir. Promptly as they

arrive I'll whisk them aboard myself. A brown-haired lass in the company of two mid-sized children you say?" the man asked.

Laurence and Elizabeth took the two youngest children up the gangway while George shook the man's hand, leaving a crown in the man's grasp. The jostling movement up the embarkation ramp jostled the toddler from his nap.

Now that Paul was awake, he seemed an endless source of questions. Elizabeth held his hand as she did her best to answer her nephew's queries. Little Lizzie stopped walking as she leaned against the rail and gazed down into the water between the mammoth ship and the pier.

"Where put the Carcars? Water cold? Is swimming?" Paul asked, not even waiting for an answer before the next question.

They paused briefly at the top of the gangway as a steward asked to see their tickets. A brief glance at the tickets, and he nodded.

"One ticket mine?" asked Paul.

The steward glanced down at Paul, "Indeed sir. Your ticket is the six hundred and forty-second one to board this fine ship. Enjoy your journey."

A wave of his hand had them being escorted along the passageways by one of the crew. Everywhere they looked they saw crewmen assisting passengers. Each one wearing a crisp White Star uniform. He held the cabin door open while they all entered.

Paul's questions continued with each new sight, and Elizabeth did her best to keep up with them. Most of them she could answer with simply a smile. Others she attempted to answer.

"Yes, all the doors look the same, now don't get lost," Elizabeth said to one such question.

"Let's go out on deck. Maybe we can see if Bessie has already arrived," George urged.

The five of them pressed through the crowds milling about every bit of the deck. At last they found an open spot of railing near the stern of the ship.

George gripped the rail in rising tension as he scanned over the crowd lining the dock. Every new motorcar that arrived brought with it the hope that his family would step out of it.

"Wait here. I'll be but a moment," George said as set off through the crowd once more.

Squeezing through the throng of passengers lining the rail, George finally found a man wearing the White Star uniform. Like all the others he had seen, the man was fielding a steady stream of questions. George's patience had vanished in the anxiety of his wife's late arrival, and he stepped between the crewman and another man waiting to ask his own question.

"Excuse me, my good man. I need to speak to someone in charge," George said.

"What seems to be the problem, Sir?" the crewman asked.

"My wife was delayed slightly. She is arriving in another motorcar, along with two of my children. Is there any possibility that we can delay our departure by a few moments to allow for her imminent arrival?" George blurted out.

The man stuttered for a moment. He'd grown accustomed to the usual questions, and didn't have a reply ready for such an event as George's question.

"I'm terribly sorry, Sir. Let me escort you to

someone that may assist you."

Waving off a few more people trying to ask questions, the crewman led George forward, toward the bridge of the ship. They were within sight of an officer wearing the stripe on his sleeve, when George heard the call go out.

"Stow the gangways!"

His heart sank. He was making this trip alone. George pressed his way back to the rail, trying to return to Elizabeth and Lawrence, while he kept one eye scanning the crowd down on the pier. Maybe Bessie had arrived while he was gone and they were making their way on board at that moment. George tried to convince himself that somehow she would still arrive in time.

George had just made it back to Laurence when he caught sight of her, sending his heart racing, but a look down revealed the widening distance between them. His wife had missed the boat.

George reassured himself that Bessie was resourceful. She would find a way to meet them before they reached open water. If all else failed, she would be in his arms again in a week or so, with the kids dancing around them comparing stories. There were other ships that made the crossing between England and America, such as the Carpathia that had brought them on the first trip.

He turned to point their mother out to Lizzie and Paul, and then had to search for her face once more. Now they were all waving to the other half of their family. He loved her so much. He knew she would be taking his absence hard, but she was resourceful for sure. It was one of her traits that he found endearing.

They stood leaning on the rail as the tugs moved the ship out to the center of the channel. Once there, the little boats nudged it toward the channel opening and the open sea beyond.

The going was slow until a soft rumble could be felt through the ship.

"I believe they've started the engines at last," said Laurence.

Rippling waves went out from beneath the Titanic, tossing all of the smaller ships tied up along the piers. One wave hit strong enough to even toss another ocean liner. They watched as the smaller liner pulled hard enough to snap her moorings, and drift out toward them.

The name SS New York was visible as the other ship drifted close enough that George felt he could almost touch it. Along the railings he could hear as others sucked in a breath, waiting for the collision. The tugs managed to keep them apart as the Titanic made for open water under her own steam.

Paul and Lizzie were exploring both rooms as fast as they could, while trying not to irk their Uncle. They opened every cupboard and door, and giggled while jumping on the beds. Both of them gasped in amazement while turning on the water at their own private sink, right there in the room.

It wasn't long before one of the porters came knocking on the door with their trunks and cases. George dropped another shilling into the man's hand, and held the door open for the trolleys. Three crewmen unloaded the trolleys and departed in mere moments.

While looking through the luggage they realized that they were missing a few things. Of course the remainder were back in England with Bessie. They had to make do with what they had.

"Want my Keykey," Paul said.

"It's with Mother. You will get it in a few days," George said, "I'm sure of it."

"But I want it now!" Paul said.

Paul burst into tears. George knew from experience that it was near impossible to get Paul to sleep without the stuffed monkey. Many a night Bessie or Mary would tell him stories in Keykey's voice until Paul closed his eyes.

George smiled at Paul, "How about we go find you a new Keykey to celebrate the voyage? I'm sure there's probably a shop on this ship, and they will have something."

CHAPTER TWO

April 10th, 1912 – R.M.S. Titanic

The ship turned east once it left the harbor, and George kept his place at the rail until England shrank to an indistinct line on the horizon. George shook his head to clear his worry and doubts. He needed to find a solution and not spend the time wishing she had made it aboard.

Many of the other second class passengers still milled around on the open deck, but the crowd had cleared enough to make walking easier. George left Lizzie and Paul with Elizabeth as he sought help. He found the same officer who'd tried to help him earlier, and asked him for a favor.

"I know we are stopping in that French port before we head on our way to America. I'd like to go ashore and send a wire to my wife. It's vitally important."

"That really won't be possible unless you plan to stay in Cherbourg. You see, we'll be dropping anchor in the deeper water. The boats will bring out the passengers who will board, and return to shore with the ones disembarking."

"Could it make a second trip?"

"The Captain will be raising anchor before the boats

even reach the shore. We have a duty to adhere to the schedule."

George sighed as he turned away. Inwardly he told himself that Bessie was resourceful. She'd find a way to meet them in Queenstown. They had talked about waving at St. Colman's Cathedral to bid farewell to the Isles. He wound his way back to where Elizabeth and Laurence were pointing out the sights to his Lizzie and Paul.

Laurence quipped, "I dare say, I think one of my cases was on the other motorcar. I won't see it until Bess Bess catches up to us."

"She'll find a way. There's still Ireland. If not that, then she'll just be a day or two behind us getting to New York."

The cases had arrived at the cabin shortly before dinner time, giving them a chance to refresh their clothes before heading off to the dining saloon. George discovered that all the children's clothing had been left behind in England. Luckily, the shop onboard carried a few bits of clothing, and they each gained a new outfit before supper.

April 11th, 1912 – R.M.S. Titanic

Paul woke first, feeling around in the rumpled bedding for his Keykey. He shoved his feet into Lizzie's back to get her off the covers, and she grumbled a bit in her sleep. She stretched as she yawned, and turned to find his pouting face. Lizzie almost pushed him away, but saw his bottom lip trembling. With a sigh she pulled him close.

"Shh… you'll wake Auntie Beth," she whispered.

"Keykey!" he blurted out.

"I ain't got him. He's back in England with David, and Mary, and Mama. Now hush and go back to sleep."

"But… Keykey…"

"And I wish David was here. And mama. Mary would scold you to hush up. David knows everything about the ship. He could… Mama…"

Lizzie pulled Paul close and buried her face in his hair, trying to hide the tears leaking from her eyes. She had to wipe her nose with the back of her hand from the sniffles that always came from crying.

They had spent the night in Uncle Laurence and Aunt Beth's cabin, after she'd spent hours reading stories to them. Lizzie and Paul's semi-quiet exchange pulled Elizabeth out of the dream she'd been having. She sat on the edge of her bunk, and pulled on her night robe.

"You both should shush a bit. Your Uncle Laurence is still sleeping."

"We're Sorry Auntie, but Paul was missing his Keykey again."

"Here, come here the both of you," Elizabeth said as she moved to sit in the chair.

Their sniffles eased as the children crawled out of bed and settled in their aunt's lap. Lizzie had brought the blanket with her, and Aunt Beth pulled it around her shoulders to snuggle the three of them under its warmth. She could feel their tensions ease as she quietly hummed a few strains of some songs she knew.

Elizabeth held them close throughout the rest of the night, watching as the moonlit porthole brightened with the coming dawn. Her own eyes had closed several times, springing open once more each time one of the children shifted in her lap. Lizzie shifted again and slid off the lap with a soft thump and muffled exclamation.

"Is it already time to be rising?" Laurence asked from where he was still tucked under the covers.

"Uncle Laurence was up late last night. Why don't we get dressed and go explore the ship a bit before breakfast?" Aunt Beth said. "Be real quiet and maybe we can get a cup of Ovaltine."

Paul eased off her lap, and slid through the door into their father's cabin. They perked up a bit more with each step, though they nearly woke George with telling each other to shush.

When the two of them made it back out to the hallway, Aunt Beth stood waiting for them. She'd brushed her hair and dressed quickly in order to escort the children around the ship. Taking their hands she headed off to the aft stairwell.

Lizzie looked over at Paul, "Race ya' to the stairs!" and took off running.

"No fair!" Paul called, as he ran after his sister.

Lizzie ran along the hall, squealing with delight at the sound of Paul trying to catch up to her. She glanced back at him a second time and ran right into a man just stepping out of another cabin. She tripped and fell to sit on the carpeted floor. He merely adjusted his hat and smiled down at her.

"Sorry mister," she muttered.

Paul fell into Lizzie with a hug as Aunt Beth stopped to apologize to the man as well. The man tipped his hat to her, and turned the way they had come, without a word.

"Maybe we should use up some of that energy out on the promenade before a cup of Ovaltine," Aunt Beth said. "It's up the stairs to C deck. Come along now, or do we need to go back?"

They both shook their heads. Elizabeth smiled as she climbed the stairs with a child holding on to each hand. The best part of being an aunt was that she could spoil them as much as she wanted.

The sun had been up for an hour, but the wind coming off the waves chilled all of them more than mornings on Grand-mama's farm. The children ran to the railing to look down at the dark water flowing past.

"Auntie Beth, come look at this. The water's glowing right next to the ship."

Beth sat in one of the deck chairs to watch them, "How about a game? Let's see… um… See how many red chairs you can count."

Lizzie and Paul ran off eagerly searching for the red chairs. Lizzie stopped to touch each of the white deck chairs as she ran past them, though Paul spent most of his time trying to catch up to her.

Elizabeth spoke so quietly that only she could hear, "What I wouldn't give to have a pair of children just like these two. Oh, Laurence, I wish we could."

"Auntie Beth," Lizzie called as she and Paul ran up.

"They're all white. Are you sure there's red ones?"

"Well, you know, I heard there were some cozy chairs just covered in red velvet."

"Outside, on the deck?" Lizzie asked suspiciously. "All these are wooden."

"I never said they were out here on the deck. I believe they're in one of the parlors."

Both of the children's eyes grew big. They walked off, determined to find these velvet chairs. They returned to Aunt Beth a half-hour later, still not finding the red chairs.

"We only found yellow ones and white ones."

"You look like you've both run the length of the ship and back. I think it's time to see about that Ovaltine."

Lizzie and Paul both nodded eagerly, and each took one of Beth's hands to pull her out of the chair. They hopped more than walked as they pulled their aunt toward the dining room.

The staff was still setting out the tableware when they arrived. Only one other couple stood waiting to be seated. Just as soon as a few tables were ready, the waiter led them off to be seated.

"Auntie Beth, how come they nailed the chairs to the floor?" Lizzie asked. "Hey, wait. These are red!"

"I forgot about these ones being red leather. I was thinking of the chairs in the other parlor."

Lizzie was still trying to scoot her chair closer to the long table when the waiter stopped to ask if they were ready.

"What is on the menu this morning?" Elizabeth asked.

"Well Ma'am, we are serving buckwheat cakes with grilled ham and eggs. There's plenty of maple syrup to top off the cakes, and coffee or tea on the side. Of course, we also have milk for the little ones."

Paul piped up, "Ova'tine!"

Beth smiled, "Yes, I did say that you could have some. Didn't I?"

"I will bring two glasses of that for you then."

Their plates were just arriving when George and Laurence settled into empty seats across from them. Neither one looked like they had slept very well.

"I talked with a steward this morning," George said. "The ship will be anchoring in Queenstown in a few hours."

"Keykey?" Paul asked.

George let out a sigh, "I wasn't able to find one last evening. I'm sure your mother will be meeting us in Queenstown, if at all possible, and she will bring your toy."

"Anchoring?" Elizabeth asked.

"Something about the pier not being able to handle a ship of this size, I believe. It'll be just like France where a boat will bring the new passengers out, and head back to shore with anyone getting off."

"How can the pier not handle it when they built the bloody ship there?" Laurence muttered.

"Bloody! Bloody! Bloody!" Shouted Paul, drawing glares from other diners nearby.

"Hush now, and eat your cakes," George scolded. "That was loud enough your mother likely heard."

After the meal, all of them returned to the Promenade deck to watch the waves. The children bided their time testing the view from various chairs and playing tag between the other passengers. Several hours later they heard the shout go out; land had been spotted.

George, Laurence, Elizabeth, and the children were standing at the railing right above the boat platform. They watched the first tender bring out the load of new passengers, craning their necks to see every one of them as they stepped onto the platform.

The first tender emptied with no sign of Bessie and the other children. George gripped the railing tighter as the boat pulled away carrying a handful of passengers ashore, and making room for the second tender to tie up.

He left the others still watching over the railing and made his way to the boarding platform on deck E. He made it there in time to get a closer look at the passengers stepping aboard. There was still no sign of his beloved wife and children.

Those coming aboard were all dressed in the plainer clothing of third class. Farmers and workers looking for a new life in America. Most of them possessed only the bags they could carry.

As the last of them stepped from the boat onto the landing platform, George stepped into the empty passenger launch.

"Sir, have you made arrangements for your cases?" asked the deck officer standing by the boat.

"I'm returning shortly," George said.

"We will be weighing anchor at 1:30 p.m. sharp."

The passenger tender pulled away to have its spot quickly taken by a couple other small boats. A dozen men carrying travel cases stepped onto the platform and began hawking their goods to Titanic's upper class passengers.

George jumped ashore the instant the small boat touched the dock, not waiting for it to be tied. He rushed back and forth a few times, before asking one of the dock workers where he could find a telegraph.

He made his way into the White Star office, and found a line of men already waiting for the telegraph operator. Many of them were reporters anxious to get the word out to their papers about the famous ship.

George filled out his own telegram and stood waiting behind the others. Every minute felt like an eternity as the line barely moved. When the clock gong announced one, he could wait no more. George laid his telegram in the box with a few coins and ran back to the docks.

The two large motor launches, Ireland and America, were tied up to the pier. One of the boatmen finally agreed to three crowns to make a special trip back out to Titanic with George aboard.

Laurence, Elizabeth, and the children were waiting when he returned. All of them clamoring for his attention.

"No, she wasn't there. I sent word out by telegraph. She'll have to catch the next ship over," George said.

"I'm afraid that you missed dinner, dear chap," Laurence said. "Hope you can last until tea."

"Perhaps I'll be hungry by then," George replied. "Right now I fear I would just stare at the sandwiches."

Beth started to say something, but it was drowned out by the ship's whistle. Immediately, the small boats still close by answered with their own whistle. From somewhere farther forward came the sound of bagpipes playing a melancholy tune, like a farewell to Ireland.

"What's that noise?" asked Lizzie.

"Those are bagpipes," Uncle Laurence told her, "playing a song I can almost remember."

"It's been a busy day, so far, I think I'll put the

children to bed for a nap," Beth announced.

"I want to watch the ship go for a while," Lizzie said.

"We can watch the waves go by for ten minutes, and then it's off for a nap," Aunt Beth told them.

"Thank you so much for your help with them. I need to go searching the shops to see if I can locate a certain stuffed toy," George said.

The children waved to all the small boats as the giant ship made its way back to open water. In half an hour the last of the fishing boats were far behind, with only ocean before them. One spot looked just as wet as the next, and it wasn't long before both of the children were yawning.

Beth led them back to their own cabin, and tucked them both into one of the beds. Paul was asleep before she kissed his forehead, and Lizzie closed her eyes only moments later.

Elizabeth quietly closed the door, and went to the next cabin, where Laurence awaited. He had spent much of the night walking the deck with George, and looked as though he could snuggle in for a nap himself.

"Laurence, dear, could you be so kind as to listen in on the children? I was hoping that your sister would be here, and I could look in on the library. I hear they have close to five-hundred books aboard."

"I'll keep an ear out for mischief, my love. Don't get too lost in the books."

Beth gave him a quick kiss before heading off to the library. As she walked into the room, the sight took her breath away. Everything was done in expensive mahogany, even the large bookcase that covered an entire wall.

She stared at the large collection of books before

stepping close enough to see the titles. There were so many choices before her that it was difficult to decide. Just as one book seemed like the one she just had to read, she'd spot another title.

Elizabeth pulled one from the shelf that was nearly two-inches thick. She opened it in the middle and held it close as she inhaled deeply. The smell of new books was one of her favorites. There was just no other smell like fresh ink and paper.

Elizabeth jumped at the sound of a woman laughing behind her. She felt the blush warming her cheeks, and used the book to hide behind as she turned around.

"I love the smell of books too. My husband doesn't really understand it. All he smells is dusty old places. My name is Mrs. King. Please, call me Jessie," The woman said.

"My name is Beth. Beth Barlow. I finally found a chance to visit the library. Paul and Lizzie are napping."

"I saw you on deck with your children earlier. They must keep you busy," Jessie said.

"I'm actually their aunt. Their mother is still back in England. She couldn't make it to the ship in time. That leaves me to take care of them since I don't have family of my own."

"Here, try this one," Jessie said as she pulled out another book. "It's called Howards End. I really enjoyed reading it."

"I've not heard of this Forster before. This should be good to spend a few hours with. I should be returning to my cabin. The children will be waking soon," Beth said.

"Those children are lucky to have you," Jessie said. "We lost our Samuel not too long ago. He would have turned three this month."

"I'm terribly sorry to hear that."

"Everywhere I looked reminded me of him. That's why my husband Ben hired on aboard the ship. Now we can return to America, where there aren't any memories to haunt me."

"I hate to leave you here like this, but the children will be waking soon. I'm very glad to have met you. I'm sure we can talk about dusty books another time."

Laurence was tinkering with a wind-up car when she returned to the room. He had half a dozen of the mechanical toys he'd found while they were in England, and wanted to have them all working perfectly before the ship pulled into New York. He insisted that they worked perfectly before he relegated them to sitting on a shelf.

"I see you found your way back out of the library," Laurence smiled at her.

"Yes, I even found something to keep me busy for a day or two. I shall be next door for when they wake."

Elizabeth settled into a chair and cracked open the cover of her book. Soon she was caught up in the story about an English woman and her husband. Nothing short of fire, shipwreck, or wailing children would pull her from the book world.

All too soon the third option occurred. Lizzie and Paul awoke and begged her to go out to the promenade once more. Beth set a hair ribbon between the pages and pulled their jackets from the wardrobe. They followed the same path out to the promenade, only this time there was no tripping over strangers.

Lizzie set up a game of chairs with Paul. She would count the empty ones while he counted the ones with people. The game lasted until Paul counted seven people. That was all the numbers he knew.

The children soon met Lottie, who was a little older than Lizzie. She had set up a tea party with folded paper cups to serve tea to her beautiful doll. They spent more time chasing down cups that blew away than actually sipping imaginary tea.

One of the times Lizzie had to run after her cup, she returned with Eva and her big stuffed bear. Paul snuggled up to the bear, calling it Beer Beer, despite Eva's insistence that he was actually named Clarence.

They had lost track of just how many rounds of tea they had all had when Aunt Beth found them laughing at Paul's attempt to carry Beer Beer.

"Paul? Lizzie? Come along now. They have just announced that it is time for tea."

"We have tea. See?" Lottie told her.

"Yes, but do you have biscuits and sandwiches to go with your tea?" Aunt Beth asked, "They may even have honey cakes in the Dining Salon."

"That's better than the mutton sandwiches David's getting!" Lizzie exclaimed.

CHAPTER THREE

April 10th, 1912 – Southampton, England

"You must be bleeding mad! Pembroke?" Mr. Hammond exclaimed.

"I'll thank you to mind your tongue around the children, Mr. Hammond," Bessie said. "Your contract was to see my family onto the Titanic. Half my family has not made it aboard. You have the chance to fulfil the promise by getting us to the ferry at Pembroke."

"But do you know how far that is?"

"Not as far as meeting the ship in New York."

Mr. Hammond drove the few streets over to the company office where arrangements were made for the trip to Pembroke. David and Mary watched eagerly as he pumped the handle that filled the glass topped stand with petrol.

"How much can it hold?" Mary asked.

"He's already filled it to ten gallons. Now he's filling it again," David said.

"I figure to put another five in the tank. That should get us to Pembroke," Mr. Hammond said.

Once he finished draining the petrol pump reservoir into the motorcar's tank, Mr. Hammond stashed a couple cans of oil into his tool caddy. He circled the motorcar, double checking the straps, before telling Bessie that everything was ready.

The driver merged into the flow of vehicles winding their way out of the city, and soon enough had them cheering as he passed a few loaded wagons. The afternoon traffic seemed less hurried, though Bessie's nerves felt stretched tighter than a harp string. Mr. Hammond grabbed at every chance he found to slip between the slow moving wagons, and even passed several other motorcars that weren't in the hurry they were.

When they reached the sign pointing the way to London, he turned west. From here on out it was all new scenery for the family. No sooner had they passed the mile post announcing Salisbury twenty-three miles than David announced he was hungry.

"We were s'posed to be eating pudding on the boat with Lizzie. I should'a gone with them," David complained.

"I'm hungry too, Mother," Mary added. "Barely had two spoons of porridge this morning, before HE dumped my bowl so we could pack the cases."

"I thought you were done with it," David responded.

Bessie raised her voice to be heard over the sound of the motor, "Mr. Hammond, how long until we reach the next town?"

"I'm guessing we'll get to Salisbury right about one-thirty or so, Mrs. Corbridge. 'Course, if you're hungry, you might want the Hedgerow Tavern. It's right about three miles from here."

Mary and David bounced from one side of the motorcar to the other as they counted sheep and horses; anything to take their minds off their rumbling tummies.

At last, Mr. Hammond pulled to a stop in front of a two-story clapboard tavern boasting flower boxes under each window. From inside came the sound of singing. Bessie smiled as the tune brought back childhood memories.

Mr. Hammond stayed with the motorcar as she led the children inside. Here they found the source of the singing, as an elderly man started another tune on the old piano. Leaning against it were what looked to be his wife and daughter, both wearing aprons.

As soon as the daughter spotted them, she spun away to pat her hand on a table and motion for them to sit. She wiped her hands on the apron and stood beside the table.

"What'll it be, mum? Got some fine mutton and rye sandwiches. Top it off with a round of butter beers."

"Have you got cakes?" David asked.

"Maybe split one of those sandwiches for them. Save the cake. They can have some when we reach the ship in Queenstown," Bessie told the young woman.

Bessie pulled a crown from her handbag and laid it in the woman's hand.

"Two shillings would do it mum. Not sure I could split a crown," She said.

"Other than that, I've got one shilling and a few pence. Well, besides a few more of those crowns anyway. George usually handles the money. Add a sandwich for me and our driver then. That should cover it," Bessie told her.

The tavern girl brought out four plates with stuffed sandwiches and chips. She set three of them on the table and headed out the door with the fourth. In a few moments she returned and served them up mugs of the butter beer.

They were halfway finished with the sandwiches when she also set a plate of tarts on the table. The scent wafting up from them told Bessie they were fresh from the oven.

"I ain't got much for cakes, but here's a few apple tarts."

"That's okay," David said. "Lizzie didn't get any cakes either. I'd have known."

"You always say you got this twin power thing. What's she thinking now?" Mary teased.

"I'm working on it. Hey, I knew when Lizzie burnt her hand on Grand-mama's steamer, didn't I?" David replied.

"Just finish your sandwiches. We have a long way to go," Their mother told the children.

The tavern girl laid a bundle wrapped in cloth on the table, along with a small jug.

"Willy, I mean Mr. Hammond, told me what happened at the dock. You got a ways to go in a hurry. I packed some more sandwiches for you and here's cider to keep you going. I hope you make it in time."

Bessie hurried the children back outside to where their driver sat in the idling motorcar. Within moments they were bouncing along the gravel track once more.

Just shy of two o'clock they rolled through Salisbury, dodging around a few farm wagons, and out the other side before the number of horses the children counted could be settled. The argument lasted another mile in which seven more horses were added to the count.

Midafternoon, Mary excitedly pointed ahead to where a few colourful pennants flew by some equally colourful wagons parked along the side of the road. A small cook fire roasted what looked to be half a lamb.

"Is that a circus?" Mary asked.

"Them's Gypsies," Mr. Hammond called over his shoulder. "They camped out by my uncle's place last month."

"Can we stop at the circus?" David asked his mother.

"They are more like travelling performers. They move from town to town selling fortunes and potions," Bessie told them.

David and Mary stared at the colourful sights as the motorcar rolled past. It was easy to tell the gypsies, dressed just as colourfully as their tents and wagons, from the few town folk milling around them. David swore that a dog tied to the second wagon had to be a werewolf.

"How do you sell a fortune?" Mary asked.

"How come they move all the time? They could move next to us and stay there. That'd be fun," David remarked.

"From what I understand, they don't really like staying in one spot for too long, or perhaps it's that people start accusing them of all sorts of stuff," Bessie told her children. "Anyway, I've never heard of gypsies in America, so take a good look."

A few minutes later, the motorcar slowed as Mr. Hammond matched speed with some other motorists winding along the road in Bath. He took the opportunity to pour a bucket of water over the motor's radiator. They left the cobblestone street behind for more of the open farmland as they drove on toward Bristol.

"Hey, I bet we beat the Titanic to Queenstown!" Mary exclaimed.

"Henry said it was the fastest ship anywhere in the world. How can we go faster?" David exclaimed.

"Well, motorcars can go faster than ships, except we have roads to follow. The ship is still on its way to France right now. So we have a good head start on them," Bessie told them. "The difficult part comes at Pembroke, where we have to get our own boat."

Passing through Bristol they almost missed the sign pointing them northward to Gloucester. Even Bessie marveled as they crossed the Severn River on the old stone bridge. They were truly in the west now. Mr. Hammond stopped at a grassy field where they enjoyed another sandwich.

"I can't believe Miss Sally sent us along with some of her cider," He said.

David drew a sigh from his mother when he displayed his mouthful of food to his older sister, thrilling to the look of disgust Mary had. Mary shoved half of her sandwich into his mouth to cover it up.

"You can play all you want when we get aboard the ship," Bessie told them. "For now let's get going before we miss it again."

The children turned it into another game to guess which they'd see next; a motorcar or a horse and wagon. After they'd passed a dozen or so wagons on the road they were passed by a fellow in another motorcar.

David and Mary cheered on their driver as he struggled to chase the faster one. At last he conceded defeat and slowed a bit.

"Sorry children. He must have one of them racing motorcars. Some of them get up to fifty miles an hour on the cobbles, I heard," He told them. "Old Bessie here works hard without much complainin', but she's not much for hurrying that much."

"Aww," They replied in unison.

Bessie's tension grew as the day wore on, and the sun began to dip low before them. Other than a couple times to eat, and the handful of stops for the loo, she thought they had made good time. David and Mary's enthusiasm for the trip had waned, and they spent their time staring at the scenery they passed.

The pale orangish-red of dusk seemed very disheartening to her as they drove through Cardiff. Bessie pulled a blanket from the basket next to her and draped it over the children who had tired of counting horses. They snuggled against each other, the scenery forgotten for now.

The moon rode high in the sky, and the streets seemed far less busy than most of the other towns they had driven through, when they finally pulled into Pembroke. Signs pointed the way to the docks which still bustled with the fishermen returning from their day's work.

The office for the ferry sat dark and lonely at the end of an empty pier. Bessie stepped out and stretched before walking over to read the sign.

Her heart sank into a deep pit as she read the departure scheduled for two-thirty daily, except Sunday. They had missed the boat once more, and the next ferry wouldn't even arrive until the Titanic was well out into the Atlantic.

She walked back to where Mr. Hammond had the bonnet propped open, drizzling oil into the motor. She felt the heat emanating from the hard working machine and marveled that he leaned over it as she would a supper pan on the stove.

"I must apologize for all the fuss I've caused you Mr. Hammond. It seems this trip was all for naught. I haven't the coins to find rooms for the night, so I'll rest in the motorcar until you're set to return," She told the driver.

"Both Bessie and I will need a few hours before trying that return. I'll have to find some petrol before then, also."

"You named the motorcar Bessie?" she asked.

"For me mum. Fine woman, and stubborn to boot."

Bessie settled back into the seat and closed her eyes. The ride had been wearying, and the disappointment at the pier had left her exhausted. She just started to feel the sleep creeping over her thoughts when she heard Mary.

"Are we there yet?" Mary asked sleepily.

"Everything will be fine. Just rest for now. We'll get to America somehow," Bessie told her.

Bessie woke with a start as the motorcar bounced through a dip in the road. The street lamps had long since gone out, and only a few people were moving along on the pre-dawn roads. She looked around more as the sky lightened, thankful the children still slumbered.

Bessie's thoughts drifted off to George and how much she missed him. They had missed the nightly routine of each of the children kissing her cheek as they headed off to bed.

Bessie felt her cheek where Mary and David had kissed it last evening, and longed to snuggle Lizzie and Paul to her. It would be at least a week before she felt their kisses once more. Her thoughts were once again pulled away when David spoke up.

"Can we have buckwheat cakes for breakfast?" David asked.

"I'll have to see what we can arrange for breakfast," she told him.

"With lots of maple syrup."

An hour later, Mr. Hammond pulled to a stop before a tavern in Cardiff. He looked as though he had gotten even less sleep than Bessie.

"If you don't mind, Mrs. Corbridge, I'd like to have a spot of tea and cakes," He told her.

"Come, then. I'll buy you as many cakes as you like. It's the least I can do after all the fuss I've caused," Bessie replied.

The four of them settled around a table inside. Within short order the lady set plates of steaming cakes before them, along with glasses of milk for the children. Mr. Hammond got his cup of tea.

"Have you got Ovaltine?" David asked.

Back in the motorcar, Mr. Hammond whistled as he drove. Only about half of the tune could be heard due to the noise of the motor and the scrunching gravel under the tires.

Martha looked up from where the hoe cut the weeds around her pansies. The motorcar pulling up the lane looked a great deal like the one she'd waved to as it pulled away from her house the day before.

Martha's surprise grew as the motorcar pulled to a stop and David bounded out. Mary and Bessie were not far behind. As they climbed out Bessie had to stop and stretch before greeting her mother-in-law.

"Bessie, what on earth happened? You should be

halfway to America by now!" Martha asked.

"It's difficult to explain…," Bessie started.

"Our motorcar went boom and crash!" David exclaimed.

"It just broke for a bit, David. If it went boom you'd have been blowed to bits along with it," Mary added. "'Course that would have been fun to watch."

"Our motorcar had some difficulty. We arrived too late to join George on the ship. I'm afraid your son is off to America on his own. We'll catch the next ship on the morrow."

"He's got Lizzie with him, and I bet she got cocoa for breakfast," David said. "I can almost taste it, too."

"I'll get your cases down in a moment, Mrs. Corbridge. I just need a moment," Mr. Hammond said.

"Take your time. It's been a rough spell. I'll be by to settle the receipt tomorrow if that suits you," Bessie told him.

Bessie helped their driver stack the cases in the parlor as the children told grand-mama Martha all about the rush to Pembroke. Sitting atop the stack of luggage sat Keykey, the one who'd held them up the day before. If he hadn't been lost she and the children would have made it aboard with the rest of her family.

Mary grabbed one of the trunks and dragged it up the stairs. She took it straight to the room that the children had shared and flipped open the lid. After a moment of rummaging through the contents she yelled down the stairs.

"Mother? What should I do with Paul's stuff? I mean, here's his blanket and some trousers. I don't know why his stuff had to be in my case anyhow."

"So what? Lizzie gots my case. What am I supposed

to wear now?" David said as he stared at the pile of luggage in the parlor.

"You've got Paul's blanket? I don't know how your father will get him to sleep without it, especially if he gets frightened," Bessie replied.

"I have three dresses. You can wear one of mine David," Mary teased her younger brother. "The yellow one suits you. Wear that to Sunday meeting."

"I ain't wearing no dress!"

"You two go help Grand-mama get dinner ready. We'll figure out clothes tomorrow when I go into town. Everything of mine is aboard the Titanic," Bessie told them. "I guess I'll just have to go to Madame Trudeau's boutique, and get that hat George liked so well. Along with enough clothes to reach New York."

April 12th, 1912 – Winchester, England

Bessie hitched the horse to the buggy right after breakfast, and headed off to Southampton. She couldn't help but wince when she passed the spot the motorcar had broken for nearly an hour.

Southampton seemed like it was back to normal after the departure of Titanic. The bench in front of the sailor's home was empty for the first time since they had arrived. Even the newspaper boy had changed to talking about progress on the coal strike, which most people simply grumbled about.

Her first stop was at the bank where she withdrew the cash to pay Mr. Hammond. She took an extra twenty crowns just to buy new clothes for herself, David and Mary. Not that Mary needed a new dress, but she would fuss if David got clothes and she didn't.

A brief stop at the motorcar company settled that bill, which totaled nearly four times what George had planned on spending for that part of the trip. She added a couple extra crowns just because Mr. Hammond had made the valiant effort to reach Pembroke.

Madame Trudeau's boutique lifted her spirits somewhat, as she collected three dresses for herself, along with one for Mary. Of course, she couldn't forget the hat. It was sure to make George drop his jaw when he saw her debarking in New York.

Bessie stopped into the White Star Lines office, where she discovered that they had no other ships scheduled for at least a week. She had to explain to him three times, just how she had missed her boarding call.

"I deeply apologize Ma'am, but April is a slow part of the year. We will honor your tickets once Titanic returns, if you would prefer," A clerk told her.

At the American Lines office she found little better news. The New York would sail in five days. Its comfort was no equal to Titanic, or even Carpathia, but she would see her George so much sooner. Bessie secured a first class cabin for her family for less than the price George had paid for their second class one on Titanic.

Bessie unhitched the horse and brushed him down firmly, treating him to a handful of oats before she took her bundles into the house.

David barely mumbled a thanks for the new clothes, but Mary seemed thrilled to have a dress that matched her mother's. She dashed off to display them for Grandmama when she saw the matching hats. Martha made tarts with some of the last of her winter apples to celebrate.

Two nights later, David woke crying in the middle of the night. Even under three blankets he couldn't stop his shivering. Bessie held onto him throughout the wee hours of the morning, and read fairy tales to him by the light of the fireplace.

"We're going to make this trip even if I have to have a porter haul you up the gangway by your toe! You best get better real fast," She told him.

"I'm sorry, Mother. I'm still cold. Can we put another log on the fire?"

By breakfast his fever seemed back to normal, though he wandered around the house without much energy. A spoonful of maple usually got him to scrape every bit of oatmeal from the bowl, but this time he walked away from half of it.

CHAPTER FOUR

April 14th, 1912 11:40pm – R.M.S. Titanic

Lizzie woke with a jolt in the darkened cabin. Paul still slept softly beside her, but something felt wrong. It had taken hours for her to become accustomed to the noise of the ship enough to sleep, and now it was different. She hopped out of bed and hurried over to shake her father's arm. He opened his eyes, still half asleep.

"Father, did you hear that?" Lizzie asked. "It's scaring me."

George sat up and reached for the lamp. It took him a moment to rub the sleep from his eyes and listen for whatever had woken Lizzie. Nothing seemed strange to him. The ever-present whir or the ventilation blowers still persisted. The thrum of the ship's engines could be heard as well as felt, though maybe that was a little different.

"I think maybe they have cranked up the engines a bit, Lizzie Lou. That just means we'll get to America a tad sooner. Not to worry, you're as safe as being home in your own bed."

"But I don't have a bed anymore," Lizzie replied. "You said we had to find the house when we got to

New York."

A little bump shook the ship, followed by a rumble. The whole ship vibrated like they were going over a cobblestone road. George looked upward for a minute, as though the answer would show on the ceiling. He reached down to scoot Lizzie back to her bed.

"What was that?" Lizzie asked. A bit of fear creeping back into her voice.

"Climb back in with Paul," George said. "I'll go see what is happening."

"But…"

"Shhh…, you don't want to wake your brother."

"Let me go with you."

"Stay here in case Paul wakes. He will need his big sister," George told her.

George pulled the covers back over the two children, bending down to kiss their foreheads. The low rumbling hum of machinery, a constant since the ship left Southampton, quieted somewhat. He dressed rapidly and left the cabin. George found a few other passengers in the halls, looking just as confused as he felt. All of them mumbling versions of the same questions rolling through his head.

George made his way to the deck where several passengers were looking over the rail at the waters behind them. He looked back, following the pointed fingers. He saw the huge glistening dark shape slowly receding as the ship continued onward. One boy ran by, still dressed in his night shirt, calling out to whoever would hear him.

"Look! I got a bit of that ice!" he called.

The four men milling around on the promenade deck nearby were discussing last night's dinner, and the flavor of Windsor's new tobacco. They barely even glanced at the boy running past with the chunk of ice. They were more concerned with grumbling about being drawn outside in the cold air.

A crewmen walked past. George grabbed the man's arm. The young crewman wiped sleep from his eyes as he turned to George. He looked like he had been resting only moments earlier and had been dragged from his bed by the same noise that had rousted Lizzie.

"What's happening?" George asked.

"We brushed a bit close to an iceberg. Everything should be fine for now, Sir. I'd say go back to your cabin and sleep through it."

"But the engines have stopped, haven't they?" George asked.

"The Captain is just assuring that all is well before pressing onward. I expect they will have them up rightly," the crewman said.

George walked back to their cabin where he found everyone else sitting around the single lit lamp. Paul looked to be asleep sitting up, and Laurence and Elizabeth both yawned.

"I couldn't sleep. Wish Momma was here," Lizzie said.

"We'll see her soon enough. Why don't we all get dressed and go look at the stars. Be sure to dress warmly. There's ice floating around in the ocean," George said.

"Ice?" asked Laurence.

"I think we may have bumped into a wee chunk of one, though the steward thought it was fine," George remarked.

Beth helped the children dress while George and

Laurence pulled out their coats. Paul woke only long enough to slide his arms into his shirt before falling asleep in Beth's arms once more.

"Mine and Paul's coats are still in England," Lizzie said. "Is it really cold outside?"

"Just wrap the bed blanket around you. Your Aunt Elizabeth can tend to Paul."

Laurence was adjusting his coat when someone knocked on the door. He answered it to find a nervous looking steward standing there.

"Please come up onto the deck Sir. Bring everyone and dress warmly. It's a cold night out."

"What is the purpose in us all coming up on deck?" George asked.

"I'm sorry, Sir. The Captain has asked that all first and second class passengers be brought up to the deck," the steward replied.

"Well, if the crowd is going to be anything like it was when we left Southampton you need to hold onto my sleeve Lizzie," Aunt Beth told her.

Beth scooped up Paul and followed along as Laurence led the way to the promenade deck. People were milling around everywhere, all chattering about the cold and icebergs. The air was much colder than the weather in England where flowers had started blooming.

One of the pursers pulled life jackets from a locker, handing them out as rapidly as he could. Many other passengers started showing up carrying life jackets they had brought from the cabins. One couple arrived fully wrapped in coats and carrying large cases. They looked ready to debark in New York.

Laurence and George heard people laughing at passengers who had already put their life vests on. White

Star was famous for their compartments which kept ships from sinking, so why did they even wear them?

George was no longer sure. Something was seriously wrong or they wouldn't have woken everyone up and told them to come up to the deck. This was starting to stress George greatly. He wished Bessie was here. 'She would know what to do,' he thought.

"Ladies and children, please move toward the boats," a crewman called out.

"Father?" Lizzie asked.

"Hold tight to your Aunt Elizabeth. I'll get us on one of the boats."

Passengers started getting a bit anxious as everyone pushed their way toward the lifeboats. The crew had performed a short instruction on wearing the life jackets the day after Titanic departed, but the lifeboat practice planned for that morning had been cancelled. People were struggling to don the bulky floats, especially over heavy coats.

George could see the crew working to get a couple of lifeboats lowered from the davits. They were struggling to get the ropes untangled. Making it worse, the deck began slanting forward. This was no practice drill. The ship was floundering and now everyone knew it!

Just as soon as the lifeboat came level to the deck, several people clamored to get aboard. Some of them shoving others out of the way to gain a seat. The loud bang of a gun being fired startled them all. From the deck above, a brilliant streak of fire arched high into the night sky. A bright red star slowly drifted downward.

James Moody, 6th Officer, who was trying to calm all of the passengers down, called out, "Ladies and children first; please only ladies and children. We will load the men into later boats."

George pulled his coat tighter around his shoulders and motioned for the others to follow him. The rest of the passengers were running around in chaos, but he was determined to keep his calm so that the children wouldn't know how frightened he really was.

Laurence grabbed several life vests from the crewman pulling them from the locker. He handed one to George and one to Elizabeth before tugging his own over his head. He struggled a little, but managed at last to get the straps secured.

George waited for the next boat to be lowered into position, then led them all close to the rail. One of the junior officers stood by, trying desperately to control the crowd of passengers pressing toward the boat he was loading.

Just ahead of them, Elizabeth saw Jessica King give a hug to a crewman and climb aboard the lifeboat. Another crewman held out his arm to stop George and Laurence.

"It's ladies and children only till Captain says otherwise."

"Go ahead my dear, take the children on this boat. George and I will follow along shortly," Laurence told Elizabeth.

"Are you sure? I can wait with you."

"Go now. There'll be plenty more boats yet. You'll hardly have time to miss us," George told her.

Elizabeth pressed forward, carrying Paul and tugging Lizzie along. Everyone had tossed thoughts of civility aside as they fought for a place on the boats. Elizabeth felt relieved that there would be a friend to keep her company until Laurence caught up.

"Jessie, can you hold him for a moment? I need to help Lizzie," Beth asked.

She handed Paul over the railings to the woman she'd met in the library. Paul murmured and his little eyes opened a little. Elizabeth turned and lifted her niece just as the crowd surged once more. Beth, Lizzie, and a handful of others tumbled over the side, into the dark waters below. Lizzie even banged against the lifeboat as she fell.

"Beth!" Laurence called.

Laurence glanced around, seeking help for just a moment, before running the four steps to the railing. He placed a hand on the rail and vaulted over without a second thought. George followed him to the rail, torn between jumping over, and his boy somewhere in the lifeboat that was now lowering. He jumped in, resolving to help the others get in the lowering boat.

Jessica pulled the little boy closer to her, feeling the shivers running through him. He was frightened and cold. Her heart ached for him. She hadn't seen people act this way before.

"What's your name, Honey? Can you tell me your name?" Jessica asked Paul.

Paul gasped once as he watched Auntie Beth and Lizzie fall. He expected that any minute they would jump up and laugh as though it were a game. They didn't jump up, and everyone on the ship that was screaming. It just sent waves of terror through him.

Jessica watched helplessly as her friend tumbled into the darkness below. As the lifeboat touched the water, she looked out and saw scattered people bobbing silently in the water, but no sign of Elizabeth. None of the bobbers made any move to join the boats. As she looked closer it became clear that they were already gone.

Paul looked up to the woman holding him close. She continued talking softly to him and wrapped her arms around him tightly. He was terrified, yet he felt safe. The toddler curled up in her arms, waiting for everything to go back to the way it should be.

"Everything will be fine Honey. Are you feeling fine?" Jessie asked him.

There were two crewmen aboard their lifeboat. They pulled out the oars to row away from the liner. Jessie looked back at the ship that still held her husband. The bow was completely beneath the waves and the deck tilted enough that people could hardly stand.

"Push them away!" a seaman called, pointing at swimmers trying to cling to the boat's side. "They'll scuttle us. Hit 'em with an oar if you must."

Jessica held the boy closer, thinking about her husband somewhere on that ship. Holding the boy close helped ease the panic threatening to engulf her. She told herself that Ben was strong. He'd find them soon enough. He'd watched to make sure she had climbed into the boat before heading back into the ship.

Jessica rocked the little boy back and forth whispering calming words, wondering if he could hear what she was saying. The words were for herself as much as the toddler in her arms. She wasn't sure if he understood, but he finally started to relax.

"You will be fine. You'll be just fine," Jessica whispered in his ear.

The only sign that he might have heard her came when he buried his face against her. All around them people screamed and splashed. Not even the dying ship was quiet. The sound of steam hissing from the stacks was joined by a deep groan as the ship tilted even further.

Paul tensed up against the woman. He opened his mouth to add his own scream and nothing came out. He looked up at the woman with fear-filled eyes. She responded by wrapping him even tighter in her arms, holding a hand over his ear to quell the screams around them.

The doomed vessel cried with the sound of tearing steel and snapping deck timbers. Another loud hiss sounded, and then even the lights were gone. They had all flickered for a moment before darkening completely.

Jessica glanced back at the doomed vessel. Unbelievably, the ship broke in half. The stern part slammed down into the water in slow motion. The motion kicked up a wave that scattered the bobbing bodies and boats like they were leaves on a still pond that someone had tossed a stone into. She buried her face in the shawl.

"Please, dear Lord, I need my Ben."

Little by little the cries died down until all that remained was the sound of waves lapping against the hull of the lifeboat. Jessie looked out to see where the ship had been. Nothing remained save the twinkling stars reflected from the dark waves. White life jackets were scattered about with bits and pieces of the fabulous ship.

"Ben, you have to be there. I don't think I can go on without you," Jessie whispered.

Jessie startled at the sound of a splash close behind her. The seaman in charge of the lifeboat struggled to stand, stepping over a few limp forms in the bottom of the boat, as he worked his way to the man that had rowed them away from the sinking ship.

"I'm sorry. I just couldn'a hold it no more. I can't feel my fingers," The man sobbed.

"It's too far out to retrieve and that leaves us with just one oar. We'll just have to wait till they find us," the seaman said.

Jessie shivered and rubbed her arms, trying to get some feeling back into them. It let in some cold to keep her coat wrapped around the toddler, but she knew that he needed the warmth more than she did.

"Use the other one to make a fire then. It's sod bottom cold out here," a voice sounded from somewhere.

"Are ya daft?" another voice hissed. "The boat's wood. You'd burn up the only thing keeping us out of the water."

"It's so quiet," whispered one of the people lying in the bottom of the boat.

The hours dragged on with hope dwindling for them. Jessie jiggled the boy once when she couldn't feel his breath any longer. Relief swept through her when he let out a soft moan.

The sky brightened so gradually that Jessie only noticed when she watched one of the deck chairs float by. It bumped into a white lump that at first seemed completely out of place. She pulled the boy tighter when she realized the lump had a head and arms. The cold water had coated the face with ice.

"A ship!" the seaman yelled, from the spot where he sat hunkered out of the biting breeze.

The sky had lightened enough to see the ship in the distance. It boasted only one stack, confirming that it wasn't Titanic. A few of the men tried calling out to it, though not one could muster any loudness to their voice.

It took two tries before Jessie could add her own voice to the calls. Her shout sounded more like a half-dead sheep than a woman whose life depended upon it. Tears squeezed from her eyes to freeze a trail down her cheeks.

"I see some boats moving," someone said, their voice cracking a bit.

A motor cutter wound its way closer to them. The handful of men aboard stopped at one of the white life jackets. After checking the person closely, they moved on.

"Ahoy," the man in the bow of the cutter called out.

The people around her raised arms to signal the other boat. Jessie did her best to add her own hand. Holding the little one for so long in the frigid night had left her stiff. Her whole body ached wherever it wasn't completely numb.

Jessie couldn't believe how many pins and needles jabbed into her stiff legs as she forced them through the loop of the rope sling. With the boy in one arm, and holding the rope for dear life, they hoisted her to the deck above. She had difficulty even convincing her fingers to grasp the rope. They were numb beyond even the pain of her cramped legs. The boy blinked sleepy eyes at her.

"You must be scared and tired, little one. I've got you. You're safe," she whispered to him.

Once on deck, two of the crew helped her step free of the rope sling and handed her off to a couple people standing nearby. These people looked more like passengers than crew. She barely registered her surroundings as they led her off to a big room with scores of other rescued people sitting around.

A young man pressed a steaming cup of cocoa into her hand as he helped her find a seat at one of the tables. As she looked around, she realized the room was a large dining hall. They had shoved all the tables into half the room, making room for blankets in the other half.

She guessed there were a hundred people already sitting around hunkered over their own mugs. Most of them were using the mugs to warm their hands as much as drinking the warm cocoa to heat them up from the inside. She held the cup gently against the boy's lips, and he sipped a little.

Once her fingers warmed enough, Jessica pulled the blanket tighter around herself and the boy. She stood and slowly made her way around some of the others that had been rescued, trying to recognize someone. A few of the faces looked familiar, but most looked as though they had been in the first class section. The wife of a crewman didn't get to venture into such elite company aboard the ship.

Jessica quickened her step a bit with the sight of a uniform. Just as she neared, he turned to face her. It wasn't her husband. It took her a few moments to recall the man's name. She'd met Jacob a few times, though they had said little more than a greeting to each other. There were so many people on the ship that she could only remember a few names.

"Have you seen my Ben? I mean Ernest, Ernest King. Some folks called him Ben," Jessica asked, hesitantly.

Mr. Gibbons just shook his head. He'd looked at her as though hoping to see someone, but now he stared into the empty mug cradled in his hands.

Jessica heard the shouts as they brought another boat alongside. She hurried over to the side and looked down into a boat that seemed fairly empty. These boats could hold sixty people, or so Ben had told her, and she counted far less than that many. Some were climbing the ladders, while others had to be hoisted as she had been. Still, none of the faces belonged to her Ben.

Jessica found the man handing out mugs of cocoa and took another. With mug in hand, and the little one tucked tight, she sat on a blanket to watch them unload the lifeboats. Each time one came in, she would stare at every face, hoping that it was her Ben.

Finally, the word was shouted that all the boats had been found. There were none left alive in the water. She watched as they lifted the last rescue boat from the water. Painted on the side was the ship's name; Carpathia. She hadn't even thought to ask the name of the ship she was on now.

Jessica stretched the blanket out and lay down in the dining saloon turned bunk house. She started to doze off until she heard the soft whimpering coming from the form she cradled.

"Shh, Little One. I have you. You're safe."

The toddler turned his face up to her, with eyes as big as shillings. She could tell that he was trying desperately not to cry as tears welled in the corners of his eyes.

CHAPTER FIVE

April 16th, 1912 – Winchester, England

Bessie once again hitched Junie, the horse, to the wagon and headed into Southampton. She had a long list of necessities. David still needed another few pair of trousers to make the trip across the ocean. She had vowed that nothing would keep her from sailing in two days' time.

She had hoped that she would miss the morning rush of everyone trying to make it into the city on a Monday morning, but the crowd reminded her of the one from that day the motorcar broke down. Wagons and motorcars crowded the streets as soon as she reached the outlying buildings.

Today there was no rush, so she let the horse wander along with the general flow of merchants and farmers. She turned down into the business district and found another crowd hovering around the newsboy.

Bessie hadn't even seen that many people trying to get a paper when the first stories of Titanic came out. The youngster was hidden behind a wall of men and women scanning their papers as though terrified of what they were reading.

"Titanic struck iceberg! No lives lost. Rush of liners

to the rescue!" yelled the newspaper boy.

"All passengers taken off in record time!" called another lad, not even a block away.

Bessie gasped, and hopped off the wagon. She nearly had her foot crunched by the wheel as the horse continued plodding along the cobbled street. All thoughts of trousers and sweet cakes vanished from her thoughts. Her family was all that mattered.

She dropped several coins into the lad's hat, not even caring that she paid ten times the price, as she pushed through to grab her own copy of the news.

Bessie joined the throng of bystanders scanning papers, trying to glean all the news she could of her family. The headlines glared at her just like the boy had said. The vast ship had struck an iceberg, but at least her family was safe.

Reading the first few paragraphs told her most of the story. Titanic had struck an iceberg late on Sunday. All the passengers had been pulled safely from the boats, and the grand ship itself was being towed to Halifax.

Junie had plodded along until the street curved. Bessie found her trying to nibble the flowers on a vendor's wagon two blocks from the newsboy. She'd already munched twenty pence worth, or so the woman claimed. Bessie handed over the coins to quell the yelling.

Scores of people were lined up outside the White Star offices waiting for news as she drove the wagon past. Bessie took comfort in knowing that her family was safe. They'd all have wild stories to tell each other for years. She assured herself that George could handle a little trouble, and Elizabeth was there to help him if need be.

She stopped into the shop to retrieve the trousers for David and a dress for Mary. Bessie put her bundles in the buggy before moving another street over. She had a few coins remaining, and decided to indulge the children each with a few pennies of their favorite sweets. George would be spoiling Lizzie and Paul to keep them happy during this bit of a mess, so it seemed only fair.

Standing almost right in front of the very shop she sought stood another news boy. This one stood shouting a very different story than the last boy. Once again she found herself pushing through to snatch her own copy of the paper as she tossed a penny into his hat.

"Titanic sunk! 2358 lives in peril!" He shouted.

Thoughts of sweets evaporated as the certainty that her family was safe dissolved. This paper claimed that the massive ship had sunk the previous evening. Some of the people were still in boats by the last account, while most had been taken aboard Carpathia. Still they claimed that everyone was safe, but Bessie's certainty was cracking.

Bessie drove the wagon around to where she could see the White Star office. Where there had been a few score of people, hundreds now jammed the street in front of the office. A pair of constables stood by, trying to quell the crowd that was getting louder by the minute..

She momentarily considered prodding Junie to charge through the crowd and scatter them, but the poor horse knew only slow and slower. She could flick the reins all she wanted if someone was rubbing Junie's nose. The horse would ignore the reins in favor of the attention to her nose, especially if they had an apple.

She knew right away that she'd not even get to the doors, let alone talk to one of the clerks inside. Bessie cracked the reins and prodded the old mare into a jarring trot. She hunched forward on the seat, calling encouragement to Junie every bit of the way back to the farmhouse. Junie slowed back to a walk only three blocks later.

Bessie didn't even stop to pull the harness from the horse as she hopped off the wagon and ran into the house. Martha looked up from where she was cutting carrots as Bessie grabbed the handset from the telephone. A rapid jabbing of her finger sent an urgent request to the operator.

"Hello? Hello. Can you please connect me to the White Star offices in Southampton?" Bessie asked into the telephone.

"I'm sorry, Ma'am, but half the town wants to talk to them. I've got eight people holding for them, and they aren't answering any of my rings," The reply came back. "Perhaps you could try their office in person."

"My family is on that ship. Or they were," Bessie pleaded

"I'm truly sorry Ma'am. My brother got a job on there as one of the firemen. One of the other operators told me they only rescued about a thousand people. The only name I heard so far is Mrs. Astor. She got rescued. No mention of the nobodies."

"Thank you. I'll ring later," Bessie told her.

She placed the handset back on the hook with shaking hands, and turned to find everyone else staring at her. Seeing the anxious looks from her children, Bessie chided herself to remain strong. She couldn't let them see her cry. She took a deep breath, willing every ounce of calm she could muster before she spoke.

"There's been a terrible disaster, I'm afraid. George, Laurence, Lizzie, Paul, and Beth are headed back here aboard Carpathia," Bessie told them.

"What happened?" David and Mary both cried out at the same time.

"Let me take care of Junie first. I'll be right back to tell you about it," Bessie told them.

She headed back out the door to care for the horse that was starting to shiver after the rush home. Bessie needed time to sort through her thoughts before facing her family to explain something she didn't fully understand herself.

Bessie took her time pulling the harness off and hanging it from the hooks. She led Junie into her stall and began the task of brushing her with straw, and then the comb. Her hands were still shaking when she finished, so she added more feed to the bucket. She had to take a deep breath when she realized she was trying to fill a water bucket that was already full.

"Ok, Mary will you stir the gravy a bit, and David can slice the tops of the buns," Grand-mama Martha told the children. "She'll be back in but a moment to tell you all about it."

By the time Bessie had brushed and cared for the horse, dinner was ready inside. She'd taken enough time to mentally sort through what she would tell Mary and David. The smell of fresh baked buns, mingled with the scent of a savory dinner, greeted her as she came back to the house.

Over dinner she told Martha and the children all the things she had learned from the newspapers. She focused more on the first story, choosing to believe that her family would be back together in a few days. The news seemed dire, but at least her family would be whole once more.

"We'll just have to postpone our trip to America a bit. At least until your father is back here with us. We'll go into Southampton tomorrow to cancel our tickets on the New York and ask when our family will arrive," Bessie told them.

"We want to go with you," Mary begged.

David nodded agreement. He still looked pale and kept the blanket round his shoulders during supper. He barely spoke more than responding to questions; most of which related to speculations about Lizzie.

After dinner, Bessie rummaged in the pantry for a few minutes, then gathered Mary and David at the front window. After wiping the dusty sill, she placed a few candles along it.

"This is for your father, George. This one is for little Lizzie, and these are for Paul, Uncle Laurence, and Aunt Beth," she intoned as she placed each candle.

"Lizzie likes the red better than the white," David said.

"The red one's shorter," Mary replied. "You can't make Paul bigger than Lizzie."

Bessie lit a match from the fireplace and carefully set the flame to each candle. With the last one, she held the match out for the children to blow out. David ended up coughing as he got the smoke in his face when Mary puffed first.

"I thought we only did that for Christmas," Mary said.

"Long ago, a father had gone out in the billowing snow to gather firewood for his family. As he chopped away, deep in the forest, the snow grew fiercer. By the time he had fully loaded his sled, the weather had turned into a blizzard. He trudged for hours in the deepening snow, getting colder with each step. All traces of his path were lost to the snow. At last, he saw a faint light to follow. His wife had lit their last candle for warmth when the final log had burned away. Her candle led him home, and his wood saved the whole family from freezing. Now we light the candles for our family to find their way back to us," Bessie told the children.

Bessie held the children close and stretched out a hand to pull Martha into the circle. Hand in hand, she whispered a prayer asking that her loved ones would find their way home. She held tight for nearly half an hour before loosening her grip.

She kissed each of the children and sent them off to bed. She knew the morning would be the start of a very long day. She listened as their footsteps trudged up the stairs and along to their room.

"I'm sure they'll have all of this sorted by the morn," Martha said.

"There had to be a hundred people trying to crowd into the White Star offices," Bessie said. "I couldn't get near it."

"I'm sure they'll have better news tomorrow. Surely those people know everything about their ship," Martha said.

Bessie didn't even make it to her bed. When morning came, she woke on the sofa with Mary and David on each side. She untangled herself carefully, and went to the telephone once more. The operator had no better news and the White Star office disconnected the call as soon as they answered. The next three times they didn't even answer.

Placing the telephone back on the receiver, Bessie wiped her eyes and wandered into the kitchen. She took her mind off her worries by fixing a big pot of porridge. Every few stirs, she would dribble a bit more of the cream into the pot, or a sprinkling of dried apple.

"Are they arrived then?" Martha asked as she walked into her kitchen.

"Hmm…?" Bessie looked up from the pot.

"You've made enough to feed all of them, including your brother and Beth. Especially if they haven't had a good meal in three or four days," Martha told her.

Bessie looked down at the pot she was stirring. Indeed, there was enough porridge in it to fill a score of bowls. She sighed and set the spoon down before dropping onto a stool.

"Mary, would you be a dear and run down to the larder and fetch me a pint of those berries? Those will go well with this," Martha called into the parlor.

"Do we have to eat all of that before we go into town?" Mary asked.

"I ain't even hungry," David said.

After they had stuffed themselves with porridge, the children helped their mother hitch the wagon. Junie still looked a bit tired after trotting the day before, so Bessie let the old horse walk most of the way into Southampton.

"We should'a called a motorcar," Mary complained.

"Last one we called blowed up on us," David replied.

It wasn't long before they ran into the first boy hawking his papers. Like the previous day, he stood surrounded by people reading the stories about Titanic's final hours.

"Boat loads of women rescued! Few men among survivors! 868 have been saved so far! 1490 are missing in this terrible tragedy!" he called into the crowd.

The next boy stood calling out names. The crowd around him anxiously scanning through the newsprint for loved ones.

"John Jacob Astor died, but wife saved! The Countess of Rothes pulled from lifeboat after rowing for hours! Sir Cosmo Duff-Gordon and Lady Lucy Duff-Gordon are in fine spirits!"

"Mother? What does he mean? I thought everybody was saved," Mary asked.

"Here, hold the reins a bit while I find out," Bessie told her.

Bessie handed the reins to Mary and climbed down to wiggle through the crowds for a copy of the paper. David hopped down to follow after her with his hand gripping her skirt tightly.

After getting her own copy of the paper, Bessie flipped through the pages. Finally she found something in the society news column. Just as the boy had said, there were many famous names listed, with half of them said to still be missing.

There wasn't a single mention of anyone near and dear to her, or even the other local inhabitants. The only names listed were some of the more prominent first class passengers; the same ones that had made the ship's journey famous in the first place.

The one thing Bessie did discover in the columns was that the RMS Carpathia was not coming to England, but instead steamed toward New York. They had reversed course. The ship was expected to arrive in New York some time the following day.

"Mother?" David asked.

With no hope of getting anywhere near the White Star Lines office for information, Bessie climbed back onto the wagon and drove it around to the Cunnard Lines office. Although the place was crowded, it was far less crowded than the White Star's.

Just as she had hoped, they had their own wireless telegraphy operator busy exchanging news of the rescue efforts with their counterpart in New York City, via ships at sea. Bessie stood in line for nearly an hour while David and Mary tugged on her sleeves. At last, she handed over the message she had composed; a plea to her parents for any news about George and her children. Bessie had asked them to meet everyone when the ship pulled into New York.

"It may be evening before I can get this through," the clerk told her. "Lots of folks keeping the telegraphers hopping."

Trying desperately to brighten the mood of everyone, Bessie scooped David into her arms and smiled at him.

"How about we stop at Marie's Pastries before heading back home?" Bessie asked her children. "She makes the best puddings. Just don't tell Grand-mama about that."

"When is Lizzie coming back?" David asked.

"Yes, and Paul, and Father, and my case of books. Oh, Uncle Laurence too," Mary chimed in.

Bessie let out a sigh as she hugged them close. She did her best to keep the tears from leaking out of her eyes as she comforted the two children.

"The ship that picked them up turned back to New York City. So we'll see them when we get there,"

"We're still going tomorrow?" Mary asked.

Bessie let her shoulders slump. Part of her wanted desperately to sail off to New York this very instant, but for the moment she couldn't even think of stepping aboard a ship.

"I'd better wait until we have word for sure," Bessie told them. "It just wouldn't be funny to sail off to meet them there, only to find they had returned here."

Both of the children looked downcast. Not even perking up with a second suggestion for puddings. They made two more stops along the way, picking up another traveling wardrobe for all the new clothes, before making it back to the farm house.

After a quiet dinner, Grand-mama told a few stories about when their father was younger. They all laughed when she got to the part where he had tried milking the horse. Her stories helped take the tension out while she told them, though the silence afterward brought most of it back. Bessie lit another pillar candle in the window, though now it was a solitary one for all the missing family.

"You said they were going to America. How will they see the candle?" David asked her.

"I'm sure they will know we lit it for them. When we board the ship we can light another one there. They'll surely see that one when we arrive."

When morning arrived, Bessie didn't even want to talk about the missing family. She kept insisting that within a day or two news would come that they had made it safely to New York. She pulled a chair over near the telephone and sat down with a book about the proper raising of fox hounds.

She spent hours barely turning the pages, glancing toward the telephone with every sound that came. David tugged on her sleeve when the old clock chimed the noon hour.

"Mary wants to make porridge, but I want buckwheat cakes. Tell her to make buckwheat cakes," David pleaded.

Bessie set her book down and went into the kitchen to solve the lunch crisis. She found Mary pulling out the second largest of the pots.

"Here, Dumpling, I'll fix you both some sandwiches," Bessie told her. "Go mind the telephone for me."

Bessie had sliced the entire loaf, and trimmed off three thick bits of the ham, when a passing motorcar let out a backfire bang. Bessie stabbed the slicing knife down into the jar of mustard and ran back to the parlor. She found Mary dutifully staring at the telephone.

"I've got them prepared for you now. Just pour yourselves a cup of milk."

"How long until Father rings us so that we can go to America?" Mary asked her.

"Just as soon as they step off the Carpathia, I'm sure your father will send a wireless telegram."

"What's a wiredress?" asked David.

"Wireless. Normally, someone sends a telegram and it gets carried all the way across the big pond on a ship. With the wireless they send it through the air to one of the ships, and that ship sends it through the air to the next one closer to us, until it finally reaches England. That's when they write it down again and bring it to our door. That means it can get here in a day instead of a week."

"What if they folded it wrong and the telegram crashes in the water?" David asked.

CHAPTER SIX

April 18th, 1912 - New York City, America

Jessica stood at the rail watching as Carpathia sailed into New York Harbor. The first thing that caught her eye was the statue that towered over the ship as they passed. She'd waved goodbye to it only five years ago, never thinking she'd see it again. She and Ben had stood at a rail just like this one, making plans for raising their family in Ireland.

She had dreamed of holding her husband's hand at the rail of Titanic, but now it was a toddler she held. He slept peacefully for the first time in days. She held a bit of hope for Ben, but knew that he was almost certainly gone. She heard several ships' whistles sounding across the water, along with the chuffing of engines as boats darted around the busy harbor. And then there were the lights of the big city. Even in the pouring rain they sparkled across the harbor.

Other passengers crowded the rail next to her. Many of them had been plucked from the lifeboats like she had and were now anxious to put the ocean behind them. The others that had boarded in New York only a week prior watched as the ship bypassed the Cunnard docks, heading toward the White Star pier.

The ship tied up long enough to offload the thirteen lifeboats they had taken aboard during the rescue. They then reversed course back to the pier. Crowds lined pier 54 as far as she could see. Despite pelting rain, it looked like half of New York had come to welcome the ship.

The noise of the crowd felt like it had when Titanic steamed out of Southampton, but this crowd grew silent as the gangway rolled out. For Jessica, it felt like the silence as the shouts in the water had slowly died out. A shiver went up her spine and she pulled the little boy closer to her.

One by one, Carpathia's passengers filed down the gangway, shaking their heads at questions too quiet for Jessica to hear. At last, word came that it was time for the seven hundred survivors to go ashore. Of course, she had to wait as the first class people went before the others.

As the first one of Titanic's survivors stepped off the gangway, people crowded around. A knot of people formed that slowly let the bedraggled passengers through. For once, Jessica was happy not to be among the first class elites. She wasn't ready to share her grief with the world. Let them all go away so that she could grieve in peace.

Around her gathered the few crew members and third class passengers that had managed to be rescued. So many of the faces she had come to know aboard the Titanic were gone. She pulled her coat tighter and hurried down to the pier. She barely had both feet on firm ground when the questions began.

"What's your name, Ma'am?" came the inquiry from a man hunched over a pad of paper with pencil in hand.

The reply came to her lips before she could stop it, "Mrs. Ben King. I mean Ernest. Mrs. Ernest King."

"Is he still aboard?"

Jessica clamped her lips and shook her head. The boy stiffened a bit in her arms. She ducked her head and pushed through the crowd. She looked up again as the crowd eased a bit. There had to be a friendly face somewhere. She'd hail a taxi and go anywhere but here.

She spotted her old neighbors standing next to a long line of ambulances and hearses. It surprised her, though Ben had told her that he had sent them a telegram announcing their move to America. They had secured a house right across the street from them in the old Bennett neighborhood. The street she'd never thought to see again.

She saw their worried faces and worked through the milling crowd to reach them. Thankfully, they both simply hugged her without asking anything. With Joe on one side, and Carol on the other, they walked the block to where he had parked his motorcar.

"I borrowed our neighbor's touring sedan because there's no way we'd all fit into the roadster I have," Joe told her. "I had counted on…, well, the roadster is only good for two people anyhow."

"You'll love the house. There's even a spot for a bit of a garden just outside the kitchen," Carol told her.

"Thank you both," was the only response Jessica could think of saying.

The boy woke up as the car made the third turn, and began crying. Jessica ruffled his brown hair, wiping the wet strands from his face. He looked up to her with his lips trembling and the only thing she could do was to smile. She put all the reassurance she could into her upturned expression. Jessica held onto him as the crying slowly eased off.

"That's... Never mind. It'll wait till we get there," Carol said.

"Shh, Little one. I've got you," Jessica told him.

They drove for a bit before the lights of downtown began to fade. Coming back to the hustle and bustle of a large city that never slept was a big change for her. She swore they must have added at least twice as many lights as when she had left it behind for quiet Queenstown.

At last, Joe pulled the motorcar to a stop in front of a row house. The two-story home hid most of its size by being long instead of wide. It was too dark to see much of the details through the rain, but Jessica saw enough to know the neighborhood had changed only a little in the years she'd been gone.

Joe held the door as she stepped out of the motorcar. Now that he was somewhat awake, the boy looked around at the adults towering over him. The house was different. The road was different. Even the people were strange to him. He grabbed tight to Jessica's hand as the only person he knew.

"I left the door unlocked so that Ben could carry you into your new home. It's... well, you'll see it better tomorrow," Joe said.

Jessica walked slowly beside as the boy took in all the new sights. At the door, she gave him a minute to stare into the parlor before she picked him up. Joe and Carol followed behind her, settling themselves on the sofa, as Jessica carried him up the stairs.

"Second door on the right," Carol called after her.

Jessica took the boy into the bedroom and laid him on the bed. He fell asleep as soon as his head touched the pillow. She stood smiling at his sleeping form before pulling off his shoes and dragging the blanket over him.

The room contained just the essential furnishings of a small dresser next to the bed. She and Ben had dreamed of a room like this for Sam, and that was likely why Joe and Carol had picked this house. Now she had to go face them with all the news about Ben as well as Sam.

Jessica walked softly back out to the parlor where Joe and Carol sat on the sofa. The furnishings had been critical to buying the house, since Ben had only been allowed to bring three cases on the ship. Now she didn't even have those. Carol looked up at her entrance.

"So, just who is he? I mean that can't be Sam," Carol asked.

"Carol…," Joe hissed at her.

"Oh posh. She had to have known the question was coming. I mean Sam would be bigger than this boy, and I don't think he looks all that much like Ben."

Jessica dropped into the rocking chair with a sigh, like all the air had been taken out of her. She took a moment to get her worry, fear, and grief in check before she answered.

"Sam was doing so well; right up to the beginning of the year. He caught a cold that just wouldn't go away. We laid him to rest about the end of February. After that, Ben got taken on the ship and it was the best excuse to begin a new life back here," Jessica told them.

"Your letters never said anything about another child," Carol prompted.

"Everywhere I looked reminded me of Sam and watching as they shoveled the dirt into the grave. I couldn't take it anymore. We vowed to start over here, where there are only good memories," Jessica said.

"Ben mentioned some of that in his telegram," Joe said.

"I went into the library on the ship one day and found this woman smelling a book. It made me laugh because it's just how Ben described what I'd do with a new book. We struck up a conversation though she never said her last name," Jessica said.

"Yes, go on," Joe said.

"I ran into her again when they were lowering our lifeboat. I'd said goodbye to Ben and I was already in the boat. He promised to catch up to me. This lady I'd met in the library, she handed the baby across to me so that she could…," Jessica told them, pausing as the tears welled up.

"She handed you her child and walked away?" Carol asked.

"No, she turned to help his sister in. The crowd suddenly the crowd pushed them all off into the water. She and the girl screamed as they fell. I'm sure he watched them fall. He hasn't said one word since then."

"You should have left him with the White Star people. They could have figured out who he belonged with," Joe said.

"You wouldn't have believed it if you saw it. People shoving everyone out of the way to climb into the boats. A steward had a pistol out to keep them back. I'm not sure, but he may have even shot one of the men. I heard the gunshot go off. Some of them even tried jumping into the boats in the water from the main deck."

"Somebody must be missing him," Joe said.

"His father was on the ship. If he had been rescued, then he would have been on the Carpathia with us. I took the boy around as I searched through all the survivors. Nobody claimed him. He didn't reach for anyone but me the whole three days," Jessica explained.

"Don't you think he has other family out there? Somebody has to be looking for him," Carol asked.

"She never told me her last name. I'm all that he knows right now. I mean, I searched through all the survivors and there wasn't anybody that claimed him," Jessica said. "None of his family made it to Carpathia. Of that I'm sure."

"Well, what is his name?" Carol wanted to know.

"Ben. His name is Ben," Jessica said, silently deciding in that moment.

"I suppose I shouldn't ask about your husband, Ben," Joe said.

"Ben hugged me, and insisted I get on the lifeboat when they were only putting ladies and children on them. He promised that he'd be on another boat just as soon as he could. I searched every time they brought in another boat. I think he broke his promise," Jessica broke off as the tears let loose.

Her sobbing was answered by soft whimpering from the bedroom. Jessica found the little boy standing in the doorway with tears running down his cheeks. She picked him up and held him tight as his body shook with each wracking, sobbing breath. Jessica cried right along with him.

"It's okay. We will be okay little Ben. I'm here with you," Jessica told him.

Joe stood and helped Carol to her feet. They both stood watching Jessica and the boy for a moment before Joe spoke up.

"I know it's late. We'd best be on our way and let you get whatever sleep you can. We're all tired. Carol will come by in the morning to help you get settled," Joe told her.

"I really need to thank you both for everything. This house. Your help. Everything," Jessica said.

"There's fresh linens on the bed at the end of the hall, too. I didn't have a chance to find you any dishes so I'll bring breakfast over as soon as your door opens," Carol told her.

Jessica stood at the door watching as Joe and Carol walked to their own small house across the street. She knew it was a miracle to have such good friends living just two-minutes' walk away. She stood listening to the rain patter, letting her thoughts drift for a few minutes. His sniffle brought her thoughts back to the present once more.

"I'm going to call you Ben, my love," Jessica told him. "I can't keep calling you boy. It's just us now."

He just looked up at her with his sad eyes. Jessica carried him back to the bed and laid him down once more. This time she lay beside him and held him close. Jessica hummed softly. Sometimes following a song, sometimes just letting the humming go where it wanted to go. Sleep closed her eyes about a minute after his.

Jessica woke to the sun shining on her face through the bare window. Little Ben still slept soundly in her arms. She carefully untangled herself and stood up. Listening carefully for him to stir, she toured the rooms. The upstairs seemed huge compared to the Queenstown cottage, with two bedrooms and even a small office that Ben could do his…

She felt her chest clench up with the thought that he would never see this house. There would never be a score of canvases with his charcoal sketches scattered around the little office. For now the room sat bare. She closed the door to it to hide his absence.

Jessica scooped up little Ben into her arms and descended to the main floor. Here the house seemed a straight through shot, with the parlor leading into a dining room and a kitchen behind that. An alcove off the kitchen boasted a double wash tub and scrubbing rack. This was an indoor luxury that had taken half the back porch at the Queenstown cottage.

When she opened the front door, she spotted Carol sitting in a rocker on her front porch across the way. Carol waved to her and disappeared inside for a moment. Right away Carol was walking across the street with a basket dangling from her arm. Jessica held the door open for her.

Carol unpacked hotcakes and a couple of boiled eggs from her basket, along with plates to hold all of it. She even pulled out half a jug of milk for them to share.

Little Ben devoured an entire hotcake by himself while managing to get syrup all over his face in the process. After half a glass of milk he curled up in the basket to nap some more.

"Where did all this come from? The house, the furniture," Jessica asked. "I thought we were going to have to search for a house when we arrived. Then when the ship… I didn't know what I'd do."

"The house came available when the last people moved west. They made it to Utah and found a place there. Joe gathered all the furniture from people in the ward," Carol told her.

"All our money was in the cases on Titanic. I'll need a job before I can even buy a loaf of bread," Jessica said.

Tears formed at the corner of her eyes and she felt the breath catching in her throat as she tried not to burst into an hysterical mess. Little Ben needed her to be strong.

"Hush, it's what friends are for. We'll go shopping in a bit, so that you won't starve. I saw an ad for a maid at the Travelers Hotel in this morning's paper. You could try that."

"Last night all I could think of was to take in mending or something. I can wiggle a needle better than most," Jessica said.

"I'll put the word out in the ward."

"I'll go down to the Traveler's Hotel first thing tomorrow."

CHAPTER SEVEN

May 16th, 1912 - Winchester, England

Martha found Bessie sitting in her usual spot next to the telephone. She had sat in that chair every day since news of the sinking had come. Bessie ate dinner with the rest of the family, but quite often she would have Mary bring her something for lunch. She held onto hope that someone would telephone with news of her missing family.

"Are you ready?" Martha asked her daughter-in-law.

"What? Ready?" Bessie asked.

"Today's the day they bring in the ones they've found," Martha reminded her. "I asked Mrs. Tingle to pop by and keep an eye on David and Mary while we're out."

"Yes, yes of course," Bessie replied. "It slipped my mind."

Bessie and Martha climbed aboard the wagon and drove it into Southampton. They stopped once at the post for Martha to send out a letter before continuing the trip.

As expected, there was a line waiting at the White Star offices. A man dressed in one of their uniforms stood at the door directing people to go three blocks farther; to one of White Star's transfer warehouses.

Bessie drove on to the warehouse, which had its own crowd gathered at the doors. After pressing their way through the crowd they found themselves among the hundreds of people in the sorting room.

Tacked along the wall were hundreds of photographs. The people pictured within them had been in the water so long that it became difficult to recognize them. Many of the photographs were accompanied by listings of personal goods the people had carried.

The women stared at pictures, and read lists, trying to find any resemblance to those they had lost. After searching through dozens of such pictures Bessie grew frustrated enough to seek out a clerk marking packages.

"Where are the bodies? I heard they would be brought in today. How am I supposed to tell anything from this?" Bessie asked.

"All the bodies they recovered were taken to Halifax, Ma'am," the man replied.

Just then a wail went up from one of the women still staring at photographs. She tore one of them off the wall and shoved her way to the poor clerk who looked as though he wished to be somewhere else.

"My Joseph!" The woman screamed. "You've got my Joseph! Bring him out now. I want to bury him proper."

"All of those you see have been taken to Halifax and buried there. I've been instructed to tell you that you can make arrangements to have them brought back for twenty pounds," The man cringed as he relayed the news.

"Twenty pounds?" she yelled. "First you drown him, and now you say I must pay to have my Joseph brought home?"

“I’m dreadfully sorry.”

“You’re sorry?” The woman yelled, waving the photograph in his face. “My Joseph is dead! Think how sorry he is to have taken on with your lot!”

Bessie watched as the woman stormed out of the warehouse, still spouting off in her anger and waving the photograph she held. Fearing that she too might find her family on the wall, Bessie went back to carefully look at the photographs. Martha stood beside her giving an equal scrutiny to find her son and grand-children.

One by one they both looked at the photographs and lists, hoping they would find what they sought and dreading it at the same time. A few spots were blank where the photographs had been taken away, but by the time they reached the last one she had seen more than three hundred frozen faces. Not one of them belonged to her missing family.

Bessie began silently crying when she reached the last one and Martha helped her out the door. Martha drove the wagon back to the house since Bessie couldn’t even see the road through her tears.

She wiped them away as the wagon turned up the long drive to the house. She didn’t want any of her children to see her this way. Bessie knew that they needed the little bit of hope that she herself held onto.

Back inside the house, Bessie headed into the kitchen and pulled out the large stew pot. She whistled softly as she filled it half full of water and set it on the stove to heat.

“Mary, will you slice up two onions, and have Lizzie get me a good handful of carrots up from the pantry while I go get a chicken?” Bessie called up the stairs.

David spoke up from the parlor, “Lizzie’s not here

mother. You know that."

"Well, then you can get me the carrots, my dear," Bessie replied.

Bessie headed out the back door with the big knife in her hand. The children set about preparing the vegetables as she had asked. Mary was starting on the third onion when Bessie returned with the other part of her soup.

Bessie soon had the chicken simmering and the vegetables sitting ready. With a bit of stirring the soup began filling the house with its savory aroma. Bessie set about making small balls of dough to drop into the pot, along with a bit of cream.

"George, the soup will be ready in about ten minutes," Bessie called out.

"Mother!" Mary exclaimed.

Bessie stopped stirring the pot and stared at Mary for a minute. She placed the spoon on the counter, and ran up the stairs. She didn't stop until she was sitting in a chair looking out the window of the library.

David ran up the stairs after her and touched her elbow. Bessie's blank expression cleared, and she turned to her little boy.

"Mother? Are you okay?" David asked.

Bessie patted his hand, "I'll be fine. I just got something in my eye."

Bessie sat there until the lengthening shadows engulfed the entire room. She jumped a bit when Mary turned on the light. Bessie turned to see her daughter standing in the doorway with a bowl of soup in her hands.

Bessie ate the soup with Mary sitting to the side watching her mother. Neither one said much until the bowl was empty. As Bessie finished the last spoonful, Mary pulled a hand from her pocket.

"Grand-mama told me that I couldn't give this to you until you had finished your dinner. It's kind of like how we have to finish our dinner before we can have a biscuit. I helped her make these. She had me cut up the figs."

"Thank you, Dumpling. Sometimes I forget what I'm doing. The soup was delicious," Bessie told her.

"That was the soup you made, Mother. I even made sure there were three dumplings in your bowl."

May 18th, 1912 – Winchester, England

As Bessie came down the stairs, she overheard Martha talking on the telephone. She'd heard her mother-in-law talking on the telephone a few times, but this time what caught her attention was the name she heard.

"…Yes, that will be G – E – O – R – G – E. Yes, same date. 1879."

"Mama Martha, what are you doing?" Bessie asked.

Martha put her hand over the mouthpiece, "I decided to set a date for the service," She told Bessie. "June is a good time of the year."

"But…"

"I'm not going down to the bay to toss lilies off the pier. We'll have a service and lay them to rest in the family plot. You and George did so much for me these past few years with my Thomas passing away. I don't think I could have managed if it weren't for your help. I need a stone to go and talk to him," Martha told her.

"But what happens when he comes home and sees it?"

"If so, he'll have a good laugh. You know how Georgie was."

June 10th, 1912 – Winchester, England

"Grand-mama Martha!" David yelled from the front door. "There's a motorcar coming on the driving lane."

Mary and Grand-mama Martha joined David on the front steps to watch as the motorcar rolled to a stop. There was a traveling wardrobe, and a few trunks strapped to the roof, that reminded the children of what their motorcar had looked like as they dashed all the way to Pembroke.

"Those aren't father's trunks," Mary said. "Who is it?"

"I am quite sure they would appreciate a hand getting to the front door," Grand-mama Martha told the two. "Why don't the both of you go help them?"

Before David could open the door on the motorcar, it opened itself. Out stepped Grandfather Henry. Right behind him was their Grandmother Elsie. David stopped in his tracks, completely surprised.

"Grandmother? How did you get here?" Mary asked.

Grandmother Elsie chuckled, and replied, "On a boat, of course. Our house was just a couple of miles down the lane, at least before we moved to America. You didn't think we'd get lost coming back, did you?"

"David, why don't you run and fetch your mother. I'm sure she'd like to greet our guests," Grand-mama Martha asked.

David ran into the house yelling loudly for his mother. Even from the front yard they could hear his voice echoing in the upper hallway. When it ceased they assumed he had found his mother. Elsie smiled.

"Why don't you come in? I'll have tea on in a moment and we can talk in the parlor," Martha told them. "I'll put you in Stephen's room. He'll be gone for a few more weeks at least."

Henry helped the driver unload the traveling cases from the motorcar as the others went into the house. He had moved them as far as the entry when Bessie came down the stairs.

"Mother! Father! It's so good to see you again," Bessie exclaimed. "Is George with you? He hasn't been here lately."

Henry started to say something and stopped with his mouth partially open. Elsie turned back from the parlor to give her daughter a hug.

"He's not coming home," she told Bessie.

Bessie paled, "What do you mean? He must come home! Doesn't he realize how much I need him? Here. Now."

"This isn't one of his business trips for the company, my dear. You already know why he isn't coming."

Bessie broke out in tears, "I'm sorry. I know. It's just sometimes…"

She hugged her father, burying her face into his shoulder. Henry tried bending to set the cases down, but Bessie held tight. At last he simply dropped the cases to put his arms around Bessie.

The whistling of the pot from the kitchen broke the mood and everyone moved on into the parlor. Martha poured them each a cup of tea, while Mary brought out a plate of small sandwiches.

"It's a good thing we wired ahead yesterday," Henry told them. "Three other people were standing around trying to find a motorcar to hire."

"How big was the ship you came on?" David asked.

"The New York. It's a fine enough ship, even

without all the glamour," Grandfather Henry told him.

They traded stories of the events from both sides of the ocean for nearly an hour. Bessie watched from her chair, adding her own bits from time to time. Martha kept the teacups filled and Mary did her best to ensure everyone finished their sandwich enough that she could give them a tart.

"Tis a shame George missed your visit," Bessie said an hour later.

"Bess…," Her father started.

"Mary, would you help her back upstairs?" Grandmama Martha asked. "I fear she is tired again."

Mary took her mother's arm and led her up the stairs. David sat staring at the floor with an angry expression, paying no attention to what the adults whispered between themselves. Nobody spoke up until they heard the sound of the door closing upstairs.

"Martha, how long has she been like this?" Elsie asked.

"It happens more often than not, unfortunately.

It's been going on since we got the news," Martha replied. "Most days she knows what happened and she just sits."

"How does she not know that monstrosity of…," Henry started, changing his words when Elsie placed a hand on his knee. "I mean how can she not see the truth?"

"There are days she sits staring out the library window, asking if there's been any word from George. Most of the time she doesn't even mention the others," Martha said.

"Just keep telling her that they're gone. I'm sure you could convince her."

"Have you ever tried to convince someone the sky isn't blue?" Martha asked.

"But the sky is blue," Henry replied.

"In your world you see a blue sky. In her world George is coming home," Martha told him. "I've tried telling her. Each time I get through that blue sky I watch her heart break all over again. How many times do you think I can bear breaking the heart of someone I love?"

"What about the children? They know, don't they?" Henry asked.

"I'm right here," David spoke up. "The ship went glug, glug, glug, and now they're all gone." He jumped up, and ran out the back door.

Grand-mama Martha sighed and related a bit more, "Mary has been acting fine, but I think she's just holding it together for her mother's sake. I don't think she's even cried. At least not that I've seen."

"So, what does she do then?" asked Elsie.

"She's been burying herself in books every chance she gets. I don't know what she'd do if I hadn't collected all those books over the years."

"Martha, thank you so much for all you've done for our Bessie and the children," Elsie said.

"Elsie, don't mention it. She's my family too, and so are Mary and David," Martha replied. "I was so blessed that they were able to come before Thomas passed. They helped me so much."

"Yes, George didn't hesitate to pack up everything to come over here. Bessie refused to let him handle it alone. She knew it would take months or more."

"When Thomas became too ill to tend the chores, I knew he wouldn't be long for this world. Stephen is away so much that he didn't know much of what was happening. I finally had the chance to spoil my grandchildren. It made Thomas happy in his final days."

"David seems to have taken it hard, but I guess that's expected. He's so much bigger than when I last saw him, but still so little," Elsie said.

"After he found out about the Titanic sinking, he refused to talk about Lizzie being dead. Then he stopped talking about Lizzie altogether. I've caught him talking to Lizzie like she was sitting next to him a few times, though he never saw me watching," Bessie told them. "He used to tease his sister mercilessly and be the one to crack jokes about everything, especially if it was something unpleasant. Now he's… He's just not the same boy without his twin."

The next morning, Bessie came down the stairs humming a tune as she wandered around the parlor straightening the curios and photographs. She brightened even more when she found her mother, Elsie, sitting at the table.

"Don't you just miss England, Mother? I thought today seemed a great day to go shopping in Southampton. You haven't taken me shopping in forever."

Bessie and her mother rode into the city to spend a day simply shopping. Martha stood on the front porch watching them head down the lane. Inwardly she hoped this would be the turning point for Bessie, to let go of the hope that her family would return.

When the women returned several hours later, Bessie had reverted to her somber mood once more. She went up the stairs and threw herself face down on her bed. Nobody saw her again until the morning when she came down for breakfast. She gave her father a hug and went about setting the table for the meal.

Two nights later, after the children had gone to bed, the adults sat around the parlor relaxing with a cup of tea. Even Bessie seemed in good spirits as the conversation wandered over various benign topics. Eventually the talk turned to the time years before, when Henry and Elsie had lived nearby with their children, Bessie and Laurence.

"Martha, do you remember when George first asked Bessie to go with him to the dance?" Elsie asked.

"Do I ever. He had such a crushing on her. She was all we heard about for weeks. Thomas laughed the whole time he built that swing for the old walnut tree," Martha replied.

"I really had to keep a straight face when he showed up to take her on the outing with a streak of green paint down his cheek from painting that swing," Henry said.

Bessie stood up and slammed her cup down hard enough to slosh some of the tea onto the little doily under her cup. Tears ran down her cheek as she once again sought refuge upstairs.

"She was doing so well. I thought it would help," Elsie said.

"No, I am grateful that others remember him too," Martha said with tears in her eyes.

"We'll see how she holds up the day after tomorrow," Henry said.

"The two men I hired have cleared out the brush. We'll put his stone next to Thomas' and the children next to his. If you're still up for it, there'll be room for Laurence and Elizabeth as well," Martha told them.

"When we return home we'll set a marker for them. It'll make visiting it easier," Henry said.

June 17th, 1912 – Winchester, England

Mary descended the stairs to find David sitting on the dining room table. She stood there for a moment, staring at him as though he should know what she was thinking. At last she spoke up.

"David…"

David glanced at the nursery rhyme book in his hand, as though surprised by its presence. With a growl, he scrunched up his eyes, and threw the book at the back window.

"We should'a all been on that ship! At least we'd all be together!" He yelled at Mary.

"David, Lizzie wouldn't want you to…," Mary started.

"Don't go mentioning her like that. How do you know she's dead? She could be alive somewhere! We ain't got proof of nothin'. I should'a been there to help her get into the lifeboat."

"You're right. We don't know what happened. You know Lizzie'd want you to be happy though," Mary tried comforting David.

"Do you need help getting that bow tied?" Grand-mama Martha called down the stairs.

David glared at the stairs and yanked on the knot at his throat. He displayed a great impression of someone strangling themselves before Mary stepped forth.

"Here, let me help you with it," Mary said.

She pulled him close and gave him a quick hug. Then she set about fixing the loop of cloth around his neck. After the third try she got the tie to look more like a bow than a big knot.

"We'll find out if she survived. If she did, don't you

think she would've tried calling us? Father would've told her that we'd follow on quick as we could. You know that," Mary told her brother.

"She'll call, just you see," David replied. "Maybe she's still swimming back to England."

"Now you're sounding like mother."

Grandmother Elsie came down the stairs, followed by Grandfather Henry. She took a minute to look over the children and licked her fingers to smooth out a particularly difficult patch of David's hair.

Martha and Bessie were half-way down the stairs when the knock came at the door. David pulled away from his grandmother's fussing and ran to open the door.

"That will be Father Sheppard, most likely," Martha said.

With everyone gathered in their best clothes, Martha led the way to the far corner of the lot. Mary picked up a handful of dandelions along the way, and handed half of them to David.

A small square had been cleared and four stone markers stood waiting. One was old enough for the moss to grow along the side, but the other three were newer. One for Martha's beloved Thomas, and the two very new ones.

The first read George T. Corbridge and Bessie B. Corbridge. It listed birth dates for both, and April 15, 1912 for George, leaving Bessie's ending blank.

The last stone looked a bit simpler, with names for Elizabeth 'Lizzie' and Paul Corbridge, ages five and two. Keykey sat leaning against the smallest stone with a ribbon tying him from falling over. The knot on it looked a lot like David's tie had, before Mary fixed it.

Father Sheppard took a stand before the stones and turned to face the family. He held his bible in front of him with a thumb wedged between a few pages. He stared at the book a moment before looking back up to the waiting faces.

"It's the hardest part of my tasks to stand before someone's final stone. Especially when I was the one that joined the family together. Be comforted that their trials are done, and they stand beside our great father in the heavens above," Father Sheppard began.

He opened his book to the 10th chapter of John and began reading one of the verses. When that finished, he turned to Ecclesiastes and read from that section as well. As he finished that section, David mumbled softly.

"I'm not ready to laugh or dance."

"And now I leave it up to the mother to drop the first bit of soil on the… well before the markers anyway," Father Sheppard said.

"My children are alive. I know they are," Bessie called out.

"Bessie, please, you are scaring the children," Grand-mama Martha pleaded.

Mary ran forward to drop half of her blossoms on the marker for Lizzie and Paul, and the other half on her father's marker, before wrapping her arms around her mother. When she shook her head back and forth there were little wet spots on Bessie's dress from Mary's tears.

David followed Mary's example, except he saved one flower to set on grand-papa Thomas's stone. After a minute of hugging, the children each took one of their mother's hands and began to lead her back to the house.

Bessie pulled away from David and Mary, walking firmly back to the headstones. She stood looking down at them for a moment and then reached down to untie the ribbon holding Keykey in place.

"I know they're out there somewhere. I can't have him finding his Keykey tied to a dead stone," Bessie said firmly.

Martha shook her head at the sight and sighed. She spread the tulips she had gathered from her own flower garden before the stones and whispered her own little goodbye to each of them.

"Dinner will be at four and you're welcome to tea in the parlor while you wait," Martha told Father Sheppard.

Bessie cradled the stuffed toy in one arm and took Mary's hand once more. She waited until David clasped Mary's other hand before leading them back to the house. Neither of the children said a word, though they both kept looking up to Bessie.

As they reached the back door of the house Bessie came to a stop. She pulled her children close to her in a hug, kissing the tops of their heads. Bessie kneeled and waited until they looked at her to speak.

"I have to accept that your father is gone. He would have done anything to be back here with all of us. I can feel Lizzie, and especially Paul, out there waiting for us to find them. I will never give up on any of my children no matter what."

CHAPTER EIGHT

November 14th, 1912 - Bennett, America

Jessica walked into the bedroom to find Ben sitting on the floor amid the scattered wooden blocks. He seemed to like the blocks, though he had never said a word about it. In fact, it was one of the big concerns Jessica held.

"Ben, what have you done here?" Jessica asked.

She did her best to put a happy note into her voice and a wide smile with spread arms to catch his attention. It was the way she assured herself that he really wasn't deaf. He looked up at her and hurriedly stacked a few more blocks.

"That looks great, Ben. Now it's time to get dressed."

Ben hopped up and ran to the dresser. He climbed on the edge of the bed and pulled open the second drawer. From there he grabbed a pair of socks. He plopped down and started to pull on the socks.

"Is that the left sock or the right sock?" Jessica asked him teasingly.

Ben looked at her and then stared at his socks. After a moment, he switched which sock he held and pulled the other onto his foot. As he went back to the drawer to pull out his small clothes, Jessica added a bit more.

"Maybe we should call it backward day. Wear the trousers first and then the small clothes."

Ben dropped the garments and picked up his trousers. He pulled them on and struggled to get the thick padded small clothes to fit over his trousers. He pulled them as far up as his knees before he kicked the stack of blocks and just stared at Jessica.

"No, you're right. They won't fit that way. We'll just have to put them on in the normal fashion. Pull them off and Mother will get them on you right."

Ben yanked off the clothes in a flash and started dancing around from foot to foot. He hurried to the door of the room, only to come right back and shuffle around in front of her.

"Really? You have to go right now?" she asked him.

He nodded energetically at her and looked down at the diaper laying where he'd thrown it. Ben let out a screech and hopped around some more, holding onto his crotch.

"You know there's three inches of snow on the ground and you're bare on the bottom half," Jessica took one look at the tears welling in his eyes and grabbed the blanket off the bed. "Always an adventure with you. One of these days you'll use words instead of screams to tell me what's going on in that head of yours."

She wrapped him up in the blanket and hurried down the stairs, carrying his little form. She set him down just long enough to open the back door before whisking him across the back yard to the outhouse. With a bit of jostling, she managed to unwrap him, set him on the seat, and wrap the blanket back around him. He squirmed around a bit on the frozen seat before letting out the pent up liquid.

"Well, it certainly is faster without the trousers on you, but we'll not make this a habit. After all, it isn't bare bottom day."

Back inside the warmth of the house, Jessica helped Ben pull his trousers over the padded small clothes. Finally dressed, they headed down the street to the market several streets away.

They had only walked two blocks before running into Mrs. Fairmont. Jessica had bumped into her briefly a few months before, but the woman had been too busy and gave a greeting and a goodbye in one breath. This time she stopped to chat.

Mrs. Fairmont knelt to stare at Ben, "So, this is your little one I'd heard about. How old are you, um…"

Ben wrapped his arms around Jessica's leg, holding tight with a fearful look in his eyes.

"His name is Ben."

"Well, he should be big enough to tell me that himself, or do you plan to say his wedding vows for him as well?"

Jessica could feel his grip on her leg getting tighter, "He'll talk when he's good and ready. For now it's enough that he knows he's loved. He still has years before he starts school, and many more before some girl takes his heart."

"If he were mine," Mrs. Fairmont started.

"Well, he's not. He's my little Ben, and he's just right the way he is!"

Jessica pulled Ben along as she continued on her way to the market. She could feel the eyes on the back of her neck, but dared not turn to check if Mrs. Fairmont was still staring after them.

The bell attached to the door chimed as Jessica walked into the market with Ben in tow. Her nerves were still on edge from running into Mrs. Fairmont, and she nearly missed the greeting from Mr. Mallory, the shopkeeper.

"Yes, good morning as well. I need a few things for the holiday coming up. I know it's still two weeks, but if I don't put in an order while I have a few coins then there won't be much," she blurted out.

"Not to fear, Miss King. After what you done for fixing up my girl's wedding dress in time, I'll have you a bird all set to pick up on time. Now what else you be needing?"

Jessica browsed through the produce, picking out a few items for their dinner. Eggs on toast was becoming the constant dinner, but today she could steam up a zucchini as well. It was tough to makes the coins stretch out until the next mending job.

While she was digging the coins from her little clutch, the shopkeeper placed a piece of candy next to her sack of flour and winked at Ben. Ben reached up to cautiously get the sweet and popped it into his mouth just as Jessica looked back up.

"What was that?"

"Just a ha-penny sweet I had sitting here. My gift."

Jessica set the coins on the counter and loaded the items into her take along bag. She did her best to keep a constant stream of words going as they walked home. Ben gave her a wide-eyed look when she neighed at the horse they passed. He almost even smiled.

December 3rd, 1913 – Bennett, America

Jessica stood at the sink washing the last of the dinner dishes when Ben walked up behind her. She heard the soft sound of his footsteps and waited for the wail and tugging at her apron.

"Mother?" came his timid voice.

The cup slipped from her hand and shattered as it struck the edge of the sink. Pieces scattered everywhere in the blink of an eye. Ben gave a shriek and ran from the room before the last of the shards settled.

Jessica silently cursed to herself. She had been waiting for this day for so long, and still it startled her when he finally spoke. She took a deep breath, set the dish cloth on the counter, and stepped over the bits of glass.

She quelled her nervousness about frightening him back into silence, but with the sound of the shattered glass, there was a shriek from her little one. She found him sobbing into his pillow.

"Ben, it's okay. Nobody was hurt. It's okay, sweetheart."

Ben released his grip on the pillow, and wrapped his arms around her. He clung to her tightly and she could feel his little body just shake with every gut wrenching sob. She wanted to cry herself, but wouldn't let him see.

Finally he tried his voice once more, "Mother?"

"Yes Ben. I'm here for you. What did you need?"

"I forgets," He replied timidly.

"Why not make another picture while I go clean up the mess I made in the kitchen? After that we can go to the store. Uncle Joe and Aunt Carol are coming over for dinner."

Ben pulled out his tin of crayons and set to work on a new masterpiece as Jessica returned to the shattered glass. It took her ten minutes to find the last of the shards and get the floor swept once more.

With her chores finished, and a new picture tacked to the wall, Jessica bundled Ben into his coat. They had a bit farther to walk this time, as Jessica now had to replace her broken glass. They were down to two glasses, and Joe and Carol were due for dinner.

Two blocks after the fabric shop, Ben's legs were tired and Jessica thrilled when he actually asked her to carry him. He used words instead of the hopping with arms stretched upward and whining. She hoisted him to her shoulders and whinnied.

"I'm Ben's horse now."

"Horsie!" Ben giggled.

Jessica was fairly tired when she finally set him down outside the department store. She had lost a lot of energy three blocks earlier, but wasn't about to set her boy down as he gleefully named trees and lamp posts and motorcars they passed. Nearly two years of silence had finally ended.

"Keykey, Keykey!" Ben exclaimed, hopping up and down as he pointed to the window.

It took her a moment to spot the stuffed monkey among the other toys in the store's Christmas display. Jessica tucked the idea away in her mind, though she had no idea how she could purchase the stuffed animal without Ben knowing about it. Nor could she figure out how to afford it on the little left over from her mending and washing money.

Despite all the toys in the window, Ben still clung to Jessica's hand as she gathered the few items she needed, including a new set of glasses for the evening's dinner.

Standing in line, Jessica racked her brain trying to figure out the name of the man ahead of her. He looked so familiar, and yet his name eluded her until he glanced around to see her.

"Jessica King? I hadn't realized you were back in the states. I mean after…," he said.

Suddenly the name popped into her brain, "Frank Strong. Yes, we were moving back here when the ship," she cast a glance down at Ben worriedly. "Afterwards, Me and little Ben here got a house in the Bennett neighborhood. How's um… Laura?"

"Laura developed cold feet and moved to Frisco. I never married. I'm sorry about Ben. He was a good man."

Jessica was searching for another nickel to pay for her things when Frank leaned over to drop a dollar on top of her meager pile of coins. He turned without a word and walked out the door. Jessica and Ben arrived home to find Joe and Carol sitting on their front steps. A short pine tree leaned against the house next to the door.

"Unca Joe!" Ben called as he ran toward them.

The couple cast a glance toward Jessica.

"He found his voice today," Jessica shrugged as she replied.

"Well, I found this tree just sitting here," Joe spoke up. "We should get it inside before it takes root here on the porch."

After dinner, they popped a big kettle of corn and Carol showed Ben how to thread the kernels onto the needle. Hours later, they had a garland wrapped around the tree and a few hand-colored paper ornaments dangling from the branches.

"Unca Joe? Help me write Santa Claus. I need a Keykey."

Joe cast a glance at Jessica, who nodded.

"Well, Santa sometimes has a hard time reading the letters, so why don't you draw him a picture instead?"

Ben fell asleep under the tree, still clutching the drawing of a monkey.

January 6th, 1914 – Bennett, America

"Hello pretty lady," came the man's voice.

Jessica looked over to find Frank Strong leaning against one of the lamp posts. For the first time since Christmas, she was out alone. She'd left Ben with Carol so that she could go pick up some shirts that needed mending.

"Frank, um… Hi."

"Would you care to join me for a coffee? There's a diner just around the corner."

"I…, I have an appointment to get to."

"Great! I'll tag along and we can go for coffee afterward."

Jessica was hesitant, but couldn't think of a reason he couldn't tag along to her appointment. She rounded the corner and found the address she was seeking: a non-descript door leading into a stairwell. At the third floor she paused at two doors.

"This one over here is the one you're looking for," Frank said as he moved past her to insert a key.

"I'm here to pick up some shirts. How did you…?"

"I know. Two buttons and a torn pocket. I've got the shirts right inside. Now, about that coffee."

A few hours later, Jessica started on her way home, thoughts swirling through her head. One cup of coffee had led to two and the counter girl just kept refilling it.

She stopped home just long enough to set the bag with Frank's shirts just inside the door, then headed across the street to Joe and Carol's home.

She gave Ben a hug and kissed his head as he sat on Joe's lap listening to another one of his stories. Jessica found Carol wringing out a dress in the laundry. She helped run the last two shirts through the wringer.

"Carol, can I talk with you?" Jessica asked.

"What's going on?"

"Someone approached me earlier today. Well, it really isn't the first time."

"Someone?" Carol asked with a raised eyebrow.

"His name's Frank Strong. He knew Ben from before we went over to Ireland."

"Does this someone want more than a friendship?" Carol asked.

"I'm all alone. I need the help. I think I will take him up on the offer. There's Ben, and the house, and I think I'm getting shorted on the coal. I just…"

"Jessie, no one is going to blame you," Carol said. "You have a young child at home."

"He invited us to lunch tomorrow."

"He cooks?" Carol asked.

"At the diner. I don't think his apartment even has an ice box in it. The cook at the diner knows him on sight."

Jessica spent an hour trying on her three dresses, until she settled for the green one with matching bonnet. It took her another hour to get Ben ready for the lunch.

It was Jessica's turn to startle him, as he was busy staring at his pocket watch.

"Hello," she said.

Frank fumbled with his watch, nearly dropping it, before sliding it into a pocket, "I'm glad you both could make it."

"You're sure you want Ben here with us?"

"Its important that he knows who his mother is with," Frank said.

The three of them sat down to an extended lunch, finished off with brownies for each of them. Jessica was thrilled that Ben and Frank got along so well.

As Frank told a story about his childhood, Jessica let her thoughts drift a bit. She imagined a scene of Frank building a tree house for Ben. It was one of the things her Ben had talked about doing for their son, until he got so sick.

She shook off the old memories and focused back on the present. The memories were precious, but they brought with them a sadness she tried hard to let go of.

She was skipping nearly as much as Ben as they made their way home after the lunch. They had parted with the promise of another lunch two days away. She could hardly wait.

Another lunch led to yet another and a walk down by the river. There was a trip through the park where the pond was still frozen enough to skate across.

Pretty soon, Jessica was planning a wedding. She never thought she would get married again after her husband, Ben, went down with the Titanic. She could never forget Ben, but this opened a whole new chapter for her life. She was overjoyed to find someone with whom she could share her life and who could help raise Ben.

She devoted all of her spare time to designing her wedding gown. There was no way she could afford to have someone else make it for her, so she sketched bits of the pattern on butcher paper. Bit by bit she sewed the whole thing herself. Seven revisions later, it was ready for her big day.

Her dress had batwing shaped sleeves with a fishtail train that was made from Chinese silk and gold thread brocade. The main bodice was cream wool cashmere edged with a gold thread. The neckline went high, with lace over the bodice.

Jessica spent three weeks putting the dress together and ended up purchasing a wide-brimmed hat topped with ostrich feathers.

Joe and Carol took Ben for the honeymoon, as Frank whisked her off to Atlanta. Spring was just starting to bloom there, and the warm southern charm made it a wonderful experience. By the third day of the trip, Jessica felt the emptiness of missing little Ben and called him. He spent twenty minutes telling her about the trouble Keykey kept getting into.

Knowing Ben was doing fine helped Jessica relax enough to enjoy the remainder of the trip with her new husband. They drove past mansions and dreamed of what it would be like to live in such splendor.

CHAPTER NINE

September 9th, 1912 – Winchester, England

Mr. Barlow slid the travel wardrobe down the stairs, one step at a time, while his wife stood at the bottom hugging her two grandchildren.

"You really should take the train back to America, Grand-mama. You can't trust them boats," David told her.

"I would, but they still haven't extended the rails that far, so I'll just have to swim part of the way if need be," she replied.

"Then you better sleep in the life boat. I read in the paper that's what they figured out. There weren't near enough boats to hold everybody."

"The Lusitania has been hopping back and forth to New York for nigh on a decade. I'm sure they have enough boats by now," Henry Barlow told his grandson, "Now, if you'll open the door so that I may get this out to the motorcar before your grandmother thinks of anything more to stick in here."

"I only put in four pints of Martha's currant preserves."

"And those books you found in the market," he added.

"Come along children. Help me load the basket for the picnic," Grand-mama Martha called from the kitchen.

Mary headed to the kitchen, dragging David along behind her by the collar of his shirt. Together they carried the large basket out to the motorcar and set it between the seats.

Bessie came out to the motorcar as everyone was finding their places. Martha sat in the front with the driver, leaving a place for Bessie in the rear.

"I…, I can't go," Bessie announced, closing the door on them. "I just can't look at a ship right now. Goodbye Mother. Goodbye Father. Have a…, I'll write. I promise."

"We love you, dear. I'm glad you've gotten over most of the pain. Your children here need you very much," her mother told Bessie.

Bessie handed three envelopes to her, "Post these when you reach New York."

"The orphanage again? I thought they wrote back that no children had been brought to them."

"This is another orphanage, and I'm sending a letter to the Senator William Smith that talked to all the survivors."

As the motorcar turned down the lane toward Southampton, Bessie sat down on the front steps. She buried her face in her knees and let the tears fall to the ground between her feet.

She had done it. She'd managed to hold the tears back until nobody could see them. An hour later, she kicked some dirt over the mud her tears had made and went inside the house.

"I hope they bring back George, Lizzie, and Paul with them," she muttered to herself.

December 20th, 1913 – Winchester, England

Bessie opened the front door to find Mr. Clark standing there with a medium-sized pine tree in his grasp. Suddenly, the season seemed very real to Bessie. She'd seen the decorated windows and heard some singing on her recent trips to Southampton, but this brought it all into focus.

She shook her head to clear it and told him, "Come in, Mr. Clark. I haven't seen you since you patched the barn roof."

"Good afternoon Ma'am. Where shall I put it?" He responded as he pulled the tree through the door.

Mary and David fairly ran down the stairs and moved furniture in the parlor so the tree could stand in front of the window. As soon as the screws were tightened on the base of it, they raced out to the barn in search of the box of decorations.

Mary dug down into the box and pulled out a knitted stocking with her name on it. Her excitement died when David pulled the second stocking out that read Father. They both stared at it for several minutes before David spoke.

"Mother can't see that. She'll throw out Christmas."

Together they pulled out all the stockings and buried them beneath the hay in the corner of the barn. David had an extra hard time letting go of the one for Lizzie. They folded the top back on the box of decorations and carried it into the house.

March 18th, 1914 – Winchester, England

Bessie finished out the letter, folding the bank note within the pages, before stuffing it into the envelope on the desk. She sealed the envelope and added it to the three others in her small bag hanging from the coat tree.

Bessie called up the stairs, "Mary. David. Lizzie. Hop to it. We need to make the post before noon to get these letters on the next ship."

She slipped the strap of the bag over her shoulder and hefted the large picnic basket sitting on the entry table. The wagon sat ready outside the door, with Junie already hitched for the trip into Southampton.

"Lizzie's not coming," David said as he and Mary came out of the house.

Bessie took a deep breath and held it for several seconds as she fought to hold the feelings down. At last, she opened her eyes and forced a half smile as she climbed into the driver's seat.

"The three of us will have a picnic in the square after I get these posted," Bessie told her children.

"Who you sending letters to this time?" Mary asked.

"Some of the same people I've posted to before. They never sent back any news. I've also hired an agent to close out our house there. Grand-mama needs us here, so it's about time that we settled in."

"Lizzie liked it here, too," David said. "It should make her happy."

Bessie ignored David's comment. During her good days she had tried to dissuade him from believing Lizzie was around, to which he insisted that he talked to her all the time. During other times, the mention of Lizzie brought her searching frantically for her lost family members. Today fell in the good times, but she decided to avoid any argument.

"I heard that the Godfreys got themselves another horse. I'm sure they'll let you have a ride on her if you ask. Junie's good for pulling the wagon, but really doesn't know what to do with a saddle," Bessie commented.

"We were going to ask if we could go riding it next week," Mary said.

June 5th, 1914 – Winchester, England

Bessie flung the rope upward and watched as it smacked into the beam, falling once more to land at her feet. Lately everything seemed so overwhelming, and now, not even the rope would cooperate with her. She picked up the loop and coiled the rope back into her hand for another try.

"There is an easier way to do that, if it's what you really want," came the voice behind her.

Bessie dropped the rope in mid-throw and tangled her feet in the remaining rope as she turned around. She spotted Stephen leaning against the post just inside the door as she fell to a sitting spot. For a lone brief moment she thought it was George, but George had Martha's red hair, while Stephen had Thomas' brown.

"What are you talking about?" she asked, trying to calm her nerves.

"You miss George. I get it, but do you really think this is fair to your children? You remember them? The ones sitting inside the house right this minute?"

"What do you care? You never really come around here much anyway. What are you trying to do, take more money from your mum?"

Stephen rolled his eyes, "You really have no idea what goes on, do you? Yeah, I messed up a few times, and your precious George was the favorite, but I knew what's going on when he never really did."

She stared at him a minute, formulating thoughts before asking, "How do you know what's going on?" Her eyes narrowed a bit, "And why are you here this time?"

Stephen slid down to sit, leaning against the post, "I've come to make a proposition. It's something I've thought about for almost two years now. I will marry you to help you out. This would simply be a business arrangement, not expecting anything from you. You and the children could stay here or come to Southampton with me. I'm a sailor, so I wouldn't be home much, but it would be a place for you."

Bessie untangled herself from the rope and walked over to sit on an upturned bucket, "Is this a way to get more money out of your mother?"

"You're right. There were a few times that I messed things up and they came to my rescue, but that's all changed now. How long do you think my father's savings could last after he couldn't work any longer? For the past several years the money has been going the other direction. It's been me keeping this place going."

"And now you think to take the final piece and have everything George had that you couldn't?"

"There was this girl I really fancied. She lived not too far away, but I couldn't bring myself to talk to her. She was the most beautiful girl around and my heart ached for her. George knew how I felt, so he went and talked to her. The next thing you know he's built a swing for her and painted it green. He did it to tease me and ended up falling for her."

"You were never around and when you were you merely tolerated me."

"How could I look at you? What could I have said that wouldn't have hurt both of your happinesses? I stayed away because I loved you both and couldn't bear to hurt either of you. Just think it over, please. I need to go talk with Mother. And best to coil the rope so no one will guess what almost happened."

Stephen walked back to the house, leaving Bessie to think over his words. She sat on the hay pondering those words and fidgeting with the end of the rope she still held. So many thoughts tumbled through her head that she couldn't focus on any single one.

"Stephen, You…!" she yelled, as she stood.

Shaking fingers pulled the knotted loop from the rope. She bunched it up and threw the rope to the side of the barn. Her children wouldn't find her dangling off a rafter, at least.

June 30th, 1914 – Southampton, England

Stephen answered the door when she knocked. It had taken asking directions twice before she stood before the moderate townhouse. The width barely fit two windows and the door, but it went up four more floors.

"I'm sorry, I didn't know which floor was yours," Bessie stammered.

"Come in, please," Stephen said, as he stood aside holding the door for her.

Bessie stepped into the parlor decorated in a simple manner, far different than the fluff Martha had in her home. The furniture looked comfortable, though with far less stuffing than her mother-in-law enjoyed.

"Stephen, I…," Bessie began, only to be interrupted by the ringing telephone across the room.

"Pardon me a moment to settle this call. I'll be quick," Stephen said.

He strode across the parlor and picked up the telephone receiver. As he listened for a moment, it became obvious that his mood changed. The smile slowly drooped to a frown.

"I hadn't looked at it yet. What does that have to do with you, Miro?... But I need you there… When are you leaving?... For how long?... I'll have it drawn up for tomorrow then. I'll see you then. Good day."

Stephen slowly set the receiver back in its cradle and drew in a deep breath. After the second breath, he brought half the smile back to his face and looked up to Bessie.

"Bad news?" she asked, hoping to delay her reason for being there.

Stephen nodded, "It seems somebody shot the Archduke in Austria."

"It sounds bad, but what does that have to do with you? Austria's halfway across the continent."

"Normally I'd think nothing of it, but Miro, I mean Miroslav, is Second Mate on Lizzie's Dream. He's Serbian, and I guess it was a Serbian that shot the Duke. He's expecting trouble to come of this and plans to head home."

"You're the Captain of the boat?" she asked.

"I guess you were expecting me to be a simple sailor, right? Actually, I hold interest in four boats. I don't think you came here to listen to my woes, though. Would you like a spot of tea? I don't have a housekeeper, so the biscuits are courtesy of the baker down the street."

Bessie sat on the edge of one of the chairs as Stephen brought out a small plate stacked high with biscuits. He brought her a cup and filled it, then remembered to slide a saucer under the little cup. At last, he sat with his own cup of tea that he drizzled some milk into.

"Stephen, I…, I don't know how to soften the words any. Your offer is very tempting, and last week I might have said yes, but deep down I know it wouldn't work. It would solve some problems, but bring on others that could very easily be worse. The town is full of gossip. Tongues would wag. I couldn't protect the children from that."

"Just how will you do it? I know George had money stashed away, but hardly enough to keep you going for much more."

"I'll hire on as a housekeeper somewhere."

"You're in the pink then. I seem to have just such an opening here."

"For the little girl who lived down the lane? I appreciate the generosity, but it simply wouldn't work. Thank you. I'll be fine now."

Bessie stood and walked over to the door. She waited while Stephen set his cup down and came to open it for her. As she stepped out, she turned to him once more.

"Thank you again, Stephen. You should visit your mother more often," Bessie said as she gave him a hug.

August 5th, 1914 – Winchester, England

"Mother, have you seen this?" David said as he paraded into the kitchen holding the daily newspaper high.

"Will you wait a minute or three? I need to finish this letter to the Mayor of New York City," Bessie replied as she scribed another line on the page.

"Great Britain declares war on the German Empire!" he exclaimed.

Bessie finished her writing, blowing softly on the drying ink. She set the letter aside and turned to her son.

"Now, what was that you said about the great German chocolate?"

"You weren't even listening. It says here that Great Britain declared war on the German Empire! We're supposed to go out and sink all their ships, just like…," David let the words trail off without finishing the sentence.

Bessie grabbed the newspaper from her son and scanned down the page rapidly. Her lips silently formed random words along the way.

"This is terrible. Stephen had mentioned some Duke in Austria getting shot. Russia is fighting Austria and Germany invaded France. Now even England jumped in to stop Germany in Belgium. How could one man drag half the world into a war?"

"If we were in America we wouldn't have to worry about no war," David said. "We should'a been with them."

Two weeks later, Stephen arrived at the door. He carried a duffle strapped over his shoulder and looked a little worried as he stepped into the parlor.

"Mother, Bess, I've decided to join up. I leave for London on the evening train, along with half my crews. They agreed to let the twenty of us into the same brigade, so I'll be shoulder to shoulder with the same blokes that I take fishing."

"This is so sudden!" Martha exclaimed.

"They need everyone they can get and I really don't have anything to tie me here," Stephen said as he cast a glance at Bessie.

"You best be putting that bottle down when they start shooting at you," his mother told him.

"I'll write as soon as I know where they will be sending us."

Martha insisted that he stay for one final dinner before catching the train. Over dinner, hardly anyone spoke after David told Stephen that he should'a taken his fishing boat out to sink the German Navy like the paper said was needed. Stephen gave one final hug to everyone, and again promised to write, as he headed out the door. He handed an envelope to his mother.

"Keep these safe. I won't need boats till I return."

Stephen's first letter home came on the same day the newspapers announced that Japan had entered the war. The letter told them how much he enjoyed that final dinner and missed his mother's cooking.

We lost William Tolman; seems the bloke had flat feet. They have us training at Heaton Park, now, and expect we should be done by spring. I guess I was expecting to rush over there and put a stop to this business by Christmas. Little David and Mary can split my pudding.

Stephen.

Bessie found herself watching the newspapers once more. Martha made a small stand to hold an electric candle for the window and then added five more electric candles for the ones lost on Titanic. She painted the stick of the big one blue for Stephen. This way they kept the candles burning without burning down the house.

That first Christmas was difficult, and felt empty without Stephen, even though he had missed most other Christmases when there wasn't a war. Bessie went back to saying a prayer over the candles and insisting that George would return soon.

Martha knitted Stephen a pair of mittens when his letter mentioned the cold, and then knitted another dozen for his pals. She filled the rest of the box with as many biscuits as she and the grandchildren could make.

"Grand-mama, what's a Zeppin?" David asked.

"Where did you see that word?" Mary asked.

"It's right here on the paper. Zeppins spotted over London. Turn out lights. Do we gotta turn out the candles?"

"Those are Zeppelins," Mary corrected him. "Big balloons that carry people. It says they're dropping bombs on people in London. I hope they don't come here."

Toward the end of January they received another of Stephen's letters.

Dearest Mother, Bess, and my niece and nephew,

We had heard rumors of it, but today they brought in a man that had lost an arm. He talked about how they stopped shooting for Christmas day. They even sang songs with the Germans.

I'd given up the bottle, you know that, but now I'm struggling once more. There's not much else to do when not marching in the mud. I'm sorry I haven't been as good a son as I should have been. I love you.

Stephen

The postman delivered Stephen's letter in May, along with the newspaper detailing how the R.M.S. Lusitania had been sunk by German submarines off the coast of Ireland.

This snapped Bessie out of her sullen demeanor long enough to write a letter to her parents. They had sailed on Lusitania when they went home.

Mother, and all,

We got word today that we will be marching out in three days. We are finally getting into the thick of things, and going to Bulougne-

sur-Mer. I think that's in France. I love you, and the guys are saying that they want more of the biscuits you make.

Stephen

His final letter came in August, two days after the man had shown up to tell Martha he had been killed. She ripped the envelope in half and then had to hold the torn pages together to read it. When she finished reading, Martha let the tears fall for several minutes before marching over to where Bessie sat in the parlor.

She thrust the letter in Bessie's lap, raised her chin, and spoke quietly but firmly.

"We haven't been very lucky lately, but we are Corbridges. We will pull through. Snap out of it. Stop looking for your dead lost children and focus on what you have here in front of you. Mary and David still need a mother!"

CHAPTER TEN

April 8th, 1919 - Southampton, England

Bessie pulled the iron off the stove and made another pass at smoothing the ribbon. Satisfied that the last of the creases were smooth, she tied the ribbon into an oversized bow around the bonnet. Next, she set about stringing a matching ribbon around the rim of a parasol.

Her own hat showed enough of its worn nature that Mrs. Peters insisted that she enter and leave by the rear of the shop when she came to work.

"I can't have my patrons seeing that thing walking out of my shop. It'd ruin what little business I have," she'd said.

Bessie had found work as a housekeeper, only to have the family's son return home crippled. He'd found himself a young French girl that came with him and she took over her job.

She worked for another family as the gardener until the stable boy ran the horses through the garden. Somehow she took the blame for it. Now, three times a week, she drove into Southampton to put hats together for Mrs. Peters.

The Model T had been a leftover from the hundreds the army had purchased and used. The end of the war meant they needed a new home and Bessie happily ignored the two holes in the door.

Bessie tied the last ribbon into the shape of a rose and pinned it to the side of the last hat in the stack. She took a moment to straighten the other hats on their stands before calling up the stairs.

"That's the last one. I'll be heading home now and I will see you tomorrow, Mrs. Peters."

An indistinct reply came, though Bessie couldn't catch the words. Bessie assured herself that if it had been important that Mrs. Peters would have hurried down the stairs to tell her about some urgent need.

Bessie shuffled through the stock room and closed the stock door behind her as she exited into the alleyway. It had taken her a week of practicing before she could start the motorcar without calling on David to help her.

She set the controls on the column and turned the key to magneto. Then, gripping the fender for leverage, she gave the handle a crank. The crank bucked, knocking her off her feet, but the motor sputtered to life.

Bessie dusted off her dress and climbed in to navigate her way back to the house in Winchester. To her surprise, both of the children were sitting on the front steps as she pulled the motorcar up to the house.

Mary held an envelope aloft, "Mother, you'll never guess!"

Bessie felt a burst of excitement mixed with a feeling of dread as she caught sight of the envelope. She had sent out scores of letters to everyone she could think of, and only a few had responded. Her last letter had been sent nearly a month previously. The only thought she held was that the letter had some news of her family.

"You're home early, David, is everything fine with the Norris' gardening?"

"I think he's running out of things to have me do around there. I had the hedge trimmed in two hours, then spent an hour setting up her tea table," he replied.

Bessie shut off the engine, and set the hand brake to prevent another instance of chasing the dead car down the lane, before she plucked the envelope from Mary's fingers. Both of the children hopped up and down awaiting the contents of the letter.

"It's from Grand-mama in America!" David blurted.

The paper gave way and Bessie pulled out the pages written in a style she didn't recognize. Her mother had been praised for her penmanship, but the letter looked to have been scrawled by a young child.

My dear Bessie,

I know that you'll likely receive this during your week of sadness, however I wanted to write this letter while my hand wasn't shaking as awful as it had been want to do lately. Your father was upset that he hadn't seen you in five years, though I reminded him it had been a tad longer than that since we had come home from the trip to England. Your father spent the day in bed for the first time in at least fifty years, but he managed to telephone the White Star offices and book a cabin for your trip. That's his way of saying that he'd like a visit from you.

Bessie's fingers clenched the pages as she quickly skimmed the rest of the letter. Her mother's handwriting and the little things in the letter frightened her nearly as much as the prospect of boarding a ship to sail across the Atlantic.

Her father would never have missed a day of work, aside from the infrequent holidays they enjoyed. Lawrence should have been the one to get such a letter, asking him to return home, but he was gone. Bessie knew she had no choice but to make the trip.

Bessie led the way inside with her children following close behind. She took a seat in the parlor, motioning them to sit as well. Even Martha came in from the kitchen to hear about the letter.

"They are asking me to come for a visit. I'll take Mary with me and we'll board the ship for New York in a week," Bessie told them.

"I still need to finish school. That'll take another month. Why does David stay here while you take me? I mean Gramps are nice, but maybe we could go after school is out?" Mary pleaded.

"Mary, you are not old enough to take care of yourself. Unless you stay with Martha and get a job somewhere, you have to come with me."

"David is not coming. I'm older than him. Why isn't David coming?"

"David has a job. He is working while I am gone to help support us. I'll have to leave Mrs. Peters, so that will be less money coming in."

Martha broke in, "How about you let her stay? I have heard of someone close that needs a housekeeper. They know Mary and would be grateful to have her. The Hansens down the road. She will be able to come home at night."

Bessie bit her lip to suppress the anxiety rising in her. She desperately wanted to never set foot on a ship again. She knew there was no choice; her parents needed her soon. Martha and the children also needed the money to support the family here.

"Why don't you go visit them tonight? That way we'll know if you're coming with me or staying here," Bessie told her.

"Supper will be ready in a couple hours, so try not to tarry overly long," Martha told her.

Mary walked down the road to large Tudor her Grand-mama had told her about. It sat back from the road behind large flower gardens. She spent a few minutes admiring the rose-covered trellis that let into the garden before making her way to the door.

Her knock was answered by a boy she recognized immediately. He was in the class ahead of her at school, and the object of many girls' dreams. She'd seen a few girls talk to him, but he always walked alone.

"Um…, hello Edward. I came for…, uh…, is your mother at home?" Mary stammered.

"Allow me to let her know that you're here. It's Mary, right? Mary Corbridge?"

Mary felt her tongue fumble with the words and settled for nodding. Edward trotted off toward the rear of the house, casting a glance behind him before disappearing into the hall. A few moments later, a tall woman entered the parlor. She paused to look Mary over from head to toe before speaking.

"Hello Mary, How may I assist you? My name is Catherine Hansen, though you doubtless already know whom you are calling on," she said.

"I uh…, my Grand-mama told me that you were looking for a housekeeper and I've come to ask for the position."

Mary caught sight of Edward peeking around the corner of the hall, watching him quickly duck out of view. She'd let her attention wander and missed the first part of what Mrs. Hansen spoke.

"… Wouldn't you agree? I'm sure that my standards might be somewhat different than your grandmother's. As such, I'll hire you on temporarily until I discover your abilities for myself."

"Sounds wonderful; when do I start?" Mary asked.

"I'll expect you at 9:00."

"Mrs. Hansen, Ma'am. I have schooling tomorrow, but I can stop by afterward."

"Very well. I mustn't interfere with your schooling. Arrive promptly after the release bell."

"Thank you for this chance. I won't let you down."

She caught sight of Edward, once again peering around the corner at her, before Mrs. Hansen opened the door to let Mary out. Mary alternated between walking and skipping as the thrill of being an adult with a job mingled with the trepidation of the responsibilities that encompassed.

By the time she had reached home, she had settled on being thrilled for the chance to prove herself and vowed to impress Mrs. Hansen. She also crossed her fingers that she'd get the chance to talk to Edward. She was doing good for being almost fifteen!

April 14th, 1919 – Winchester, England

Bessie opened her travel case on the bed. It had spent four months packed from her original trip, left sitting in the corner of her room, before Martha had chided her into unpacking it. Now here she was packing it once more.

She pulled the cloth divider aside and froze for a moment. Sitting in the bottom of her case was Keykey. The stuffed monkey brought memories and feelings flooding back faster than she could stop them. Her vision blurred as tears welled in her eyes.

"How I'm going to be missing you when you are gone," Martha said from the doorway.

Bessie wiped at her eyes, pulling the cloth back over Keykey, before turning to her mother-in-law. She had wallowed in the grief before and didn't want Martha to see her like this again. She still missed her children and George but couldn't let Martha see it overwhelming her again.

"I know, Mother, however…, I'm torn. My children need me here, but my parents need me as well. I need to be brave for my children. They'll be fine here with you."

"I know Bessie, I know."

"I arranged for a motorcar to fetch me in the morning."

That evening, Bessie pulled the children close to her after supper. She held onto them tightly as she whispered a prayer to keep them safe. At last, she let them loose and stood back to look at them intently.

"I know that you'll both be good for Grand-mama and work hard to keep the family supported while I'm gone."

"Mother, please, you're going to make me puke if you get teary-eyed again," David said. "I'll work so hard that Grand-mama won't even miss you."

"David!" Mary exclaimed as she slugged his shoulder.

"Mother knows what I mean. I won't be here in the morning as I need to be there for the new calf they're expecting. Little Dora already want's to name it Cow Norris. Who names a cow?"

"Everything is fine, Mary. I'm worried about leaving the both of you here while I go to America, but I know that you'll both be fine," Bessie told them.

When morning came, Bessie found a plate of pancakes sitting on the dining table, along with a note under a vase of tulips fresh from Martha's garden. Mary had already left for school, while David was dealing with the calf before classes.

Bessie scooped a bit of applesauce over the breakfast and enjoyed her last meal in England. She finished breakfast with barely time to lug the travel case down the stairs before the motorcar arrived. Ten minutes later she sat watching the hedges roll past her window.

Southampton seemed like any other day and Bessie felt almost disappointed that the town hadn't lined the docks to wave her off. Even the crew of the RMS Baltic seemed almost bored with the few passengers queuing up for boarding.

Most of the bigger passenger liners were still attached to the Royal Navy after being used to transport troops or serving as hospital ships. Nobody had wanted to sail across while the Germans were sinking every ship they could find. The war had ended, but people still remembered stories of RMS Carpathia and HMHS Britannic.

Bessie found her cabin and settled in right away. The porter brought her case a few moments later. She didn't even venture out when the ship's whistles sounded the dropping of the lines almost two hours later.

The sound brought back the memory of standing on the dock watching George pull away with Paul and Lizzie. The memory left her soaking the pillow with her tears. Eventually, the tears stopped though her eyes had puffed out.

Bessie kept her head down as she made her way to the restroom to splash cold water on her face, though she didn't run into anyone else on the way. When she was finally satisfied that her eyes wouldn't give her away, she made it down to the dining parlor for the afternoon tea.

After returning to her cabin, she sat staring at a painting on the wall until the thought crept up that she needed to unpack her clothes.

When she opened the case, she found a wooden whistle that George had carved a dozen years before. David had promptly grabbed it to carry around for a while, though he had lost it soon afterward. She hadn't seen it since their first trip across from America. Right under it was Keykey, holding a tulip that had been flattened from the press of clothes in the case. It was obvious that David and Mary had both stuffed things into her case to help her spirits. She almost burst into tears once more.

The second day out at sea, she stepped out to look across the water only to rush back inside as the sight threatened to break her hold over the fears she had pushed down.

Bessie spent most of the voyage wandering the passageways or sitting in the parlor. Most often, she sat alone at the meals as the ship carried only a fourth of its normal compliment of travelers. The few that talked with her invariably quickly reached the point of asking how she enjoyed the open ocean view. She left several of them shocked that she couldn't even look at the sea.

She ventured out on deck once more as the RMS Baltic nudged up to the pier in New York. As soon as the gangway dropped into place, she hurried down dragging the travel case behind her, not waiting for the porters.

With firm ground under her feet once more, Bessie began to relax as she walked up the pier to the few waiting taxis. Her hurried steps carried her ahead of the other passengers and she reached the first car to find the driver dozing in the seat. She set her case down and shook his arm.

"I need to reach the train depot, please."

"Which one ya need? Ya got the New York Central, Ya got the Delaware line, Ya got the Baltimore one, ya got…"

"I need the one that goes up the Hudson River toward Poughkeepsie," she told him.

The trip across town seemed longer than she remembered, but she soon she stood in the depot reading the departure time table. The Baltic had arrived in the morning so she needed to wait nearly an hour and a half until the next train northward. Bessie bided her time nibbling some biscuits the Americans labeled cookies and sipping a few cups of tea.

Soon enough, the train whisked her northward, the wheels clattering along the track in an almost hypnotizing fashion. As soon as her eyelids drooped the car would lurch sideways, jolting her awake once more. She felt almost as grateful to step off the train as she had been stepping off the gangway of RMS Baltic.

The ticket clerk helped her telephone the taxi company and soon she stepped from the motorcar to stand before a house she hadn't seen since Paul was an infant. She and George had preferred living closer to his work in New York City, where David and Lizzie were born. Her parents had visited them a few times at their city home, though they preferred the quiet countryside.

Bessie set the case down and pulled the bell cord, readying herself to hug her father when he came to open the door. She startled when a strange woman opened the door.

"Um, this is the Barlow home, isn't it?" Bessie asked, worried she had knocked on the wrong door.

"I'm guessing by that trunk you have sitting there that you're Bessie," the woman said.

"Yes, but who would you be?"

"Please come in. I know they're expecting you," the woman said as she stepped aside, holding the door open.

Bessie pulled her case through the door and settled it just inside the parlor. With another glance at the woman, she headed toward the kitchen where her mother usually spent half the day.

"They're on the back porch," she told Bessie.

Bessie went on through the kitchen to the screened porch where she found her parents sitting in rockers overlooking the garden.

Unlike their visit to England, they waited in their chairs as Bessie came to hug them both. Her father let out a soft gasp as she hugged him tightly.

"You're hurt?" she asked, stepping back to look at them.

Her father smiled at her, "Just a touch of the age settling in my bones."

"Unless I pulled a Rip Van Winkle, you're not even sixty five yet. This is still 1919, is it not?"

"Somebody forgot to tell my bones that story," he chuckled.

The laugh dropped into a hacking cough for a minute before it stopped. He folded his handkerchief to cover the spot he'd coughed into and stuffed it back in his breast pocket.

"How much are you paying her, Father? I know you have never liked having staff around," Bessie said. "You never mentioned her in the letters you sent each month."

"If you must know, I give her ten dollars a month. She comes over to bring us lunch and then back again for supper when she takes our laundry. It's been a blessing for your mother."

"Your letter said you weren't feeling well, but I never imagined you like this. When you summoned me home, Papa, I didn't expect to find a housekeeper. Why didn't you tell me you needed help? We could have come sooner."

"Where are the grandchildren?" her mother asked.

"David's had a job tending garden for nigh on a year now, and Mary just hired on as a housekeeper to help ends meet. It seemed better to let them stay there since I didn't know how bad things were here," Bessie told her.

"Tis a pity. I would love to tell them more stories about you growing up."

"Don't change the subject. Have you called the doctor on this?"

"It's just a bit of coughing and I'm somewhat tired. An old people disease sort of thing. Everyone catches it if they live long enough," Henry joked.

"I'm sorry I made it sound so dire in the letter," Elsie said. "I wasn't sure what it would take to get you on a boat to come visit."

"Luckily, the trip was uneventful and gave me plenty of time to think things over. I apologize that I haven't come to see you sooner, but after…, well, after everything…," Bessie said.

"Well, you made it safe and sound."

"I'll put my things in my old room, and then I'm calling the doctor," Bessie told them.

"I'll be alright. Nothing that a bit of rest won't cure," Henry told her.

Bessie watched over them as the coughing became worse in the few weeks following. Elsie withered to the point that she no longer came down the stairs, so Bessie took her meals up to her. She hardly even finished a bowl of soup most days.

A week later, Bessie was helping her father make trips between his bed and the toilet, though he refused her help for more than supporting him as he made the trip. He would close the door in her face to do the deed alone. Both her parents had become bed ridden and withered by the day.

Finally, Bessie could take it no more and picked up the telephone. It took a bit of talking with the operator to find the right doctor, but ten minutes later, Doctor Swenson agreed to be there within the hour.

The doctor arrived a few hours later with his bag of tools and medicines. He looked at both of her parents with a lot of mumbling as he did so. At last, he looked at Bessie.

"How long have they been coughing up blood?" he lifted the handkerchief from Henry's hand, showing how half of it was bright red.

"I thought it was only once in a while. He's lost a few of them, though now I see why."

"I'll take this back to my office to perform a test on it, but I'm completely convinced they are both suffering from Consumption. You need to be washing everything in boiling water. Wash your hands every time you touch them. Absolutely keep the children away from them."

"My children are in England."

"Even better. A whole ocean between them. This is deathly and very contagious," the doctor told Bessie.

Doctor Swenson left Bessie with a big bottle of pills and instructions for her to give them to both her parents and take some herself. The pills seemed to do little good for Henry and Elsie. Bessie watched them become mere shells within the week.

She believed the pills weren't doing any good, but the first time she coughed, Bessie became frightened and took extra pills herself. Her parents lasted only two weeks after the doctor visited. She called him once more the day before they passed, but he told her there was nothing more that he could do for them.

Bessie felt barely alive herself as she went about the task of burying her parents. She only let herself cry at night; during the day she focused on making all the arrangements so that she wouldn't have time to think about the loss. She even burned their bedding and clothes, fearful there might still be some trace of the disease that had claimed her parents.

She filled two travel cases with the family bible and every photograph she found. Everything else she turned over to an agent, along with the house.

When she could do no more, she called a taxi to take her back to the depot. Her world seemed to be shrinking and she feared losing the last of her family.

Once the train deposited her back in New York, Bessie rented a room. She spent three days visiting every orphanage and shelter she had written letters to, though none had any word of her lost Lizzie and Paul.

When she could find no place left to search, Bessie purchased another ticket to take her back to England. She felt an increasing anxiousness to be with the last of her family.

CHAPTER ELEVEN

June 24th, 1922 – Bennett, America

"Mother?" Ben asked.

"What is it, Sweetheart?"

"You adopted me, right?"

"Yes, you are adopted; you were an orphan from the Titanic sinking," Jessica told him. "I told you the story a hundred times."

"How old was I?"

"I believe you were three. We gave you a new birthday on the day I found you. We made April 15th be your birthday."

"Then you don't really know how old I am?"

"No, I really don't know how old you are, but it doesn't matter Ben. It doesn't matter how old you are. You are loved and I know your parents and relatives loved you. Now let's think of happy thoughts."

Ben walked away, shaking his head. Something wasn't right with that story, but he couldn't figure out what. He didn't feel like an orphan, at least he didn't think he did. Ben had no idea how to tell his mother that he thought there was more to the story that she wasn't telling him. Every time he brought it up she found a way to talk about something else.

"Some of the other boys call me a runt. They think I made it all up about being on the Titanic, just so I could get ahead in school."

"Why don't we go down to the Majestic this afternoon and see a moving picture? I saw where they had a new one called Oliver Twist."

The excitement of seeing a motion picture nudged away the doubts lurking in his thoughts. His mother could only take them once or twice in a year.

"Will Frank, I mean Papa, come with us?"

Jessica shook her head, "It'll just be the two of us and we can make it back home in time to fix his dinner. He won't be home until nearly 8:00, like normal."

"He could come if he didn't work for Mr. Scrooge," Ben said as he left the room.

"This isn't a Christmas book," she called after him.

Ben went into the back yard and picked up his well-worn baseball. He didn't bother with the mitt since there was nobody to throw the ball back to him. At the far side of the yard stood a stick board figure Frank had helped him make with an old box. Right next to it was a milk crate nailed to the fence at waist height; the strike zone.

Ben squinted at the crate and mimicked adjusting his non-existent cap. He spit off to the side, wound up, and threw the ball. It smacked inside the crate and bounced halfway back to where he stood.

"Strike one!" he called out.

Ben spent an hour playing in the backyard before his mother called him in. After a few dabs at his face with a wash cloth they walked the mile to the Majestic Theater. The marquee above the door proudly announced Oliver Twist and a handful of times it would be showing.

Next to the entrance they had pasted a poster showing a boy about Ben's age wearing somewhat ragged clothes, but a happy smile. There were only a few people in the line for the show. About ten minutes later, the usher escorted them to their seats near the front.

The moving picture show started to the sound of the pianist playing a lively song. She faltered halfway through the opening scene as the book fell from her stand and she scrambled to get it back and resume playing. Ben split his attention between her and the screen until the exciting part began.

It didn't take Ben long to notice a connection to the lead character. They were both orphans, though Ben enjoyed a much better life. For one thing, he didn't have to scrub floors for a bowl of gruel.

Oliver made the best of his situation, even though he kept getting tossed into awful spots. Ben watched as Oliver struggled through the hardships with barely a bowl of gruel and sometimes a place to lay. He quietly laughed at the thought of sleeping in a coffin when Oliver tried to be an undertaker, letting out a soft cheer when the young boy ran away from the hardships and abuse.

They walked most of the way home quietly as Ben thought about the moving picture. He tried to imagine himself in place of Oliver. At last the biggest of his questions bubbled forth.

"I didn't have a locket when you found me, did I?"

Jessica looked down into his bright eyes, feeling many more questions behind the first. She hadn't known what the moving picture was about until they watched it. His words connected enough that she understood why he wanted to know about a locket. After several steps, she finally replied to the question he'd asked.

"I'm afraid that when she handed you over the railing it was just you in your night clothes. I'm sorry. No locket leading to a rich father came with you."

"Well, I'm glad I'm not in England with those awful workhouses."

They stopped at the market on the way home and Jessica picked up a few things for their supper. Their conversation drifted away from the moving picture, into such things as baseball and racing cars.

Ben stopped in front of the sweets display as Jessica inspected some vegetables. He stood there trying to decide the best way to spend the nickel in his pocket while the merchant looked on. He could get a whole handful of the hard balls, but then there were the caramels.

"Mr. Harris? I think I'll get eight of the caramels."

"You know, if you get the whole nickel's worth it's three cards."

Ben pulled the coin from his pocket and laid it on the counter like he was letting go of a childhood treasure. The merchant piled enough caramels on the counter that Ben had to use both hands to pick them up. He was still trying to fit them into his pocket as Mr. Harris counted three cards from the roll and carefully cut between Lefty O'Doul and Wally Pipp.

Ben's heart skipped a beat as he took the strip of cards from Mr. Harris. Right in the middle of the strip was his all time favorite. Babe Ruth, looking as though he was going to launch another home run over the left field fence, smiling back at him from the card.

"Mom, I got two New Yorker's!"

"You spent that whole nickel? You know there won't be another one for almost two weeks."

"I know. Maybe I can trade Red Faber to Thomas."

"You know what? I'll buy that one from you for a penny, but you can't spend it on candy."

Ben thought for only a moment before handing over the card. He pocketed the penny and handed her a caramel from his bulging pocket, "Here, Mom."

Ben rattled on about baseball for most of the way home. He named players and talked about how they played. For the most part, the names all blurred together as Jessica listened to the excitement in his voice. It sent a thrill through her every time he called her mom. Slowly, the anxiety over his questions about being an orphan faded.

At home, Ben ran to his room to pin his new cards to the wall of his room. He had eight of the New York players now and a small stack of guys from other teams in his sock drawer. He used those cards to trade with Thomas and Marcell whenever they had a New York player. Marcell dreamed of getting a card for every single player.

Jessica pulled a cigar box from the top of her wardrobe and dropped the Red Faber card into it, on top of Frank Snyder and Eddie Collins. Her joy for the cards had nothing to do with the sport. They shared the box with a lock of hair from his first barbering, a rock he'd painted to look like her, and three teeth the tooth fairy had exchanged for nickels.

She sighed contentedly and returned the box to its spot before heading into the kitchen to fix the fried chicken dinner Frank had asked for that morning; one of her husband's favorites. Cooking wasn't her favorite thing to do, but she did her best to keep her boys happy.

Jessica's thoughts drifted off as she floured the various bits of chicken. It had been a decade since Elizabeth had handed the toddler over the railing, but sometimes it felt like just yesterday. In her mind she watched Elizabeth tumbling into the cold sea and heard the screams once more.

Her thoughts continued along this path, dredging up the empty, sick feeling she'd felt while searching Carpathia for her Ben, and the unjustified anger over his broken promise to catch up to her. Jessica slumped into a chair and buried her tears into flour covered hands.

She was still sitting like that when she heard Frank's key in the door. Jessica used the corner of her apron to dab at her eyes as she headed to meet him. Ben was one step behind her as the door opened and Frank stepped in.

Frank pulled her close for a kiss and all the dark memories eased away. Frank would never replace the Ben she had lost; she loved them both. Jessica relaxed in his arms, bringing good memories up to drive out the dark ones.

"Mom took me to see the moving picture Oliver! It's about an orphan just like me. It's about Oliver getting pushed around all over the place, but he has to do all sorts of hard stuff. I think I got it better than him," Ben blurted out in one breath.

"You sure do, son. You sure do. You have the best mom in the world," Frank responded as he kissed his wife again.

"Supper will be ready in a few minutes. I was just about to drop it in," Jessica told them. "Both of you go wash up."

"You've got a bit of it on your eyebrows," Frank chuckled.

Frank nudged Ben off to the bathroom where they both washed up for supper. The sound of sizzling chicken spurred on their appetites, and they were both seated before the last piece was ready for the table.

Frank offered grace and Ben silently mouthed the wish that he had his own locket with a picture of his first mother. Frank always got the first spoon of coleslaw, but there was still plenty by the time his mom passed the bowl to him. Ben ended up getting a drumstick. Those were his favorite pieces because they had a built-in handle.

As he finished the drumstick, he held forth his plate and exclaimed, "please Sir, I want some more."

Frank held the bowl of coleslaw, "Is that really the way to ask for this?"

"That's what got Oliver sold to the Undertaker," Jessica reminded him.

"You're not gonna sell me, are you?"

"Depends on how much they want to offer. Better eat the other drumstick so you aren't too skinny. Skinny kids are cheaper."

"I'm just glad I don't hafta scrub the floor and put wood in the stove for a bit of gruel. Chicken tastes better," Ben laughed.

"Mallard is delivering the coal tomorrow. Maybe you could practice shoveling it into the bin," Frank said.

"Maybe scrubbing floors ain't so bad," Ben said. "Hey, tomorrow's Sunday. Can we go watch them build the stadium?"

"They only started Yankee Stadium a month ago. There won't be much to look at yet. Maybe we can go down to the harbor and watch the ships come in. Have a picnic at the beach or something," Frank said.

The next morning, Jessica fixed sandwiches and packed the picnic basket while Ben and Frank gathered the swimming clothes, towels, and a blanket.

With everything packed into the Oldsmobile, they drove down to the harbor to watch the hustle and bustle of ships. The tugs kept in constant motion as they shoved the bigger ships into position. The freighters got shoved dockside over by the warehouses, where huge cranes waited to lift the cargo free.

Closer to downtown, the liners docked. Here, Ben could watch as people from all over the world came to visit his city. The whistles blew from a tug as it latched onto a line from the incoming ship.

"Hey, that ship's got a funny flag. That's not English, like most of them," Ben exclaimed.

Frank looked where Ben was pointing. Three tugs were pulling in a large liner. High up on the mast fluttered a striped flag with bold colors. He laughed lightly.

"Good eye. That one's French. You don't see many of those these days. Most of them were sunk during the Great War."

"I don't see what was so great about it. Kristie's dad came back missing half his arm. Joe's uncle never came back," Ben grumbled.

"Thankfully, I was only there a few weeks before they all shook hands and sent us all home," Frank said. "I barely had time to get trench mud on my boots."

They watched as the tugs shoved the ship up to the pier and the gangways were rolled up to it. Another loud whistle sounded as the ropes were tied off, holding the ship firmly in place.

Hundreds of people streamed down the ramps, and gathered in groups as the travel cases were brought ashore in big nets. A few of the later passengers simply carried their own bags, allowing them to have first pick of the taxis waiting at the end of the pier.

"Look, I can see the name on it. That says Paris. I guess that is France, right?" Ben asked.

"Right, with the blue, white, and red flag."

"I think I'll carve a ship like that. Or maybe Titanic," Ben exclaimed. "I just don't remember what it looked like."

"It was a bit bigger than this one. It had four smoke stacks on it," Jessica told him. "Everything on it gleamed."

"Was it American?" Ben asked.

"British. It was built by the White Star people. I go past their office on Broadway almost every day," Frank told him.

"What happened to all the American ships?"

"I think a lot of them were sunk in the war. Them German submarines shot up a bunch of ships," Frank said.

"Come along, you two. Let's head for the beach now. We can get some swimming time before lunch," Jessica told them.

The three of them piled back into the Oldsmobile and headed off to the beach. Frank drove around the bay, and past a Ferris wheel before they finally sighted the water once more.

He had to circle the Oldsmobile around once before he found a spot to park it. Luckily, the dressing tents were close by, and within minutes, all three of them were racing into the surf. Frank beat them to the water and scooped up some to splash them.

After about twenty minutes of splashing around in the waves they all decided on taking a break. Jessica spread out the blanket and brought the picnic basket from the car. Frank and Ben set to work piling up sand.

Soon they had a pile reaching up to Ben's waist. They began carving out walls and towers. Random shells they found became knights lining the walls. Ben found a stick and a bit of seaweed for a flag. A little crab was proclaimed king, though he soon scaled the walls to escape.

Frank placed one last shell on the wall as Jessica called them both to eat. They were all happily munching the sandwiches when the beach officer strolled by. After admonishing Frank to pull his sleeves back down to the elbows, he pulled out the measure tape to check Jessica's shorts. She had to tug them down a little so that it measured less than the six inches the law called for.

Satisfied that Jessica wasn't showing too much of her thigh, the officer continued his patrol. He didn't have far to go before measuring the next woman's suit. No amount of tugging could bring it closer to her knees. The patrolman finally escorted her off the sand.

By the time they finished the sandwiches, the tide had turned. Water crept up the beach, filling the moat around Castle Strong. They pulled the blanket further up the beach to keep it dry.

As the sun dipped closer to the skyline they called it a day. Frank loaded the picnic supplies back into the Oldsmobile, and the three of them headed home.

As soon as they arrived home, Ben ran up to his room. He pulled out a few sheets of paper and wrote a long letter to the White Star company. He asked all sorts of questions about ocean liners and particularly about Titanic. He especially asked for all the pictures they could send him.

Ben pulled out another sheet of paper. He folded and tucked it into the shape of an envelope. He stuffed the two pages of questions into the newly made envelope and folded the flap down.

He had difficulty sleeping that night and woke to the sound of Frank shuffling around in the lavatory before the sun was even risen. Ben pulled his makeshift letter from under his pillow and crept down the hall.

"Dad Frank?"

"Hmm? Aren't you supposed to still be sleeping? The coal won't get here for a few hours."

"You said you go by their office every day. Can you take this to the White Star People? I'll shovel a ton of coal. Ten tons of coal!"

"What is this?"

"I just want to know about Titanic. Don't tell mother, though. She gets upset when I talk about it."

Frank slipped the note into his vest pocket and patted Ben on the head, "I'll see what I can do with this. I'll also let her know that it'll be fine. She won't get mad."

"It's not mad. She gets real sad. I know, I'll have her show me how to make a cake for her," Ben said.

"You do that. I've got to run now. The bus will be leaving in twenty minutes, with or without me. That means running most of the way to the crossroads."

CHAPTER TWELVE

June 27th, 1922 – Winchester, England

David tied another yellow ribbon around the lowest branch of the apple tree overhanging the paved patio. One last tug and he climbed down to look over his work. Hundreds of ribbons dangled from the branches, casting a warm glow on the table below.

"I'm running out of room for these, Mother," he called over his shoulder.

"Then put some of the pink ones in the pear tree. You've hardly touched that one," Bessie told her son.

"I wish Grand-mama could be here for this," Mary said. "She liked family things."

"Don't start on the sad stuff. We all miss her doing everything she could to hold this family together. Don't make me start crying. Now hustle your bottom back in the house, young lady. This is your party, so no peeking," Bessie told her.

Mary hurried off to the house while her mother and brother finished the decorating. It took an act of will not to peek into the box that Mrs. Hansen had brought over that morning. It wasn't a secret; everyone knew it to be Mary's birthday cake. She just hadn't seen it yet.

Mary picked up her latest book and sat herself in the

parlor. She read a page or two before the distraction of wondering just what they were doing outside set her thoughts to drifting. The warbling of a bluebird outside the window jarred her thoughts back to the present and she found herself reading those same pages again.

A few hours later, Mary answered the door to find her best friend Rose standing there with Susan and Emily. They each held small wrapped gifts. Just as Mary started closing the door behind them, she caught sight of Edward walking down the lane. She slammed the door with a squeal.

"Edwards coming! What do I do?" Mary gasped.

"You might want to let him in," Rose laughed. "I saw him standing outside the chocolatiers just yesterday. You don't want to miss that."

The four girls hurried through the house and out the kitchen door. Bessie turned, ready to scold her daughter for peeking once more, but her expression softened upon seeing the other girls.

"David, can you go fetch whomever is at the front door?" Mary pleaded.

"Like I'm the dog?" David asked. "And why didn't you fetch them? You were obviously just there."

"Please?"

"Fine, but only because it's your birthday. Call it my gift to you. Now I can keep what I purchased."

"David!" Bessie scowled at him.

"I'm going. I'm going."

David returned shortly with Edward in tow. He performed a flamboyant bow, motioning Edward to a seat at the patio table. One by one he held the chairs for the girls. When he got to Mary's chair he jokingly pantomimed pulling the seat from under her. Mary sat with a thump as he shoved the chair forward instead of pulling it back.

Bessie brought the cake from the kitchen. Mary gasped when she saw the confectionary flowers adorning the sides. The top was bare, save for the seventeen candles burning there. Only two candles went out during the trip from the kitchen and David quickly relit them.

After the laughing, and the singing of the birthday song, Mary blew the candles out in two breaths. Bessie started cutting into the cake as David pulled a small package from behind a flower pot.

"I know I said I wasn't getting you nothing, but here," David said, extending the box out to Mary.

Inside she found a wide ribbon that ended in a tassel. Little flowers had been painted down the length of the ribbon.

"I kinda messed up on the lily, but, well, it's for your books," David told her.

"I like it," Mary told him as she pulled him in for a hug.

The other three girls presented her with handkerchiefs and trinkets. Each one rewarded with a hug. She turned toward Edward and her mother, wondering what they had been whispering about moments earlier. Edward pointed to Bessie before stepping back a pace.

Bessie pulled a ribbon adorned book from behind her back, and held it out, "I had to look quite a bit to find one you hadn't read, young lady. This is called Howards End, by a man named Forster."

Mary took the book and held it close, inhaling the scent of fresh paper.

"Edward, I'm sorry. I didn't mean to put you on the

spot about a gift. I'm just grateful that you could attend the party," Mary told him.

Edward chuckled as he pulled a small box from his jacket pocket, "I just thought you might want to open this one last."

The small gift rattled as Mary vigorously shook it. Something small and hard was within, but she couldn't think of what it might be. At last she pulled the paper loose and opened the box.

With a gasp, Mary dropped the box. Edward scrambled to catch the box, along with the ring that rolled toward a crack between the stones. Mary dove for the ring as well and ended up bumping heads with Edward. They sat side by side laughing for a moment, then Edward held the ring aloft.

"Mary, will you consent to be my bride? I'm sorry I couldn't ask your father for your hand," Edward said.

Bessie stumbled to a chair and sat with a thump. She buried her face in her hands and did her best to be quiet as the tears rolled down her cheeks.

"This ring looks familiar," Mary started.

"I got it from your mother. It belonged to your grandmother in America." Edward told her.

"Grandmother Elsie?" Mary gasped.

David had moved over to wrap an arm around his mother. The three girls circled around Mary, trying to get a look at the ring. She tentatively slid it onto her finger and wiggled it to catch the sparkle as the stone glinted back the sunlight. She looked up, hoping to see her mother's reaction, only to see David wrapping his arms around Bessie.

Mary looked at Edward. "She needs me."

He sighed and spoke up, "Come along, girls. I think

they need a few minutes."

Edward escorted the three girls around the corner of the house and down the lane. His thoughts drifted back to Mary as the girls bubbled over with their chatter. He had a brief moment of panic at the realization that Mary hadn't actually said yes to him.

Mary joined David in comforting their mother, who cried steadily for a few minutes. At last, she sniffed back the tears and hugged them both.

"I'm sorry I spoiled your party," she spoke softly.

"There's still the cake waiting," Mary said. "And you brought my ring back from America."

"You had best ring Edward to return for a bite of it. After all, his mother made it special. She knew what he was going to ask," Bessie told her.

"Please don't cry again, but I really do wish Father were here to walk me down the aisle. Everything will be fine."

Mary went into the house and telephoned the Hansens. She spent several minutes talking to Edward's mother before he walked in the door. She assured him that her mother was fine and insisted that he return for his share of the cake.

"And bring your mother along so that I may thank her for a most splendid cake."

September 3rd, 1922 - Winchester, England

Mary fidgeted as she stood on the upturned milk crate. Bessie pinned another fold in the dress and followed it with her needle. Every time she paused to look up at her daughter a smile crossed her face.

"I'm so nervous mother. What do I do?" Mary asked.

"You need to hold still while I get the last of the seams finished. We need to be at the chapel in two hours."

Mary's floor length dress had begun as her grand-mama's dress, complete with the hand-stitched lace for the bodice. Bessie stitched a few alterations in it to lend it a more modern look, while keeping the parts that Martha had spent years creating for when she wed Thomas.

Bessie crafted a whole new veil with ribbon and lace from the hat shop, giving Mary a flowered headband trailing the sheer lace over her flowing brown tresses.

"You look so beautiful. Your father would be proud. It seems like yesterday when you were born. Now you're going out on your own," Bessie told her.

"Are you going to be okay with this Mother? I mean, you had such a difficult time when Edward gave me the ring and you're the one what gave him the ring in the first place."

"I promise I'll try. I still have David to lean on. You just worry about what you need to do. This is your day after all," Bessie told her.

Bessie finished the last seam and helped Mary down off the crate. Her dress brushed the floor with a small train flowing behind her. Mary pirouetted once, watching her mother's smile grow as she turned.

"You'll just need to hold it up out of the mud till we get to the chapel. After that, just don't trip as you walk down the aisle," Bessie instructed.

David waited at the car and helped her step up without the slightest of sibling shenanigans. At the chapel, David stood beside her, standing in for his absent father.

He held his arm out to her to guide her down the aisle to where Edward stood. There was a moment of laughter as he led her all the way to Edward, instead of letting her walk the last two steps alone. David had become distracted watching Rose, who stood as one of Mary's bridesmaids. He blushed all the way to his seat beside his mother.

After the service, everyone headed back to the Hansen's home, to where Edward's mother had set up a reception for the couple.

Edward and Mary moved into the south wing of the house, giving them a measure of privacy from his mother. She had spent so long as the housekeeper that she was well aware of the routine.

Mary adopted a busy schedule. She prepared breakfast for Edward, as well as his mother, and cleaned up afterward. Shortly after Edward left for work, she would ride over to visit with her mother. Mid-afternoon, she returned to her new home and began the preparations for their evening meal.

Mary had practiced managing the household when her mother had fallen into such dark times. Luckily, her grand-mama had been there to guide her through some of the necessities. Mary worked diligently to put her hard-won lessons into practice pleasing her husband.

She spent hours working out a compromise between

her mother's recipe book, and the elder Mrs. Hansen's recipes. It amazed her that there could be so many ways to prepare the same meal. At last, she resolved to combine them with her own touches and label them as her recipes.

Even after several months of married life, Mary found herself still struggling to write her name with the Hansen surname. Several receipts had been signed with Mary C, followed by a scribble, Hansen. Even with the struggle to remember it, the sight of her name sent a thrill through her.

April 14th, 1923 - Winchester, England

Mary paled for a momen, and set her tea cup carefully on the saucer. She could feel her belly knotting up and willed it to last until she reached the sink. She stood slowly, bracing her hand on the chair to steady herself a moment.

"If you'll excuse me a moment, Mother."

"That's twice in an hour. Are you not feeling well? Shall I ring the doctor to come round?" Bessie asked.

"I've seen the doctor just last week. He tells me I'll likely feel a measure of this for the next several months. Perhaps seven months at most." Mary told her as she leaned over the sink.

"That long? Oh! You don't mean? How long have you known? Why didn't you tell your dear mother?" Bessie asked.

"I wanted to be certain before I told anyone. You're the second, besides Edward, to know. He's been quietly moving things in and out of the nursery. He plans to paint it next Saturday, unless they need him to pull another shift."

Mary rinsed her mouth out and returned to her seat. She cast a wistful eye at the plate of biscuits before convincing herself that nibbling on one would be fine.

"Mary, I remember when I was planning for you to arrive. Your father had already settled upon naming you Thomas. I had to remind him that you might very well be a girl. I told him that we would not be naming you Thomasina."

"It's still too early to even guess about mine. I'm hoping for a boy," Mary said.

"Not to worry. The little one won't need much

besides blankets and diapers for some time. We can start sewing things after he's born," Bessie told her.

"I just don't know whether to name him George or Edward," Mary said. "I'm thankful that I have you to help take care of the little things."

"It sounds to me like you have completely settled into your home. I half expected you to have some difficulty with living so close with Mrs. Hansen and what not," Bessie said.

"There've been a few rough patches, but we get along just fine. Edward keeps reminding her that I'm a Mrs. Hansen now as well. I'm still getting accustomed to the name. We're going to have to tell her about the nursery soon though."

"What about when he is working?"

"I've got books to read. Edward's father had stocked up a library hoping he would read more. I'm having trouble recalling it, but Father used to read to us, didn't he?" Mary asked.

"He could have. I don't remember, to tell you the truth."

"What do you remember about him, Mother? I think we should write his story down. I think it would be great for little George, or Edward, or Agatha to know something about father."

"Why do you want to bring up sadness? This is a time to be happy. You have a child arriving soon enough!" Bessie exclaimed.

"I am sure the times weren't all that bad. I can't recall a sad time with Father. I'm wanting to write all the good times down to help keep the sadness at bay."

"I came home and cried for an hour after your wedding. I was angry with George for not being there to give you away. He left me to do all the hard stuff. I know it isn't a fair thought, but I couldn't help it."

"That's it. I'll be over to write a page a day until you run out of stories to tell. I want to know everything about Father, and Grand-Mama, and Grandfather Henry, and Grandmother Elsie. I feel like I'm losing them."

"You're wearing her ring," Bessie said. "All right. I'll try to hold it together to tell you stories. You have to do the writing though."

September 10th, 1923 - Winchester, England

Mary glanced out the front window as she brushed the dust off the oddments lining the entry mantle. She caught sight of Rose walking up the lane, escorted by David. Even as she watched, Rose pulled her hand from David's as he reached to hold it. She saw the smile on Rose's face as the young woman skipped a step ahead of her brother. Mary felt the excitement of anticipated gossip. It had been nigh on two weeks since Rose had last stopped by for tea.

Mary tucked the feathered duster back in the broom closet and opened the door to greet her visitor. She wanted to run and greet them, however she feared unbalancing from her protruding belly. She settled for holding one hand on the door as they came nearer.

"Hello David, Rose," she said while giving them each a hug. "I must admit, I wasn't expecting you, David. Edward went fishing just a few hours ago."

"It's quite alright, Mary. I was just escorting Rose. Have you ever heard of a Kangaroo? It's one of them Australian animals. It's got this pocket that it shoves full of stuff. Gives it a big belly all the time. Hmm…, Miss Kangaroo has a nice ring to it."

"David!" Rose exclaimed.

"That's alright, Rose. That's one of his better ones," Mary giggled.

Rose took hold on Mary's arm, leading her down the steps. They were several strides down the lane before Rose said another word. She cast a glance back to where David stood watching them.

"Mary, do you mind me being somewhat bold?"

"Rose, we have known each other for years. I know that you like David, though sometimes I wonder about your sanity. You have my blessing, if that is what you're asking for."

"How could you have known?" Rose asked.

"I love you to pieces, but you are nearly as bad at keeping it hidden as David is," Mary told her friend.

"Really?"

"He's had a hard time taking care of too much. Whenever he gets nervous he comes up with jokes that only a six-year-old could laugh at."

Mary glanced back toward the house. David sat on the top step, idly carving a design in the railing post with his pocket knife.

"I was nervous to ask David, and even more nervous to ask you," Rose said.

"When is the date?" Mary asked.

"We haven't decided. Not till I do something about my dad. He's just now getting the hang of his crutches after losing his foot in the war."

"If I recall correctly, there's nigh but a thin wall between his room and yours. You'd have to go somewhere just to whisper with David."

"He already grumbles about us giggling too loudly. I don't know what he'd do if he heard kissing."

"You could always move in with our mother. She's got plenty of space in that big old house and she could use the company. That would put you close enough to visit your dad every day if you wanted," Mary said.

"Maybe we'll try for early summer next year. David's hoping to get on with the railway. It'd be steady work," Rose said.

"You tell him to be extra careful. I read where they lost a brakeman and a conductor not two weeks ago."

David stood to meet them as Mary and Rose walked back to the house. He slid the folding knife into his pocket and brushed the shavings away from the small rose that now adorned the railing.

"Well, what did she say?" David asked Rose.

"I told her that if he misbehaves then she can turn into another Australian animal; the Tasmanian Devil. I think they are about forty-nine percent temper, forty-nine percent teeth, and two percent cute and cuddly," Mary told him.

"Not to worry. She'll never have a reason to doubt me. We can get in one of the railway houses in a year."

"And mother's house has three empty rooms if you move out. You could have a nursery and a room for Rose's dolls if you stay there, plus Mother would enjoy the company. You know she needs you."

CHAPTER THIRTEEN

May 7th, 1931 - Bennett, America

Ben adjusted his tie in the mirror and licked his fingers to smooth out a stray curl that refused to stay put. At last he felt that he looked the best he could.

Times were tough, but he managed to hold three dollars aside for this night on the town. The coins jingled softly in his pocket as he strode down the hall toward the front door.

"Bye Mom. I'll be out late," Ben called.

"Not too late, Ben. That Griffin gang has been looking for trouble with anybody they think is Irish," Jessica replied from the kitchen. "And tell Kristie to come by for supper on Sunday."

"I'll be careful."

Ben walked the mile to Kristie's house, waving to a few of the neighbors he passed along the way. Mr. Fisher sat in the same spot on his porch that he had for more than a year; arms on his knees, holding up his chin, with his eyes staring off into nothing.

Ben called his name and waved, but the man who had worked next to his father merely glanced up and wiggled a hand without enthusiasm. He hadn't really even looked at Ben. Ben sighed as an unwanted memory surged up in his thoughts.

The twenty-fifth of October; the day Frank didn't come home. Mr. Fisher had been the one to stop at their house the next day to tell Jessica how Frank had stepped out the fourteenth floor window. Since then, Mr. Fisher usually retreated to his house when Ben walked by.

Ben looked away, trying to focus on some other thing to take his mind off the day that had been dubbed Black Thursday and how he could his mother pull their lives back together after the loss of Frank.

Ben rounded the corner onto Kristie's street. He tugged his tie once again and quickened his pace. He couldn't decide if he was more nervous or excited before he found himself standing on her doorstep. He took a deep breath and knocked on the door.

Kristie's father, James, answered the door. He stood in the door, glaring down at Ben as though trying to decide how best to be rid of him. Ben swallowed his nerves and smiled.

"Good afternoon, Sir. Is Kristie here?" Ben asked.

"And whom should I say is calling? I mean, if she is at home," James asked in a gruff voice.

"I'll be right down, Ben; Father please don't torment him," Kristie yelled down the stairs.

"Torment you? Do I torment you, Ben?" James asked in a much friendlier tone.

"You torment him mercilessly, my love," Kristie's mother, Sally, said as she walked into the parlor. "Why don't you come in Ben?"

Ben stepped inside, glancing up the stairs where he could hear Kristie moving around. He knew that staring up the stairs wouldn't make her arrive any sooner, so he shifted his focus to James.

"We'll stop at Victor's for a soda, then walk to Hampton Hall," Ben told him. "There's a five-piece band for the dance tonight. I expect we should return by nine."

Whatever James started to say was drowned out as two boys burst through the door shouting at each other. There was a bang and clatter as the one boy tossed a bat into the closet just inside the front door.

Their shouted discussion of baseball players continued as they stormed up the stairs with all of the subtlety of rampaging elephants. Each step echoed throughout the house, ending in the banging of a door that muffled their loud discussion. Ben smiled slightly, wondering how it would be to have siblings.

At last, Kristie descended the stairs. She wore a flowered yellow dress tied with a ribbon at the waist. The way her red hair framed her face made the whole outfit seem brighter. Ben felt his jaw dropping and clamped it shut again before he looked like a fool. Ben's jumbled thoughts worked to find the words.

"See? I told you that yellow dress would be just the thing tonight," Sally told her.

"You sure are pretty. You two have fun, and don't keep her out too late," James said.

Ben held out his hand for her, "I agree. You're more than pretty. Shall we go?"

Ben and Kristie walked arm in arm to the soda shop. Victor's always had a few people, and sometimes finding a seat seemed difficult. Tonight, there was a table just waiting for them by the window. They sat sipping soda through a long straw and staring at each other.

"I'm excited to go see my grandparents. They always spoil me rotten, since I'm the only girl grandchild. I get whatever I want," Kristie said.

"Well, you deserve the best, but what am I going to do without you around?" Ben said. "You leave in two days?"

"I'm pretty sure that you'll be doing what you normally do. Except for hanging around my house, of course," Kristie said.

"And you'll have a bunch of guys chasing after you without me to scare them away."

"I'll be back before you know it," She told him.

Just a block down the street from Victor's sat Hampton Hall. It was an old hotel that had been converted into a stage theater that now hosted events. Tonight, the marquee listed four bands that would be playing.

Ben pulled out a pair of dimes to hand through the window of the box office and led Kristie inside. The sounds of Dream a Little Dream flowed out over the couples moving about the dance floor. Ben led her straight out into the middle to dance with all the other couples.

Ben never felt happier than when he held Kristie in his arms. They twirled around the floor, laughing and talking the night away. They hardly even noticed as one band changed to another band.

The music kept everyone happy, though some of the songs were easier to dance to than others. Every few songs they would take a break to laugh over the punch bowl.

As they danced, occasionally Ben would get tapped on the shoulder as some guy cut in to dance with Kristie.

Ben would smile and reluctantly stand to the side waiting. As soon as that song would end, Kristie would make her way back to be with Ben once more. She never danced with the same guy twice and Ben spent his time on the sidelines watching her.

The moon stood high in the night sky by the time Kristie finally tired of the dancing. Ben collected Kristie's shawl from the check girl and wrapped his jacket around her shoulders.

They walked slowly back toward her house while Ben pointed out stars in the sky to keep the conversation going. He knew the names for some and invented names for the others.

At last, they stood at the bottom of the steps leading to her porch. Ben tugged her arm gently so that she turned to face him. He took a breath to steel his nerves then spoke up.

"Kristie, I was wondering if you would be my girl," he stammered. "I know you're going to be up at your grandparents for a while, but I'd feel a might bit better thinking you were coming back to me."

"Ben, I'd love to!"

Kristie stood on her toes to kiss his cheek, then handed him his jacket. Just as they reached the top step to her porch, the door opened.

"You know that it's nine-ten, young man?" James asked.

"Daddy!" Kristie exclaimed.

"It's just fine, Kristie. I'll be counting the days until your return. Have fun at your grandparents. Just not too much fun," Ben told her.

Ben walked home, still humming a few of the songs they had danced to. The streets seemed fairly empty, but he wasn't lonely. His thoughts lingered on Kristie's smile just before she turned to go inside.

September 11th, 1931 – Bennett, America

Ben glanced up from tightening the gate hinge, just in time to see the cab pass by. Kristie sat in the back seat, though she hadn't been looking his direction.

He gathered his tools and dropped them into the carrier. Ben ran around to the small shed at the back of the house and set the tool carrier on the shelf, dodging back outside before the door swung shut once more.

Ben washed his face and smoothed his hair down with just a touch of the hair cream. Satisfied he looked his best, he ran off down the hall calling out.

"Mother? Mother?!"

"What is it, Ben?" came her answer from the kitchen.

Ben found her in the kitchen kneading a loaf of bread. Flour coated the table and her apron. Jessica wiped her hands on the apron, leaving a few more pale streaks.

"I need to borrow the automobile," he blurted.

"I'm sorry dear. I need it to drive over to the Sears store. You can just walk or ride your bicycle over to Kristie's house. I mean she doesn't live all that far away," Jessica told him.

"How..., How did you know? You already knew she was returning today?" Ben asked.

"Well, you washed that smear off your cheek and your hair is combed for the first time in months. You didn't even do that when Uncle Joe and Aunt Carol invited you to go to church with them."

"Oh Mother, stop. I'm not that bad, am I?"

"It's true, Ben," Jessica said with a laugh. "But it's ok. You can wait till I get back, or you can walk on down.

She won't bite and she won't like you any less for not having an automobile."

Ben opted for walking so that he didn't end up smelling like a sweaty dock hand when he got to her house. It also gave him the chance to let all of his tumbling thoughts settle before he spoke. There were so many things he had thought of while she was away.

He was deep in his thought, composing just what he'd say to her when he saw Kristie, but he still managed to notice Griffin and a couple of his boys standing on the corner of Oak Street. Ben kept to the far side of the street, quickening his pace without looking as though he was hurrying.

He didn't have time to deal with them. He also wanted to make a good impression on Kristie's father, James. Showing up on his doorstep with a bruised eye and ruffled clothes would definitely give him the wrong idea. It wouldn't look good to Kristie either.

Ben pulled the memory from the last he'd seen of her, picturing the way the door light shone on her red hair and the mirthful glint in her green eyes. Kristie always looked on the bright side of things. It was her laugh that had first drawn him to her.

He was still rehearsing his words as he stood in front of the door. Ben took a deep breath and knocked. Only a moment later, the door opened to reveal the girl he'd been thinking of for three months, with her father standing right behind her.

"Um…, hello Kristie," he stammered.

"Hi Ben," she replied.

"Good afternoon, young man," James said.

"Kristie, can we go for a little walk? There's something I wanted to say."

"I can't let you steal her away when she just now returned home," James said. "Step inside, young man. We can discuss what you wanted to say around the dinner table."

"I wondered how long it would take you to show up," Kristie's mother called from the kitchen. "Grab the chair from beside the coat rack. Dinner will be ready in just a few minutes."

"Is there anything I can do?" Ben called back.

"I'll get the extra plate if you'll pour the water," Kristie said.

In a matter of minutes, the extra plate had been set out and Ben joined the family at the table. He helped himself to only one small piece of the chicken and potatoes. He knew they hadn't planned on an extra person. When James finished and set his napkin down, Ben gathered his courage and spoke up.

"Sir, may I speak with you in private?" Ben asked.

"If you have grievance with me, then I shall indulge you. If this involves the family, as I suspect, then speak up now."

Ben glanced at Kristie, "Very well, sir, I am quite fond of your daughter."

"I noticed something of the sort. Just what are you getting at? You wished to have your seat at the table beside her instead of across?" James asked teasingly.

"I…, I would like your permission to ask for your daughter's hand in marriage. There, I said it," Ben blurted.

"You certainly did. Just what is she going to do if you marry just her hand?"

"Dear!" Sally exclaimed. "He's trying to be serious."

"Very well, just how do you propose to support my daughter after you whisk her away from us? Where will you live? This is all assuming that she'll say yes."

"I've got my job stocking at Goodman's warehouse. We can live at my mother's house for now."

"Ben, why don't we go for a walk?" Kristie interjected.

Ben held her chair as Kristie stood, and they walked out the front door. They walked along in silence for more than a block before Kristie coughed lightly. They sat side by side on the bench near the newsstand.

Ben's thoughts swirled around in his head like a whirlwind. None of them stopped long enough for him to focus. He'd spent weeks planning what and how to say it, and now those plans lay scattered.

"Look, I'm sorry for bringing that up at dinner. Nobody tells us guys how to do it," Ben stammered.

"We picked all the peaches off three trees and canned them. I think I canned enough peaches and apples to last a year," Kristie said.

"I missed you while you were gone. I didn't know how much until you weren't here," Ben said.

"Perhaps I should tell you about the boy I met up there?"

"Boy?"

"His name is Duke. He's got deep brown eyes that sort of go to the bottom of your heart. Gorgeous reddish-brown hair and ears that flop when he tilts his head."

"What?"

"We walked around most days. I'd throw the stick and he'd bring it right back. He also liked to lick my hand." Kristie laughed.

"You tease me as bad as your father," Ben said.

"What can I say? It runs in the family."

Ben slid off the bench and knelt before her, taking her hand. With his other hand he pulled the small satchel bag from his pocket. He pressed it, lightly fingering the lump inside.

"Kristie, I have fallen in love with you. I want to spend the rest of my life with you as my wife," Ben said as he slid the ring out of the pouch. "Will you marry me?"

Kristie squealed with delight and with tears running down her face, "Yes. Yes I will!"

"It may not look like much, but I spent two months shaping this from an old silver spoon. When times get better, I'll put a real ring on your finger," Ben said.

Kristie looked at the ring as he slid it onto her finger. She saw no trace of the spoon he'd crafted it from, only a thin band that loosely circled her finger. Tiny hammer marks gave evidence of how he had shaped the metal.

"Maybe we can find a jeweler to shrink it down a little. I'm afraid I'll lose it," Kristie said.

"I had to guess at how big to make it."

"A wee bit of tape will hold it for now," she told him.

"We should go tell my mother," Ben said. "She doesn't know yet."

Ben helped her to her feet and they walked along toward Ben's house. Every few steps Kristie would hold up her hand to stare at the ring it held. Each time she did, Ben would blush.

They were still two blocks from his house when a figure stepped around the corner to block their path.

Ben knew him, though Connor Griffin usually had a pair of boys backing him up.

"Well if it ain't a couple of Micks out wandering in the good part of town. Lookin' for stuff to steal?" He sneered.

Connor stood a few inches taller than Ben and always pressed forward so that he loomed over his victims. Ben glanced around, trying to spot where Connor's back-up might be hiding, but couldn't see anyone else.

"Lay off, Griffin," Ben said.

"Ooh, getting brave in front of his Mick wench."

Ben didn't even try to consider other ways to deal with it. His one fist caught Connor in the mouth, turning his face for the second fist to crush his nose. The assailant fell to his knees and a knife went skittering into the gutter.

The two men scrambled for the knife, but Ben was faster. He came up holding Connor at bay with the blade. Griffin made a lunge, only to step back as the blade aimed for vital spots.

"Give it back you lousy Mick before I call my boys!"

"I'll gladly tell them how I took it away from you. You'd best find a clean shirt before you do. You're bleeding all over this one with proof of how weak you are."

"This ain't over Mick!" he yelled. "You steal our jobs. I won't let you get away with it!"

"You got drunk and punched your boss. Everyone's heard the story," Ben said. "Come on, Kristie. Let's get out of here."

They hurried on their way before any of Connor's buddies could come to the commotion. As soon as they were out of sight, Ben dropped the knife into a garbage can. Ben knew that Connor would find another knife before the night was out, but the last thing he needed was to get caught with a stolen knife.

Jessica wasn't home when they arrived. Three loaves of bread sat cooling on the kitchen counter. Ben sliced off a few pieces, giving one to Kristie. The butter melted as soon as it touched the fresh bread.

"Ben, I'm sorry. That wouldn't have happened if I weren't with you."

"Who knows? He might have left me alone, or he might not. It doesn't matter. I sure wasn't going to put up with him insulting my wife. Besides, I just might be a Mick at that. My hair's red enough for it," Ben said, trying to lighten the mood.

"Who's calling you a Mick?" Jessica asked as she entered. "Hello Kristie. Good to see you."

"It's nothing, Mom. Connor Griffin was just being a bit loud tonight."

"Ben stood up for me. Griffin was trying to insult me."

"Yes, I see his skinned knuckles, now that you mention it," Jessica said.

"Mom, that's not the news that's important. My hand is fine. It's Kristie's hand that needs attention," Ben said, trying to hold back a smile.

"What? You punched him too? Oh, a ring! When did this happen?"

"Earlier today. Ben asked my father and all," Kristie said as she held her hand out.

"How did you afford a ring?"

"It used to be a spoon. I talked old man Mooney into letting me do a little work with his forge. I just had to fix his bellows," Ben said.

"Tell me details. What have you planned?" Jessica asked.

"I'll have a spring wedding; maybe April. That will give me time to work on the dress. I'm sure we can get into the Park Street chapel, with Reverend Louis performing," Kristie said.

"When did you plan all that?" Ben asked.

"Right after you broke his nose. I wasn't about to let you go after you played such a valiant knight!"

"I just got as far as thinking that I'd have to work more hours and we could move in here. I mean, there's room for it."

CHAPTER FOURTEEN

January 11th, 1933 – Southampton, England

David winced as the fireman, Michael Harold, pulled the bandage tighter around his arm. David had been standing a bit too close when the boiler gauge on Number Ninety-Two broke loose. The water spraying from the broken tube flashed to steam as soon as it escaped, scalding his arm and face.

"That's about the best I can do for you, Mate. Best get home to your missus right away," Michael told him.

"We've still got to make it back to Southampton. Plus, I've got that run out to the coal yard in the morning," David said.

"You're gonna be strapped to a bed when Rose sees you like this."

"Grab my tool caddy and help me patch this thing back together," David replied. "There's a diaper full of biscuits Rose made in my lunch pail. They're yours if you don't tell her till I get back from the run."

Michael found the gauge in a shrubbery twenty minutes later and the two of them worked to get it mounted back in place. David had difficulty even holding the wrench. Every time he flexed his arm the pain would draw another wince from him.

"One look at you and Rose will tan both our hides, but at least I get those biscuits of hers. Makes it all worthwhile," Michael chuckled.

The fire in the firebox still glowed, though not hot enough to even make tea. Michael shoveled a few more scoops of coal from the tender as David nursed the flames up with a bellows. He used his good arm to prime the pump and refill the locomotive's boiler with water.

As soon as he had pumped enough water to build up some steam, the automated pump took over the task of satiating the iron beast's thirsty nature. Thankfully, there was plenty in the tank for them to make it back to the Southampton yard.

A switchman stood waiting as they pulled into the yard. He had already set the route for them. David slowed the train down to yard speed, which was about as fast as a man could run, and slid past two other freights ready to make a run to London. He brought Ninety-Two to a stop next to the waiting yard engineer.

David spotted the yardmaster coming down out of the switch tower and pulled on the steam dump for several seconds. The steam created an extra-large cloud that enveloped half the locomotive in the cold night air. David climbed down the other side, using the concealment to avoid harsh questions about his late arrival.

He turned Ninety-Two over to the waiting yard engineers and they unhitched the empty covered wagons at the west end. While they lined up a row of the ore tubs for him, David made his way to the blacksmith's shop.

Horses were one of the few things the blacksmiths didn't work on. Everything around the railway was made from iron and it took a lot of fire to shape the stubborn metal. They knew just how to deal with the burns that came with the fire.

He found William doing a minor mending job on one of the brake shoes. With William's help, they pulled the wrappings from his arm and smeared every bit of the burn with Carron oil. The stuff stank, but it helped draw out the pain enough that David could bend his arm once more.

"Now hold still. This'll sting a bit," William told him.

The blacksmith smeared more of the oil down the side of David's face and neck. There wasn't much they could do for a bandage over it without covering his eye, so they left it open to the air.

David made his way across the yard to where the hostlers and switchmen were coupling the last of the ore tubs to his locomotive. Michael had already refilled the beast's food and water bowl, as it were, and stood atop the tender munching one of the biscuits from David's lunch pail.

His arm still pained him, but he climbed back in the cab with barely a wince. The signalman stood by the switch a few hundred feet away, already swinging his lantern in the motion to proceed.

David glared at the gauge as he tapped it twice. The pressure showed good and the gauge remained attached. He pulled the throttle open a little, giving two short blasts on the whistle. Charles grabbed the handrail and pulled himself up to the cab as they passed by.

Charles plopped his bottom into the jump seat for the trip. He didn't have anything else to do until they reached the coal yards and the handful of switches there. David took the other jump seat between making adjustments of the dozen steam controls.

"What've ye got for livening up the run?" Charles asked.

"I left all my monies for Rose to go shopping and I had to bribe Michael with the only biscuits I had," David replied.

"Bribe him? For what?" Charles asked.

David pulled back his sleeve, showing the bandaging job William had done on him. The single shielded lantern and the glow from the firebox had kept his injuries fairly hidden from the switchman, but now he turned and pointed to the blistering skin on his cheek as well.

"Just so he wouldn't go calling Rose until I got this run done. I need the wages," he replied.

"So, no stakes for cards and it be two hours till we get to Bristol? I, myself brought along some of Nellie's tarts," Charles said, patting a pouch slung over his shoulder.

"I'll just owe you some biscuits if I lose. I'll make 'em myself if Rose won't. Deal me in," David said.

"Only if Rose makes 'em. You go hard on the salt. Nobody likes a salty biscuit," Michael said, pulling out a well-worn deck of cards.

By the time they reached the mine, David had garnered two of the dozen tarts and owed three biscuits to Michael. Charles climbed down to line the switches as David washed the last of the tarts down with tea from the brewing kettle.

David signaled the brakemen with his lantern and eased open the throttle. The mine seemed deserted compared to the bustle of the Southampton yards. David and his crew had to do all of the work to position the empty ore tubs, ensuring the brakes were set on every car and coupled up to the row of loaded ones. It was even up to them to top off the tender with fresh coal and water.

By the time they were set for the return trip the sun peeked over the tree tops. They waved to the morning shift of miners as the train ran through the Woolshead crossing. It was easy to distinguish the pale oncoming shift from those that looked as though they had swam through a tar pit as they headed home.

"I'm glad I don't have to work down in that hole," David remarked.

"Nah, ye' just prefer to boil your hide off," Michael joked with him.

"At least Rose won't slap me too hard when she sees this face." David winced as the smile pulled at his scalded cheek.

With the morning sun came people driving their motorcars back and forth at every crossing. The train crew didn't have time for cards. Every crossing had David pulling the whistle line. People still rushed to cross with mere inches to spare as the locomotive bore down on them. They made it back to the rail yard without adding any new scrapes to the plow.

This time there was no avoiding the yardmaster. He stood next to the rails as David pulled the line of ore tubs into the yard. David climbed down to meet him and his ever-present pocket watch.

"I heard about your adventure last night. I'll let it go that you were forty-seven minutes late pulling in. I need you on the breakfast run to London in twenty minutes."

"I've been going for nineteen hours now. I need to get home to the missus. She's due any day now. Besides, that's Earle's run, isn't it?"

"Not anymore. He dropped Seventy-Seven into the river last night, along with a dozen wagons. I've got Stuart off to tell his widow."

David ran to the yard office and rang home. He knew that Rose was waiting for him. She'd be frantic if he didn't let her know what was happening and why he was gone most of the day. Elaine picked up the handset on the third ring.

"Hi, hi, this is the house of Father and Mother and Elaine, that's me, and Edric," she exclaimed. "Who are you?"

"Most of the time I'm called father, but sometimes I'm called Honey Dear," he told his daughter.

"Only by Mother," Elaine said.

He heard the shuffle of the telephone momentarily being set on the desk. The muffled sound of bare feet scampering through the house accompanied the calls for mother.

"I'm guessing there's a reason you're not seated here for my buckwheat cakes? I even tossed on a few slices of bacon," Rose said.

"I know you are waiting for me, Pumpkin, but there was a bit of mess last night. I've got to make the run to London, but I should be home for supper."

"Don't be too late. I'll plop some tarts in the oven and the children will eat them all if you're not here in time."

"I'll tell you all about it when I get home. Hug them for me."

David set the handset back into the cradle and ran across the rail yard to where his train waited. At the head of the line sat one of the big road locomotives, easily twice the size of Ninety-Two. Little poppets hissed gently with the full head of steam built up in the boiler.

David had started at the bottom of the gang as a switchman seven years earlier and had thought it would be at least another three or four years before he could get a coveted long haul run. It was also sobering that the usual progression stemmed from unexpected openings. He would miss Earle, though he was thankful for the promotion as it were.

He spent a few minutes familiarizing himself with the bigger engine, then eased the throttle open a touch. A loud chuff and squealing wheels sounded as the locomotive gained traction. Clack, clack, clack, down the line the couplings tightened.

His tired mind poked him and he gave a quick tug to the whistle. This run had two brakemen. They sprang into action, leaping wagon to wagon, releasing the mechanical brakes. The squealing lessened as the brakes were freed.

David brought the train up to a brisk walking pace until the last of the wagons had cleared the yard, then he eased it up to running speed. With clear rails, he could easily outpace any motorcar.

He had to keep a vigilant watch for any cows that might have wandered onto the rails. As soon as he spied any of them, he would sound the whistle and apply the air brakes. As they passed, he would release the brakes and ease the throttle back up. He wouldn't need the brakemen and mechanical brakes until he pulled to a stop in London.

Fighting off the exhaustion seemed to be his biggest challenge. Every time he felt the yawn coming he stuck his head out through the window. The blast of crisp January air helped drive the sleep away.

Once in London yard, he kept himself busy shuffling his wagons for the ones heading back to Southampton. David met a few new faces in the switchmen and signalmen, as well as a yard boss that scowled at him. He earned a second scowl when David asked him to repeat what he'd said; his thick Scottish accent was difficult to understand.

They pulled back out of London by midafternoon and headed home. Most of his wagons were loaded, though a few were returning empty. The train of wagons was more than twice as long as the one he'd pulled from the coal mine. His firemen kept busy shoveling the coal to keep the machinery moving and the scenery flying by.

The closer they drew to Southampton, the less he felt the need for sleep. Rose would be waiting for him. His belly grumbled a bit with the thought of the buckwheat cakes he missed that morning.

It seemed to take forever for the brakemen to set the mechanical brakes as he pulled into the yard. He rushed off to the yard office as soon as the last one called finished. He dropped the manifest on the yard boss' desk and punched his card.

David came close to clipping fenders with a few motorcars on the way home, though he made it without a scratch. Forty hours without a rest was beginning to take a toll on him. Elaine and Edric rushed out to help him up the front steps.

"Where's your mother?" he asked them.

"What happened to your face?" Edric asked.

"Grand-mama is making supper cause mum is upstairs sleeping again." Elaine said.

"I'm not sleeping anymore. I heard you pull up. Oh my gosh! What happened to you?" Rose asked.

"I'll tell you all about it over supper. I'm famished," David said, giving his wife a kiss.

Inside, David found his mother setting a pot of stew on the table, with Jenny helping her. The smell of fresh baked rolls and stew set his belly to rumbling once more. His sister, Mary, opened a bottle of jam and set it next to the plate of butter.

He washed up as the children settled into chairs at the table. It took him a few minutes to clear the oil from his face, buried under a layer of soot from the locomotive. When he finished, he could see a few blisters on his cheek, but otherwise, it looked more painful than it felt. He ran a comb through his hair and joined the family at the table.

"It looks as though I'll have a bit of a chance at the London run," David announced. "It would mean a regular schedule and less hopping around."

"And what good is that going to do her with you out there burning your face off while your wife is home, laid up, and ready to burst with a child on the way?" Mary asked. "Little Eliza is ready to burst out of Rose any day now and I'm going to spoil her rotten."

"Mary!" Rose exclaimed.

"Well, what're sisters for? You weren't going to ask him."

David set his fork down and glared at his sister. After a moment, he sighed and looked around at the expectant faces. He gathered his thoughts and began telling them what had happened.

"The railway is still one of the best ways to earn the money this family needs, though it does have a bit of hazard to go with it. Sometimes things break," David said.

"You'll scare the children," Rose began.

"I was just adjusting the valves on the water feed when I felt it. Something shoved me back. Nobody was there, but I felt her hands shove me back. That's when the steam gauge blew off the tube. If I'd have been a step closer, like I was a moment earlier, the steam would've peeled off half my face."

"It hurts?" Edric asked.

"'Course it hurts!" Elaine told him.

"None to worry, Pumpkin, I'll be right as rain in a day or three."

David waved off a few other questions as they finished off the supper. He finished off a second bowl of the stew, and even a few of the rolls, before his hunger had been sated.

After supper the children were sent off to their room while the three adults retired to the parlor. Bessie remained in the kitchen finishing up with the dishes as they talked. Rose sat with a pillow behind her back to ease her discomfort. It was a trick the midwife had shown Mary, who shared the good idea.

"Mary, I want to thank you for helping Rose while I'm off working. I hope that Edward doesn't mind too much," David said.

"I don't mind. I mean, Rose has been my best friend since before she caught your eye," Mary replied. "Edward is fine as long as supper is on the table when it's time.

"Then could I ask a favor? Help me with my shirt. I didn't want the children to see this."

"Your shirt?" Rose asked.

With Mary's help, he managed to get the shirt pulled loose and the bandage taken off his arm. The oil had helped, but there were patches where the skin had split and begun to bleed. Bessie walked in at that moment and grabbed his arm to take him to the kitchen.

"My dear child! You're twenty-six years old. When are you going to grow up?" Bessie asked in a huff.

"It's really not that bad. It could've been a bunch worse if not for Lizzie!" David exclaimed.

Bessie stopped to stare at him as she held his arm under the water faucet. By now, the other two women had followed in from the parlor to see what was happening.

"I didn't want to say this at supper, but I heard Lizzie tell me to get back. I heard her plain as the sun, just as I felt her push me away. She was there in the cab watching over me. If not for her, I probably wouldn't be standing here now. I would've been cooked in a second if I was still standing where I was."

His mother let his arm drop and eased herself into a seat. All the colour seemed drained from her face with the mention of Lizzie. Rose started to tend to his arm, but Mary shooed her away.

David washed the rest of the carron oil from his arm himself. Mary helped Rose back up the stairs to her room, leaving mother and son alone in the kitchen.

"I know you don't like to talk about it, Mother, but I know Lizzie was there. She's in a good place. At peace."

David smeared a bit of the lard his mother kept in the kitchen on his arm and tied the washed bandage back around it. He gave his mother a hug before he headed upstairs to join Rose.

He sat on the edge of the bed, intending to talk with her some more, but the pent up exhaustion claimed him. He got as far as telling her he loved her before falling over onto the pillow.

An hour later, Rose called out as the first waves of pain hit. Mary came running and saw the drenched dress. Mary returned a few moments later with towels and a basin of water.

Mary helped Rose, knowing that the contractions were coming fast enough that the midwife would never make it in time. Twice she reached over to shake David, but he merely answered her with snores. He kept sleeping through all the noise Rose and Mary made.

David's third child came out a few hours later, while he still slept. Mary helped tie the cord and clean up the mess. Rose held onto her new daughter for a while, and then her eyelids began drooping as well.

"You name her Elizabeth and don't let him talk you out of it! I don't think he will, but you insist," Mary told her.

Mary took the little one into her arms and helped Rose lay back next to David. She sat in the rocker holding the bundled baby as Rose joined David in slumber.

CHAPTER FIFTEEN

November 17th, 1933 - Bennett, America

Jessica clutched the bag of groceries closer to her, trying to keep the chill wind from working its way through her tattered coat. She spent so much of her time mending and washing for others, she neglected to patch up her own coat. The late fall chill was doing all it could to remind her of this as she carried the fixings for the evening meal home.

She stepped into the street and looked up to see if she could catch a glimpse of Kristie in the upstairs window, forgetting to watch where her feet were going. Her foot found one of the deeper ruts and twisted under her.

She fell sideways into the path of the car just rounding the corner. Its fender caught her side, knocking her backward onto the sidewalk she had just stepped off. Part of her mind marveled at the way her groceries flew up out of the bag. The wrapped chicken even bounced to the opposite sidewalk before coming to a rest.

Jessica knocked a trash can aside and slammed into the light pole. She slid down till she sat on the curb, resting her back against the pole. Her shocked mind did little more than note the loaf of sourdough getting squished under the tire of a truck passing. With a gasp, she remembered to breathe.

Kristie set down her needlework and stood, stretching out the kinks of her overbalanced body. The weight of her belly left her feeling as though there was little she could do. She had exhausted the books in the house and begun the project of decorating a pair of towels.

Three days of pushing the needle through had left her fingers aching. Kristie stretched them as she walked over to look out the window. The gray clouds in the sky did little to lift her spirits, though she saw what looked like her mother-in-law walking along the sidewalk a half block away.

Kristie waddled over and had worked herself mostly down the stairs when she heard the squealing tires and screams. Panic gripped her and she hastened her steps. Her fears rose even higher as she spotted Jessica sitting on the opposite curb; her hair mussed terribly and a dark streak covering one eye.

"Somebody help her!" Kristie yelled, pointing across the street.

Kristie hurried to the street, feeling her child squirming inside her. She cast a glance both ways before stepping forth herself. She called for help once more as she reached the middle of the road, and still no answer. Several more steps brought her to Jessica.

"What happened?" Kristie asked, trying to keep the fear from her voice.

"I just need a minute to rest," Jessica coughed, a little blood trailing down her chin.

"I'm going to call a doctor," Kristie told her.

A spasm of pain shot through Kristie, nearly doubling her over. It felt as though a giant hand had squeezed her middle, forcing the breath from her.

"Help me up. I gotta make it home," Jessica begged her.

Kristie helped her to stand and pulled Jessica's arm around her shoulder. Kristie waited till there was a break in the cars moving along the street. She took a step, pulling Jessica along with her. Step by step they made it across the street.

"Kristie, tell Ben I love him. That I did everything I could to make him happy. He was my whole world."

"Don't be silly, Mom, he'll be home soon and you can tell him yourself," Kristie replied.

Joe came running across the street as they made it to the edge of the road. He took most of Jessica's weight onto his shoulders and guided her to the house.

Another wave of pain hit just as Kristie was helping Jessica through the front door. She nearly dropped the older woman as the spasm wracked her body.

"Kristie, don't leave me," Jessica barely whispered.

"I'm not going anywhere, Mom. I'll be right here."

Joe took over and mostly carried Jessica up the stairs to her room. He returned a moment later to lead Kristie to the sofa. He lifted her feet up so that she lay along the length of the short sofa.

"What happened to you two?" he asked.

"I think a car hit her, but I didn't see which one," Kristie told him.

"And you got hit in your condition?"

"I wasn't hit. I just went to help. Arghh…," Kristie said as the pain came one more. "I don't know. The pain. It's too early for..."

"They come when they will. You sit tight while I check on Jessica. You should be fine for at least an hour or two," Joe told her.

Joe stopped in the hall and picked up the telephone. He first called the doctor, telling the man to hurry over. A moment later, the operator connected him through to his own phone. He spoke quietly to his wife for a moment, then hung up before climbing the stairs.

"How is she? What do I need to get for her?" Kristie called out.

"You just rest for now. Carol will be here in a minute," Joe replied.

The front door banged as Carol entered. She hurried over to where Kristie struggled to stand once more. She helped her up and walked with her to the stairs. Two steps up, Kristie gripped the bannister as though her life depended upon it.

"What's wrong?" Carol asked.

"It's too early. The doctor said it wouldn't be for another three weeks." Kristie told her.

"Well, I think your little one has other ideas," Carol laughed.

Carol guided her up the rest of the way, insisting she lie down on her bed. Once Kristie was settled, she headed back to the other bedroom where Joe was watching over Jessica. She found him kneeling beside the bed with tears streaming down his face.

"Love?" Carol asked quietly.

He sniffled and looked up to her, "She's not going to make it. I told her to hold on until Ben got here, but I don't know if she will. What am I going to tell him?"

"Tell him it will be fine. She was a good woman. I know where she'll end up. He'll see her again," Carol said. "Give her a blessing. I'll go see what I can do for the living."

Carol stopped in the restroom to wash the tears from her own face before returning to Kristie. She wanted Kristie to focus on her baby, not on Jessica's fate. Carol filled a basin and grabbed a few towels as she headed back to the other room.

Kristie had sat up on the bed, so Carol eased her back down on the mattress. Together they got her dress bunched up out of the way so that Carol could help the baby when it decided to make its debut.

"Let's get you all ready. That baby seems to want to be coming awful soon. Everything feel okay?" Carol asked her.

"Between him kicking, and me feeling like I'm ready to puke my guts all over the floor, I guess it's okay."

"How much time between contractions?"

"I wasn't counting. Ungghh, here it comes again! I barely have time to breathe between them," Kristie gasped.

Carol pulled the rocker close to the bed so that she could hold Kristie's hand during each wave of pain that went through her. She longed to go into the next room where Joe was looking over Jessica, but knew there was little she could do there. Kristie needed her more.

"Hello?" came a man's voice from downstairs nearly an hour later. "It's Doctor Harris."

Carol descended the stairs to admit the doctor. She took him upstairs to the end room where Joe still sat watching over Jessica. He looked her over for a few minutes and even put his ear to her chest. He stood back up and clasped his bag closed.

"I'm afraid there's nothing I can do for her. She's gone the way of the angels," he told them.

"I heard her gasp for air not ten minutes ago," Joe said.

"That was likely her last breath on this earth."

"Can you take a look at Kristie while you're here?" Carol asked. "Just don't tell her about her mother-in-law. She's got it tough enough for now."

Doctor Harris followed Carol into the other room, looking Kristie over like he had Jessica. After asking a few questions, and being told all about how absolutely bad the contractions were, he just nodded along with them.

"I'd guess you have another three or four hours until they're about a minute apart. That's when your boy should be poking his little head out. He feels like he's pointed in the right direction, anyway."

"Three or four hours of this? Can't you make it go faster?" Kristie asked.

"Afraid not. At least until the little guy pops his head out. Then I have something to pull. Would you like me to come back then? I have to get to Mrs. Kugel. She was saying something about Nellie having spots."

"You can come back then, if you want. I should be able to handle it though," Carol told him.

"Alright. Just don't forget to call the wagon for your mother," he said.

"What's he mean by wagon?" Kristie asked. "She needs an ambulance?"

"Just focus on your child," Carol told her. "There's nothing you can do about anything else in your shape."

An hour later, Joe called Carol into the other room and they switched places. He left Carol to take care of

Jessica while he sat beside Kristie. Joe tried taking her mind off the pain by telling her stories of Ben's youth.

"… He pushed that little truck so fast that it went off the end of the walk and right into the street. 'Must have been a dozen cars that went right over the top of it without crushing it. His momma walked right out into the middle of the street, waving her scarf to scare them cars away, while he got it back. He never shoved it that way again."

Joe told her a dozen stories between the contractions. Some of them were ones that Kristie knew, but many had taken place before she had met him. Every time she started to laugh at one, another contraction would hit.

"Hello? Anyone home? Kristie? Mom?" came Ben's voice up the stairs.

"Come on up here, Son. We've been waiting for you," Joe called back down.

Ben entered the room just as Kristie moaned with the pain of pushing. Carol had returned and was helping guide the new arrival into the world.

"Kristie? Kristie are you alright?"

"Why don't you grab a couple more towels? Kristie went into labor and the baby is coming now," Joe told him.

"What? The baby is coming? The baby is here? Where is Mom? Shouldn't she be helping?"

Joe grasped Ben's shoulder as he turned down the hall, "Do what you can for Kristie. She needs you right now."

Ben glanced at the closed door at the end of the hall as he pulled the last towel from the cupboard. The thought that he should wake his mother up was interrupted by an anguished cry from his room. He rushed back to Kristie.

Carol was washing off the little form and turned to lay it in the towel Joe held. As he wrapped the towel around it, Carol went back to helping Kristie. Joe handed the baby to a befuddled Ben.

"Ben, meet your new daughter."

Ben held the baby close, studying her tiny face. For him, nothing else mattered at that moment. After a minute, he looked up to see Kristie laying there, exhausted and smiling. He kneeled to place the baby on her chest.

"I know you were set on calling the baby George, but that hardly fits now. Why not Jessica?" she said.

"You're right. George doesn't fit her. Maybe Carol. How about Carol Jessica?" Ben offered. "Mom should be here for this. Where is she?"

Ben stood and headed for the door. Joe gently placed a hand on Ben's chest to stop him. Ben could see the tears welling in the corner of Joe's eyes, turning to find Carol with tears streaming down her face. Even Kristie was crying, and it looked like more than joy for their daughter.

Ben looked from Kristie to Carol and Joe and then back at his wife. He was very confused, "What are you not telling me? What is going on?"

"Ben, there was an accident today. It's… Ben, I'm sorry. It was real bad. We did all we could for her and even the doctor couldn't do more," Joe started.

Ben pushed past Joe and ran to the closed door. He flung the door open, unsure just what he'd see. There on the bed lay Jessica. Carol had washed the dirt from her face and even dressed her in her favorite dress. It looked for all the world as though his mother had just decided to lie down for a nap.

Ben kneeled beside the bed and grasped Jessica's hand. He couldn't help but note that her hand felt as though she had been hours in the weather with the coolness of it. He held it up to his cheek, to the tears that had started in his own eyes.

Just at that moment, there was a knock on the door. The doctor had finally arrived. Joe ushered him in and up the stairs. The doctor spent a few minutes assuring himself that mother and daughter were doing well, before poking his head in to where Ben was.

"There was nothing I could do for her. She was already gone by the time I got here," he said. "The baby seems healthy, though a bit on the smallish side."

"It was supposed to be nearly a month before she had the baby," Ben replied.

"Ah, that explains a bit. I'll go home to get the papers ready. I just need names."

Joe left Ben to say his goodbyes and took the doctor downstairs. A few minutes later, the man left with names for both certificates. He promised to bring the documents back the following day.

Ben squeezed his mother's hand as he searched for the right words to tell her. Anger, depression, sorrow, and frustration swirled around inside his thoughts. For the most part he just let his tears run over their joined hands as he kneeled by her bedside.

"Why did this have to happen? I'd have gladly run any errand you wanted when I got home. Mom, I'm so sorry. So sorry I wasn't here when you needed me," Ben sniffled. "And I know there were things you never told me about my past. I guess I'll never find out now. You crossed that street a thousand times. Why now? Thank you for keeping me."

He heard the plaintive little cry from the next room and Kristie's soothing words. Ben closed the door behind him as he went back to his wife and new daughter. He stopped outside the door long enough to wipe most of the tears onto his sleeve, then stepped in.

"Daddy's here. Daddy's here," he said softly, lifting her from Kristie's arms.

"I'm so sorry about your mother," Kristie said.

"Get some rest now, my love. I've got her," Ben whispered to her.

Ben walked back and forth across the room, holding his daughter close. He hummed a few songs that came to mind, swaying back and forth as though the baby was in a rocker instead of her father's arms.

A few hours later the black wagon arrived and two men carried his mother out the front door. All the feelings he had shoved down while holding his daughter came right back up as he had to say his goodbyes once more. Thankfully they were done and gone in short order.

No sooner had they left than Carol came in the door with Joe right behind her. Between the two of them they brought a pot of soup and rolls. Kristie managed to make her way downstairs and the four of them ate in a quiet dining room. Carol Jessica slept through the first bit of dinner before letting out a wail. Kristie excused herself and treated her daughter to her own version of dinner.

After dinner, Joe and Carol walked across the street to their own house. Kristie sat down next to Ben on the sofa, leaning against him. Ben held the baby close, watching her sleep.

"She wanted you to know how much she loved you. That was all she could think about as we got her into the house. She just wanted to make you happy and do her best by you," Kristie told him.

"I know that… I know that. I loved her very much. I can't believe she's gone. I'm trying real hard not to be mad over the secrets she never had a chance to tell me. I just keep telling myself that she loved me."

"Please Ben."

"It's fine, my love. I'm mostly upset at myself. I hadn't asked her since I was a lot younger. Joe reminded me about how they believe we'll all end up together once more. Believe it or not, I felt some comfort in that."

August 4th, 1935 – Bennett, America

Carol Jessica leaned over her patchwork doll and adjusted the paper cape it wore. The circle of paper with crayon colored stars, her crown, slipped from her head to lay on the ground beside her.

A pair of crates rescued from the back alley and a Quaker Oats box, served as her castle. Her other doll, with the yellow yarn hair, sat atop the Quaker Oats tower waiting for the prince to ride in on his white horse and save her.

“Hi hi, C.J.”

Carol Jessica looked up and waved to her best friend as she walked up. Nichole didn’t sound very happy and she was almost frowning as she reached down to pluck the paper crown off the ground where C.J. had dropped it. With a half-hearted smile, she placed it on her own head.

“I thunk you couldn’t come out and play,” C.J. said.

“We gotta leave tomorrow,” Nichole told her.

Carol Jessica looked surprised, "Who I going to play with, if you leave?"

"I don't know," Nichole said.

"But my mother is having another baby," said C.J.

"Wow, a baby! But they always cry. Maybe you could come visit me," Nichole said.

"I am going to have a quiet baby," C.J. said.

“Help! Help! Come rescue me,” Nichole said as she danced the princess on top of the Oat box.

C.J. placed the prince on his folded newspaper horse, having him ride around the side of the crate castle, before he climbed the tower and rescued the princess. They were on their fourth rescue when Nichole’s mother shouted her name from two houses up the street. Carol Jessica gave her friend one last hug before Nichole ran home.

Tears were streaming down her face when C.J. ran into her own house. It took her a moment to find her mother folding laundry in the upstairs bedroom. Carol Jessica ran over and hugged her, pressing her tear-soaked face into the apron.

"What's wrong, Honey?" Kristie asked as she smoothed her girl's hair.

"Nichole is gone. I can't play with her no more."

"Oh, that is sad when friends leave. I am sure we can find out where they are moving to and maybe you can see her once in a while," Kristie said, as she hugged Carol Jessica.

"Mother, when is baby coming?"

"The doctor said he should be here in about two months. Yes, now go along and play so that I can get supper started. Daddy should be home pretty soon."

C.J. skipped out of the room and went into her own room. She picked up one of the wooden blocks and balanced it on her nose for a minute. She tossed it aside to trade it for the ragged stuffed monkey that her daddy had given her. It had only danced halfway across the toy box when she changed her mind.

"Mother? Do you know where my princess doll is?" she called out.

"Is it in your castle?" came her mother's reply.

"Oh yeah," Carol Jessica said, as she ran down to the backyard once more.

Kristie finished folding the laundry and hanging Ben's shirts in the wardrobe, before going down to the kitchen to start the supper.

Half the backyard had been turned into something of a garden. Kristie managed to find a head of cabbage that hadn't quite gone to seed and a few carrots. She even found the last of the onions, though it was somewhat nibbled by the bugs that claimed sovereignty in the patch.

Back in the kitchen, she set about slicing her finds into the soup pot. She knew Ben would grumble a little about having soup for the fourth day in a row, but there was little she could do to change it. She was just thankful for the garden stretching their budget as far as it had.

She looked up to the sound of knocking and saw Carol at the door. Carol stood there holding up two quart jars. Kristie motioned for her to come in as she scooped the last of the vegetables into the pot.

"I thought you might like these. It's the last of the peaches. I gave all the other bottles to the bishop for the storehouse. We can only take the essentials with us."

"Where are you going? When will you be back?" Kristie asked.

"I thought Joe had already told you and Ben. We have to be out of the house by the end of the week. The landlord wants to let his brother live there. Joe knows a guy in Provo. We thought he might help us find a place there. Hopefully, Joe can find a job and what not," Carol told her.

"I don't know what to say. Thank you for the peaches. We're going to miss you. Are you sure you have to move? This is going to be so hard on C.J. too."

Kristie put the pot on the stove to get the soup going and sat staring at the pot as she thought about things. She thought of every way she could gently break the news to Carol Jessica. Her little girl was losing her best friend, as well as Poppy and Grandma Carol at the same time.

Before any solution could come to mind, Ben walked in the front door and tossed his hat to the peg. Kristie hopped up, glancing at the soup in fear that it had cooked too long, but the water was just beginning to boil.

"Ben, you're home already. Is everything okay? He didn't fire you, did he?" she asked.

Ben kissed her and sighed, "No, he just let us off a little bit early. There just wasn't anything to do. He did fire Carlita and Tucker though. I'm doing what I can to make it where he needs me."

"Oh, thank heavens!"

"Soup? Smells good," he said.

"What do you think about putting Carol Jessica into the half room? She doesn't have all that much stuff to need a big bedroom anyhow. That would free up the second bedroom."

"And we need a second bedroom for the new baby?"

"Just a thought that flashed in my head. Joe and Carol are having to move by the end of the week. They're talking about going all the way out to Utah. I don't know how C.J. will take it, especially with Nichole moving away tomorrow as well," Kristie said.

"You're thinking they could move in here?" Ben sucked in a breath and thought a moment. "You know, they're supposed to be godparents for Carol Jessica and the baby that's on the way. We should go talk to them."

Ben put his hat back on and walked across the street. He couldn't help but think of all the times Joe had been there to help his mother out. Now he had the chance to return the favor a bit. When Joe answered the door, Ben could tell the hard times were weighing on the man.

"Joe, I'd like to ask a favor of you. I mean, I know you've helped us out more than I could ever repay, but just one more favor?" Ben said.

"Sure thing. Let me grab my hat. What is it you need?"

"No rush. I was wondering if you could help me move C.J. into the half room. That would open the second bedroom up so that I could have somebody stay there. I was hoping it would be the baby's godparents."

"Are you certain about this?" Joe asked.

Carol walked up next to Joe and put her arm around him, "I think He found a way to answer our prayers after all."

CHAPTER SIXTEEN

September 2nd, 1939 – Winchester, England

"Can you believe it?" Bessie said. "The Chancellor of Germany just marched his troops right into Poland. The next thing you know Chamberlain will be wanting to send men over there to kick him out."

"That's way over on the continent, Mother. I'm sure they will talk it all out and that will be the end of it," Rose said.

"Well, it says here that Chamberlain is threatening this Hitler to withdraw his troops or we'll force him to do it. It's almost the same thing they said before, only the names are different."

"Why don't we have our tea out in the garden? There's still a little bit of summer left. The children head back to school in a week," Rose offered.

Rose mixed up a batch of biscuits while Bessie heated the water for the tea. Elaine cut the bread for some cucumber sandwiches and little Elizabeth sampled the biscuits before they even made it into the oven.

With the preparations complete, the tea moved out to the garden table. Rose sat across from Bessie chatting about things of little import while the children ran off through the flowered paths.

"Mary told me how Edward just found himself a new job," Rose said. "He took on at a place called Supermarine, over in Woolston. He'll be fitting framework together on some new airplane they are building."

"It's good that he has something. Jobs seem to be difficult to find these days," Bessie replied. "But, I guess if Chamberlain gets us tangled up in this argument with Germany, all the boys will be running over there to get themselves shot up."

"Surely it won't be that bad," Rose remarked.

"That's what everyone said about the Great War. George's brother Stephen left off his fishing boats to go over there. They didn't even send pieces of him back."

"David was too young to go then. I don't know what I'll do if they call for him now," Rose said.

"You just hold onto the children and pray. It's what I had to do then," Bessie said.

"I never met him. Stephen, I mean. David said he never came round."

"He asked me to marry him once. I almost said yes. Things were somewhat dire after George… After George. I don't know why he hasn't come back. Doesn't he know how much I miss him?"

"Mother? Are you well?" asked Rose.

Bessie stared down into her half-full teacup, swirling it gently. She gave no indication of even hearing Rose's questions of concern. She had retreated back into herself once more, shutting out the world. She startled slightly when Elaine bumped her chair as she chased Edric across the patio.

"I love the sound of the children playing," Bessie remarked.

Edric climbed up into the apple tree overhanging the patio and tossed down a few of the ripened ones to Elaine. Just as he tossed the fourth one at his sister, a loud crack sounded behind him. The branch shuddered under him. Instinctively, he grabbed on tight as the branch cracked even further.

"David, get down from there now!" Bessie called up to him.

"I'm Edric," He shouted back. "David is…"

The last crack dropped the entire branch down through the lower ones, bouncing Edric off as it crashed to the stones below. Edric felt the pain shoot up his arm and pulled it close with his still good arm. He couldn't help but let out a yelp of pain.

Rose rushed over to her son and scooped him into her arms. She could plainly see where his arm bent at an odd angle, right where there was no joint. He bit his lip to keep another cry of pain from escaping as his arm jostled against his mother.

"Ooh, this looks bad," Rose said.

"You think he'll need stitches?" Elaine asked. "Grand-mama is teaching me knitting."

"Mother? Will you be so good as to watch Elaine and Lizzie? This is going to need a doctor," Rose said, as she lifted Edric into her arms.

"I can walk!" he shouted.

Rose set him back on his feet and guided him gently around the house to where their motorcar sat. She held the door open as Edric carefully sat himself in the seat. Rose ran around to the other side and put herself behind the steering wheel. She was just reaching to open her door once more when Elaine ran out with the keys for her to start the engine.

She started the motorcar, giving Elaine a kiss, before pulling away down the lane. Every little bump in the road jostled Edric, who did his best to keep from crying out from the pain. Rose drove as carefully as she could.

It wasn't long before she pulled in front of the doctor's home. She led Edric up to the door and gave him the most reassuring smile she could as she pulled the bell cord.

"I'm sure he'll have you fixed up right soon, my little climber."

The door soon opened with the doctor's housekeeper there to greet them. It took Rose two attempts to get out that Edric's arm was bent at an odd angle. The housekeeper simply led them inside to his office, where he had his nose buried in a thick book about blood ailments.

He looked up at them, "What seems to be the trouble Madam? Oh, Mrs. Corbridge. Come in."

"It's his arm. It's bent oddly."

"So it is," He replied.

The doctor had Edric sit on the edge of the table and looked his arm over carefully. He mumbled a few things, and even stuck a flat stick in Edric's mouth, before making his announcement.

"I do believe the boy has a fractured radius. Now, if you will be so kind as to stick out your tongue while closing your eyes, I will confirm this."

Just as Edric closed his eyes the doctor grasped his hand and placed his other on the boy's shoulder. He gave a sharp jerk, eliciting a cry of pain from Edric. The arm looked considerably straighter.

"Now hold it straight and don't move a muscle as I wrap it up."

"How long I gotta hold it?" Edric asked.

"I'd say about eight weeks. Give or take."

The doctor wrapped Edric's arm with soft linen, all the way from his fingers to near his shoulder. As soon as he was satisfied with the bandage, he mixed up a batch of plaster as though he were patching a wall. He dipped long strips of linen into the mixture and continued wrapping the arm. At last he stood back to admire the work.

"This thing is heavy. How'm I gonna' swim tomorrow?" Edric asked.

"Don't you dare even try swimming! You'll end up sinking like a stone." his mother admonished.

"If you get it wet, that cast will most assuredly break and then we'll have nothing left to do save chop off the arm," the doctor said with a bit of a grin.

Rose helped Edric get himself in the motorcar and started the drive back to the house. With the crisis averted, and Edric not crying out with every bump in the road, she had time to think about supper. She stopped at the market to purchase a few essentials.

*****

The man stood on the stoop waiting almost patiently for the door to open. His patience seemed to wear ever thinner with each tap of his fingers on the clipboard he grasped. The half-dozen sheets of paper it held fluttered in the light breeze.

At last the door opened. Bessie waited as the man straightened his stance, and brought his hand up in a salute. He glanced down at her a moment before dropping his hand once more.

"May I help you?" Bessie asked.

"Mrs. George Corbridge?"

"I am," She replied. "And you?..."

"My name is Mr. Wilmington. No relation, mind you. I represent the offices of the Refugee Children's Movement, in cooperation with the Central British Fund for German Jewry. Now, if you will be so kind as to sign here, here, here, and here, I'll be on my way."

"What are you talking about?" Bessie asked.

"I am here to deliver the children that you requested. Per your request dated, let me see... Ah, yes, November 27th 1938. Sign right here please Madam."

"They said someone would be around to determine eligibility. I've not heard anything more since then."

"Yes, I have just determined eligibility and present you with these children. Now, if you'll be so kind as to sign this paperwork, I'll be on my way."

The man motioned to the motorcar parked in front and three children stepped forth from the rear door of it. The oldest, a girl who looked all of twelve, gripped a case in one hand and her younger sister's arm with the other. A boy stood on her other side, gripping his own small case.

All three children looked frightened underneath their dirt smudges and tattered attire. They looked as though they had crawled halfway across Europe, through ditches and hedgerows, to be standing on her front stoop.

The ministry man climbed into the motorcar and pulled away before Bessie could ask any further questions. She had all but forgotten about sending the letter, and had envisioned receiving one, maybe two children, if she were selected.

Bessie took a deep breath and called to them, "Come along, children. We will keep you safe until your parents are able to retrieve you."

They stood at the foot of the steps, with the two youngest merely staring at the ground. The oldest looked up to Bessie, her face impassive, as she studied the woman holding the door open for her.

Finally, she nudged the two younger ones before her as she slowly climbed the stairs. She didn't look at Bessie as she passed, but mumbled something that might have been a thank you. The low voice and heavy accent rendered her words uncertain.

Bessie closed the door behind them as she followed them inside. The sounds of rattling dishes and teasing ended with a shriek. Lizzie ran into the parlor from the kitchen, closely followed by Elaine holding a large glass of water. Elaine's hair and face were still dripping. Both girls came to an abrupt stop as they saw the new children.

"Let me introduce you," Bessie said. "This is Elaine, and little Elizabeth."

The oldest one turned to Bessie, "I Abigail."

Abigail nudged her two siblings, but they remained silent. At last, she put her hand on the boy's head.

"Aaron. And she is Adalyn."

"My name is Mrs. Bessie Corbridge. This is my home," Bessie told them. "Elaine, will you be so kind as to aid me in preparing a room for our guests?"

"They're not taking my room, are they?" Elizabeth complained.

"The way I figure it, you can either sleep in the barn, or share a room with your brother," Bessie said. "And Elaine, you can set three more spots at the table."

The three hesitant children remained huddled in the parlor as Bessie took Lizzie upstairs to begin moving the girls into Edric's room. Abigail, Aaron, and Adalyn only moved a little as Elaine retrieved a chair from the telephone desk to add to the dining room table.

They looked visibly startled when the front door opened once more, and Edric walked in. His mother followed him in, commenting about the motorcar she'd seen pull away. She stopped as she spotted the new children. Edric simply walked past them and into the kitchen.

"Stop it. Supper will be ready in a minute," Elaine told him in the kitchen. "And why didn't they just chop off your arm?"

"Are you three staying for supper?" Rose asked the children.

"They will be remaining a mite longer than that," Bessie said, as she descended the stairs.

"Oh? Who are they?"

"I told you several months ago, about how I had inquired about the lost Jewish children, remember? They will be staying until their parents arrive to fetch them home. I'm guessing that won't be until all the arguing in Europe is done. They'll have the corner room and the rest of us will all squeeze up a bit."

"The rolls are finished," Elaine called out.

Abigail and her siblings remained standing together in the parlor as Edric and Lizzie ran to sit at the table. Rose promptly pointed them both toward the lavatory. They grumbled as they went off to wash up a bit.

Rose looked at the guests, "The table has room for you as well. Just set your cases over there and join us."

Abigail set her case next to the fluffy chair and spent a few minutes trying to talk the boy into setting his own case down as well. Finally, she yanked the case from his grip and slammed it down beside hers. Rose could see the glistening in his eyes as the tears threatened to leak out. The girl stood, taking both younger siblings by the hand and walked toward the table.

"Clean faces and hands at our table. Lizzie, show them where the lavatory is located," Rose told her daughter.

Lizzie groaned, and stomped off toward the lavatory once more. Abigail pulled the others along as she followed Lizzie. Abigail helped her siblings clean most of the smudges from their faces, and finally followed back to the table where everyone sat waiting.

"Hurry up! I'm starving," Edric said.

"David! I mean Edric. My word, but you remind me of your father sometimes. These are our guests!"

The three newcomers stood waiting at the side of the table until Rose pointed out the empty chairs, once again inviting them to sit. At last, they sat down and stared hungrily at the waiting food. None of them moved as Edric grabbed a roll for his plate and Elaine began spooning corn onto a plate for Lizzie.

As the three new children sat silently watching, the others scooped food onto their plates. The boy reached for one of the rolls and his big sister tapped his head. He pulled something from his pocket to fiddle with under the table and glared at his empty plate.

"Come, children, Help yourselves. If you wait too long then there may not be much remaining," Bessie told them.

Abigail reached out and placed a roll on each of their plates and then spooned a bit of the corn beside it. When Rose handed her the plate of chicken, Abigail hurriedly shoved it along without taking any for them.

"The chicken is really good. Try some," Rose offered.

Abigail looked down and shook her head. Tentatively, she took a bite of her roll. That seemed to be the signal for her siblings to start eating the food on their own plates. After a few questions from Rose, Abigail finally answered.

"Chicken buttered. Must not eat," she told Rose.

The rest of the meal seemed subdued as the family kept glancing at the new arrivals. The three of them slowly ate the meager amount that Abigail had served them. When the littlest one looked up at Abigail, Rose passed her the plate with two remaining rolls on it. She gave a nod as Abigail looked at her. The rolls vanished in a flash.

Finally, Abigail tapped her siblings and they bowed their heads. Abigail began reciting the words in Hebrew, as the others sat watching her. She spoke softly, though the words sounded loud in the quiet dining room.

"What kinda words are them?" Lizzie asked.

"Is Birkat Hamazon," she replied. "Words for a meal."

"Over here, people say Grace before the meal is eaten," Rose said.

The three newcomers remained at the table, even as Edric hopped up from his seat and ran up the stairs. Shortly afterward, Rose and Elaine began collecting the plates. Still, the new children remained seated. The boy fiddled with whatever he kept hidden in his hands.

"Go on now, take your things up the stairs. You'll have the room all the way to the right," Bessie told them.

Abigail led her younger siblings back into the parlor where they gathered their cases once more. They gripped them tightly, as though fearful that the cases would be stolen. She glanced back to Bessie, who motioned toward the stairway, and led the group upward.

"I don't know why she didn't like the chicken, Mother. I thought it tasted good." Elaine said.

"Perhaps they weren't very hungry," her mother replied.

Bessie went up the stairs and found the three children sitting outside the door to the room she had told them about. She glanced in and saw Lizzie sitting in the middle of the room playing with a doll.

"Lizzie, come on out. We talked about this," Bessie said.

"But Grand-mama, I like this room. I don't want to sleep with Edric and his stupid arm."

"We agreed that we needed to share our home. It will only be until their family comes for them, so no worries."

"I didn't agree to it."

Lizzie danced the doll around a bit more before she stood and left the room. Bessie motioned the other children to enter and pointed out the bedding on the floor.

"I'm afraid for now we only have the two beds. In the morning, I will get another one from the barn. We haven't needed this many beds since…," Bessie said, letting the sentence trail off. "The washroom is across the hall. If you need anything, just let me know."

Abigail pulled the others behind her and entered the room. They stood staring at Bessie while they clutched their cases close. Bessie left them to sort out the bedding on their own, pulling the door closed behind her.

In the morning, Edric came down the stairs first, complaining loudly about how Lizzie had drawn flowers all over his cast with her crayons. Rose set them down, and placed a large stack of hot cakes before them.

Edric forgot about the flowers, for the moment, as he struggled to eat with the cumbersome cast. He settled for eating the cakes straight from the plate until his mother scolded him for getting applesauce on his nose. As they were finishing, Rose sent Elaine upstairs to fetch the new guests.

Elaine walked straight into the bedroom to find the children sitting in the middle of the room, talking in some strange language. The boy rolled something from one hand to the other, and back again. Elaine grabbed it from his hands and ran down the stairs to show her mother.

"Mother, look what he had. This looks expensive," She called out.

Abigail ran down the stairs right behind Elaine and stood by as Elaine handed the object to her mother. Rose took it, fingering the chain and the finely crafted watch dangling from the end of it. Abigail stood by, looking terrified, as Aaron hid behind her.

"You're correct. This does look to be quite expensive. I'm sure that if you ask him nicely, he'll tell you where he found it. It looks every bit as fancy as the one your father carries to keep the locomotive on schedule."

Rose held the watch out toward the boy, who slowly reached out to take it. He looked fearful that the watch would be snatched from his grasp the instant he took it.

"Would you mind telling me about this? I am quite sure such a fine watch bears a story to go with it," Rose said.

"Es iz mayn!" the boy yelled, clutching the watch tightly.

"Why don't you tell me about it over a stack of hot buckwheat cakes with some applesauce on top?" Rose offered. "Though I mostly know English and French, with a little Latin for good measure."

Abigail, Aaron, and Adalyn settled into chairs at the table as Rose quickly fixed several more plates of the hot cakes. Lizzie ran off to play, while Edric still struggled with his cast that just wouldn't bend so his fork couldn't reach his mouth very well. Elaine sat back down to listen to the story.

"Our father owned best watchmaker in Hamburg shop," Abigail started. "I help in shop, so I learn German and some French and English. They know some German too, but not so much English. At first, things were happy. Papa make good for family with his clocks."

She fingered the small six-pointed star sewn to her dress, "Then we have to show pride for being our Jewish. German man come to tell Papa that we must move. We pack wagon and Papa take his tools. Mama left her good dishes behind.

We moved to place Papa called ghetto, where all were Jewish. We had two rooms and kitchen and other family come to share. We each family get a room. We still together and happy."

"The other family and Papa argue with soldier. Soldier hit him in head with gun. I saw, but Papa not know I saw. He got real afraid. Said we be very quiet. Papa used his tools to hide things in walls. Soldiers took everything they find.

They moved another family in with our room. I hear Papa and Mama talking with them at night when they think I sleeping. They talk about train and England. Papa cried when he found out only children go. Papa told me to trust his friend and all would be safe.

He made us drink milk so we be safe, telling us we wake up in England. He and Mama would come for us and we all go home to the big home over the shop. I made Aaron and Adalyn drink milk when they did not want. I was almost sleeping when he gave us to Zelieg. He pile smelly hay on us.

When I woke, we on train. We go for several days. When train stop we were at end by sea. I pay for ship with one of Mama's pearls. Papa stuffed all his money in my pocket, but it was gone when we got off train. Aaron keep the watch hidden, or they likely take that, too.

Papa say they will find us, but I know not how. We go wagon, and train, and ship, and motor, and several places. Now here, but not know where here is."

Abigail whispered something to little Adalyn, who ran off up the stairs. She returned in a few minutes carrying a photo that had once been framed. A crease down the middle told of how it had been hidden away while the children traveled.

With it, Abigail pointed out her father and mother holding the three children as they stood before a store. The lettering seemed to be German, though it became obvious what it was with the depiction of watches and clocks painted on the windows.

"Edric, fetch me a hammer and nail from the barn, if you please," Rose said.

Rose took the photograph up the stairs and in a few minutes had located one of similar size. She only needed a few minutes to swap the photo in the frame with the bent one the children had shown her. By then, Edric had returned with the hammer and Rose put a nail in the wall near the door. The frightened look on the children's faces brightened up a bit as she hung the photo of their parents on the wall.

CHAPTER SEVENTEEN

May 11th, 1940 – Winchester, England

David walked in the front door, dropping the daily newspaper on the secretary desk by the telephone. He shook his head as he once again read the headlines splashed across the front page. Germany wasn't waiting quietly any longer.

Two big headlines competed for the most important spot. Churchill had been sworn in as the new Prime minister and the Germans had pushed right on through Belgium into France itself. The Army was falling back as fast as it could.

Exhaustion won out over the headlines and David climbed the stairs as quietly as he could, in the pre-dawn hour. He spent several minutes scrubbing the soot from his face and arms, before crawling into bed beside Rose. As careful as he was, she stirred and kissed him as she climbed out of bed. He drifted off to the sound of her filling the tub in the washroom.

Rose and Bessie started preparing breakfast, following the rules they had learned about Jewish cooking. It required a bit of effort to change some of the age-old family recipes to keep everything kosher. David had grumbled a bit about the lack of bacon, but bacon was becoming scarcity as it were anyway. A good deal of the crops were being shipped across the channel to keep the boys fighting over there.

Elaine led the children down to the dining room, after ensuring they were all washed and dressed. They had become a tight knit group and Rose gave Edric a stern look as he and Aaron whispered their devious plans. Together, they found far more ways to stir up mischief than Edric managed on his own.

As seemed usual, Edric and Aaron raced through the meal. Both of them were done by the time Abigail was placing her second helping on her plate. The boys shoved their chairs back, ready to bolt for the back door.

Abigail called out to Aaron before he could reach the door, "Sfilus kumen ershter. es iz shbs."

He stopped and lowered his head. Aaron took a deep breath, then turned to walk up the stairs. He looked like someone walking to their execution, for all the excitement his face now held.

"Mom? What did she say? We were going out to the creek," Edric said.

"I remind him it is Sabbath. Prayers come first," Abigail said.

"Isn't it your turn to wash the dishes?" Rose asked.

"Why do I gotta work while they sit around mumbling that stuff?" Edric pleaded.

"Well, I suppose you could trade with Elaine, just this once," Rose said. "She needs to practice her stitches for a few hours."

"Ughh, I'll do the dishes," he replied. "Last time I stuck the needle through my favorite finger."

Abigail and Adalyn finished their meal and headed up the stairs to join Aaron. One of the few things the children had brought with them had been a tiny book of scriptures. The book was no bigger than Abigail's hand and filled with the symbols only the three of them could read.

They sat in a circle, in the middle of their room, as Abigail read to them from the book. The clock struck ten in the morning before they returned back down the stairs. Edric had long since finished the dishes. Aaron found him colouring pictures with the crayons.

Soon enough, the two of them went out to the barn to find more nails. David had brought home some of the cribbing used on the rail wagons and the two boys had been turning the wood into a tree fortress.

For now, it was little more than a small platform nestled in the branches of the apple tree, but it already bore a sign prohibiting girls in three languages. Edric nailed his board to the trunk as the beginnings of their fort's first wall.

Three boards later, Abigail called them down out of the tree and scolded Aaron for working on their holy day. Edric finished his board before climbing down the wooden ladder to join Aaron for more colouring pages.

After Elaine finished her stiches, and pulled half of them back out to redo them, she joined Abigail to read stories to Adalyn. Elaine helped Abigail read the words from books in the library. Abigail then translated the words into Yiddish for young Adalyn.

The end of the day saw the children lighting candles for the parents still missing in Germany. Bessie had helped them revive this tradition in the hopes that it would keep the children from undue worry. Elaine always lit one for her father when he was out on the train, and he blew it out as soon as he came in the door.

The following day seemed like the same thing, only in reverse. After their breakfast, Rose gathered her children into the parlor, where they sat around while Rose read to them from the Bible.

There had been a bit of grumbling about it at first, but Rose had seen how dedicated Abigail seemed to be. Reading to her family weekly gave everyone a bit of stability in a world that seemed destined to tear itself apart.

Bessie turned the radio on for Monday, when the papers had said their new Prime Minister would be accepting his appointment. Everyone gathered around to listen as the preliminary announcements came through. At last the announcer shifted the broadcast over to hear his speech.

"I hope that any of my friends and colleagues, or former colleagues, who are affected by the political reconstruction, will make allowance for any lack of ceremony with which it has been necessary to act. I would say to the House, as I said to those who have joined this government: I have nothing to offer, but blood, toil, tears, and sweat."

There seemed to be no one talking for a minute or so as the radio carried the sound of feet shuffling, and soft murmurs. At last, the announcer came back on the air with his own comments.

"Folks, I do believe that is one of the shortest acceptance speeches I've heard for some time. We have a new Prime Minister. Let's pray that he can lead us through this mess in short order."

As the days wore on, the news from the continent grew ever more dire. The whole family huddled around the radio in the evenings. British troops were getting pushed back across France almost as fast as they could move. Town after town fell to the German forces.

In two weeks' time, several hundred thousand British troops huddled around the port of Dunkirk as a handful of boats pulled them back across the channel. Many of the troops carried only the barest of equipment, with more than half having left rifles behind as they withdrew.

Bessie had just finished listening to the radio talking about the urgent need to bring the men safely home when a knock sounded on the door. She opened the door to find a man standing there fidgeting with his hat.

"A good day to you Ma'am. I is the Captain on Lizzie's Dream. Me and the boys want to go help get the blokes back over the channel."

"You mean the soldiers camped on the beach?" she asked. "By all means. Go and get them. But why do you ask me?"

"If you'd be so kind as to sign this paper I got. They needs the owner's say so writ down on account of the Germans trying to shoot up any boat what comes across."

"But Stephen died in the last war."

"He signed the four boats to a Mrs. Bessie Corbridge before he shipped off. Near as I know, that be you."

Bessie held the door for him to enter and took the paper from his hand. A quick glance at it showed the government seal at the top of the page. He stood waiting while she signed the paper and held it out for him. She held it tight as he reached for it.

"We will have a right good chat about this when you return. I heard not a peep about those boats of

Stephen's for twenty years. There'll be some settling to take care of. For now, go bring those boys home safe!"

"Aye Ma'am. I understands ye. Soon as the boys be back in Dover, I will."

As Bessie held the door for the Captain's departure, she noticed a car parked somewhat down the lane toward the road. Three other men stood around it, obviously waiting for the Captain's return. Bessie caught his elbow for a moment.

"What are the others called?" she asked. "The other boats."

"There be Lizzie's Dream, Paul's Seamonkey, David's Right Hook, and Mary's Joy. We'll get those boys back home and then I'll take you to see them. They all be in good and seaworthy shape. Shipshape, if you will."

September 24th, 1940 - Winchester, England

Mary finished setting the plates on the table for supper and reached for the glasses. Edward would be leaving the plant in a half hour and she wanted to have the meal ready when he arrived home. He had been working hard, lately, to finish a new project and Mary wanted to have a nice supper ready for him.

She looked upwards when the sound of aircraft engines roared over the house. She'd become accustomed to hearing them a few times a day, but usually around noon; here it was well after four in the evening.

She stopped for a minute as the sound intensified. It sounded deeper and there had to be dozens of planes buzzing around like an angry hornets' nest. This wasn't the one or two aircraft they daily tested at the plant before sending them out. Suddenly, a new noise joined the buzzing.

Distant thuds and whumps puzzled her for a moment, until the tableware rattled. She dropped the glass she held and rushed outside. Smoke was rising from the direction of Southampton and dozens of aircraft were in the sky over it. These were much larger than the ones Edward helped build.

"I thought they were only supposed to come at night. Edward is still there," she said worriedly.

Jenny joined her in the lane, "What's happening, Mum?"

"Get down deep in the larder and stay put and mind the glass bottles. I've got to go see about your father," Mary told her.

"Is he hurt?"

"Just hurry, Jen! I won't be long!" Mary shouted.

Mary pulled her bicycle from the carriage shed and peddled over to Grand-mama's house. She hopped off the bicycle, letting it fall against the stair railing as she bolted to the door. Mary knocked, then walked in to find Rose reading to the children in the parlor.

"Is David home?" she asked between gasping for breath.

Rose set the book down and helped Mary to a seat, "He should be back in a few hours. What's the trouble?"

"They've bombed Southampton," she gasped. "I saw the planes and the smoke. Edward is there! I've got to get to him!"

As she said this, they could hear more of the soft whumps in the silent room. The distant drone of the airplanes, and the soft thuds, as the bombs found something to erase from the face of Southampton, sent fear into everyone.

"Children, down to the root cellar this instant! I'll be taking Aunt Mary to sort this all out," Rose told them.

"I'm coming too," insisted Edric.

"You'll do as you're told. No arguments or there won't be pudding for a month!"

Mary pulled open the barn doors to find the cowling of the old model T car, a remnant from the last Great War. Bessie had bought one when the army had put them for sale and drove it for years. Now it spent most of its time inspiring imagined adventures for the children.

Mary spun the motor crank while Rose fiddled with the magneto switches. After several minutes, the car roared to life with a few bangs and a cloud of smoke from the rear. Mary set the picnic basket and dolls to the side as she climbed in next to Rose.

Darkness was settling in as the women turned the car down the lane toward the main road. Far ahead, over the tree tops, they could see the big planes turning for another pass over the city and the sparkle of explosions between them as the gunnery crews sought to bring their raid to an end. Numerous plumes of smoke rose to create a pallid cloud over Southampton.

The closer they drew to the city, the louder the bombs sounded. They had barely reached the outlying shops when the roads became so congested with people fleeing amid scattered rubble that Rose could drive no closer.

A constable stood atop the remains of a large truck that had been smashed by one of the bombs. He pointed for them to turn the truck around.

"I must get to the Supermarine factory. My Edward is there," Mary yelled to be heard above the other noises.

"Very sorry, Ma'am. That place is gone. That were their first target. There's nothing left of it. Now they're aiming for the shipworks and the rail yard, near as I can figure. There's no way through here."

"But my Edward!"

"Any that the crews find will be sent up to Upton. Look there," he told her.

"The rail yards? My David's on the train from London. Any word?" Rose asked.

The constable had already turned his attention to another group that was pushing their way through from the centre of the city. One of them was an older man that wore a sling for his arm. Blood dripped down from a cut on his head.

The two women looked at each other a moment and then Mary hopped down to help the old man climb into the passenger side. She joined the rest of his group as they sat in the back of the old truck.

Rose managed to get the truck turned around and soon they were bouncing along the cobbled road toward Upton. As they drove along, the noise and chaos dwindled a bit, though the thumps of the bombing continued.

Night was settling in, but Mary watched the glow over the city increase. They were too far away to see the individual flames, but she could tell that the heart of her fair city was slowly turning to ash. As she watched, another set of explosions added their own flames.

Rose followed the other vehicles that converged upon St. Boniface. At last she found a spot to stop amid several other cars. A crowd had gathered outside the doors and they scrutinized every person brought in.

Mary and Rose aided the old man out of the truck and through the crowds. Most of those outside were doing just what Mary wanted to do; they looked into the face of each new arrival in the hopes that it would be someone they knew.

Rose and Mary squeezed their way inside the lantern-lit church and found most of the pews filled with people laying on blankets. Every one of them showed signs of the violence still dropping on Southampton. Further toward the altar, Mary watched one of the priests giving a prayer over one of the people before he stood and folded a blanket over the face.

They inched along the pews, stepping around blankets on the floor. Everywhere they saw women and children, as well as men. Rose chocked back a sob when she came across a boy that looked terribly like Edric, only the boy was missing half of his leg.

Each face that wasn't Edward or David brought them new hope and each new arrival brought a resurgence of the anxiousness twisting their insides like a rung-out dishrag.

Two hours later, one of the sisters bringing water to the injured paused in her rounds and looked upward.

"Shhh! Do you hear that?" she said.

"All I hear are the sounds of these people," Rose told her.

"Precisely. The planes are gone," she replied. "Now we can bring the lights back up."

Rose pitched in, helping the sisters sort through the injured people, bringing the worst cases to the altar where a priest kept busy offering last rites. The simple ones they sent on their way to make more room.

Mary shook Rose awake at quarter to five in the morning, when seven more injured were carried in. The litter bearer announced these men had come from the factory in Woolston.

Rose and Mary hurried over to search the faces once more. The second litter held Carlie, one of Edwards pals on the line. A metal bar stuck up through his right side, with towels wrapped around it to hold the blood in.

Mary gasped and ran along the line of litters, stopping at the sixth one. Edward lay there with half his face covered in a torn rag. The shirt she'd sent him to work in was torn and had been used to strap a board to his leg.

"Edward!" she cried out.

He opened his eyes to look up at her, "What are you doing here, Love?"

"Just look at you! I mended that shirt just last week!" Mary scolded as she grabbed his hand.

"It's not as worse as it looks. A bit of rest and I'll head back to work tomorrow," he said, forcing a smile.

"You'll phone in sick is what you'll do. You're not going nowhere till I say," Mary insisted.

"Then you best say to go home. I think I need a bath."

CHAPTER EIGHTEEN

December 7th, 1941 – Bennett, America

Ben pulled the Chevrolet to a stop in front of the house. Kristie stepped out and opened the rear door, letting the girls tumble out in a rush to the house. Their shoes crunched through the thin layer of snow covering the walkway to the door.

"Change out of your church clothes before you do anything else," she called after them.

"Yes, Mama," came the simultaneous replies from Dot and Tatiana as the front door banged shut behind them.

"C.J., will you help me break up some ice to make the ice cream?" Kristie asked. "I'll get Lily changed and be right down to start the cream going."

"Hungry, Momma," Lily said.

"I know dear. We can break our fast soon. Supper should be ready in just a bit," Kristie replied.

Ben gathered the family bible and scriptures from the front seat and the little tote bag from the rear seat. He dropped a few of the crayons that had spilled out back into the bag. He sighed as he saw Tatiana's sock doll in the bottom of the tote.

After Joe died, Ben took the leap and began attending church services. With many Sundays of stern looks and hissed warnings to be quiet, Kristie had convinced him to let the girls color after the meeting's halfway point. Tatiana's sock doll wasn't supposed to be in the bag, even if the girls had used crayons to color the face on it.

Ben carried the things inside the house and set them on the stairs. No sooner had he set them there than Dot and Tati raced down the stairs. Dot jumped the last three steps, winning the race and tumbling into the sofa.

"Girls, go help your momma get supper ready. Everybody's hungry," Ben said.

"I'll snap the beans," Dot said as she ran for the kitchen.

"No fair. I was gonna do that," Tati said.

Ben pulled a tattered box of old papers from the top shelf of the closet and settled in the seat by the small desk. He pulled out a sheaf of papers that he had looked at so many times that the corners were all curled.

He walked over and turned on the radio before settling down with his list. As the tall console warmed up, the squealing subsided and the static hissing sound became a commercial for the Sears, Roebuck and Company. They were offering the latest in stoves, just in time for the holiday cooking season.

Ben had read the list so many times that he could name every one of the people listed on the manifest without looking. Every Sunday, it was the same routine. He'd pick a name and try to find some kind of connection to living people. His finger settled upon a Mr. Davidson of Montreal.

He pulled the box back to his lap and searched out the directory for Montreal he'd acquired several years earlier. There were five listings for Davidson and his marks showed where his letters had not yet been answered.

Ben paused in addressing the first envelope as the radio let out the sounds for the start of the World News Today program. John Charles always started with the latest news of England and the bombings there.

Today he began his broadcast with an urgent bulletin, "The Japanese have attacked Pearl Harbor from the air and dropped bombs and torpedoes on all naval and military activities on the island of Oahu, principal American base in the Hawaiian Islands."

The news stunned Ben. He remembered watching the soldiers marching off to the last war and sometimes not returning. Kristie's father, James, had been one of the lucky ones to return, though he limped from the shrapnel in his leg and half his arm remained somewhere in France.

"Honey?" Ben called out.

"What is it?" she asked, coming from the kitchen.

"It's unbelievable! The Japanese attacked Hawaii! They dropped bombs on all those ships there. That means we're going to war!"

"You can't. I mean, our girls. What would I do?" she asked.

"My name's been in the hat for a year now. If they call I'll have to go, but only if they call. Having a leg that can predict the rain, like your father's, isn't something I look forward to," Ben said, trying to lighten the mood. "And I prefer both arms to hug you with, but if they call me, I'll have to go."

"Come along and offer the prayer. Everyone is starving according to Lily."

Ben slid the stack of papers back into the box and returned it to the top of the coat closet. Titanic's legacy, or at least the part that concerned him, would have to wait until after supper. The aroma of Kristie's fresh-baked rolls set his mouth to watering.

Ben sat at the head of the table and held out his hands to his two nearest daughters. With the circle complete, he began the prayer adding in a bit to comfort the families that lost men that morning.

"Who got lost?" Dot asked.

"War is a terrible thing that tears families apart," Ben mumbled.

Dot grabbed the bowl of beans and spooned some onto her plate, "I made the beans. Everybody gots to have some."

Her bright smile did wonders to drive away the fear edging into Ben and Kristie's moods with the news. Soon, the whole family was laughing and chattering about building snowmen and stringing garlands.

Ben helped C.J. clear the dishes from the table and scrubbed the baking pan while she washed the other dishes. Kristie took the other girls into the living room to begin cutting the paper strips. They had hundreds of strips cut and colored when Ben brought the ice cream tub out.

C.J. did most of the gluing, while the other girls colored the strips as rapidly as they could. Ben looped the chains across the windows, and draped them along picture frame nails, until the colorful chain crossed two walls.

"Ooh, watch Momma," C.J. said, as Kristie began folding some paper.

Kristie folded her paper into a long triangle, then carefully snipped odd shapes into the edges. The girls had seen it every year and still they watched closely. At last, she unfolded her paper to present them with a lacy snowflake.

Tati already had a bit of thread ready to tie a loop to the decoration. Soon, more snowflakes began taking shape as fast as the scissors could be passed around, though Lily still needed a bit of help to craft hers.

Most of the ice cream had been eaten by the time Ben hung the last of the snowflakes. The desk and radio had been moved aside a bit to clear a spot in the corner by the windows. Ben promised them that next Saturday they would all go find a tree to fit the bare spot.

They sang one last song before shooing the children upstairs to bed. Ben and Kristie cuddled on the sofa and admired the decorations as they listened to the girls quieting down for the night.

"What if they call your name?" she asked softly.

"Then I get to march through the mud in some far off place. I suppose I'd be sending you postcards every other day."

"I just… I just don't know what would happen. I mean, Daddy talked about how he was hunkered down in a hole when the mortar hit."

"Maybe I should join the Navy. That way I'd avoid muddy holes," Ben said.

"How can you even think of ships after…, you know."

"I'll put my trust in the Lord for what I should do. It's all I can really do."

The next morning, Ben dressed and left for work just as the sun was rising. When he arrived at the warehouse, he had to work his way through a cluster of men surrounding the time clock. At the center of the crowd stood Mr. Kitomi holding the remains of his torn card.

"Go on! Get out of here! We don't want you anywhere near us!" yelled Cramer.

"Yeah, I got a cousin in the Navy," chimed in Gronsky.

"Gronk, what's going on?" Ben asked.

"Ol' Slant-Eye here thinks he can come to work like nothing happened after his buddies attacked us," Gronsky replied. "He's lucky we don't toss him in the river, or ship him to back home to China."

"Kai's worked here for three years. He works harder than most of you other blokes," Ben said.

"Well if you like him so much, you can just take off too. We don't want no enemy sympathetics here," Cramer spat.

"I'm the floor lead. I say he stays," Ben said.

The foreman stepped between some of the men, "Not any more, you're not. Now both of you get out of my sight."

"You can't do that! I've been here ten years!" Ben exclaimed.

"Just did. Ain't having them bombs dropping on me cause of a spy or nothing."

Mr. Katomi followed Ben out the door. This is where their paths split. Ben climbed into the Chevrolet, while Mr. Katomi headed through the gate on foot. Ben caught up to him a block down the road.

"Climb in, Kai," Ben called as he pulled the car to a stop.

"So sorry, Mr. Strong," he began.

"Hop in. It's still a few miles home."

"I know nothing about it. They say I bomb them. I bomb nothing," Mr. Katomi said.

"You haven't listened to the radio? Well, got news for you! The Japanese military bombed Pearl Harbor, Hawaii yesterday."

"Was not me. I right here in New York."

"I didn't think you had. You may dress a bit funny, but I know you're honest. Like that time you lost an invoice and spent four hours looking for something you'd stuck in your pocket. Boy, did you turn red when you found it."

"So sorry got you fired."

"Get this straight. It wasn't you that got me fired. If you need anything, give me a call," Ben said.

Ben dropped Mr. Katomi outside his house before driving the last bit to his own home. His thoughts were still jumbled as he pulled to a stop. Christmas was not the time to lose a job. The thought flashed through his mind, wondering if what he felt was anything like his stepfather had felt on Black Thursday, before stepping out of the fourteenth floor. He shoved the thoughts aside and went in to face Kristie.

Kristie sat on the sofa with Lily on her lap. They were both staring at the radio. She looked up at the sound of him entering and waved for him to sit beside her as the announcer commented that the President was coming. The noise on the radio died down as the unmistakable voice of the President began.

"Mr. Vice President, Mr. Speaker, Members of the Senate, and of the House of Representatives: Yesterday, December 7th, 1941 – a date which will live in infamy – the United States of America was suddenly and deliberately attacked by the naval and air forces of the Empire of Japan.

The United States was at peace with that nation and, at the solicitation of Japan, was still in conversation with its government and its emperor looking toward the maintenance of peace in the Pacific.

Indeed, one hour after Japanese air squadrons had commenced bombing in the American island of Oahu, the Japanese ambassador to the United States and his colleague delivered to our Secretary of State a formal reply to a recent American message. And while this reply stated that it seemed useless to continue the existing diplomatic negotiations, it contained no threat or hint of war or of armed attack."

They listened on as Roosevelt listed off several other places that Japan had attacked since Pearl Harbor. He vowed that America would last through the current crisis to come out victorious and ended by calling upon congress to declare a state of war.

As the President's words died away, and the radio erupted with the shouted voices of the people sitting in the congress all trying to be heard over one another, Kristie looked at Ben as though suddenly realizing he was home.

"What happened? You haven't even been gone all that long," Kristie said.

"They fired Kai just because he's Japanese. I thought for sure they were going to haul him out to the alley and beat him or something. I said they couldn't fire him, so they sent me packing too. I'm sorry dear. Maybe I should've stayed out of it."

"You wouldn't be you if you didn't stand up to people. Like when you broke Connor Griffin's nose that night for making fun of my Irish."

"But that didn't get me fired. I have a family to take care of."

"WE! We have a family! You wanted to put your trust in the Lord. I think maybe you ought to listen to him! We'll get through this together."

Ben left again after lunch. This time he walked to save the cost of gasoline. With no idea of when he might be hired, every penny counted. He walked toward the waterfront and the string of warehouses there. He couldn't go back to his, but there were a dozen others that he could try. Hopefully, one could use an experienced man.

Ben returned home tired and a bit dispirited as the sun began setting. None of the warehouses were looking to hire anyone new. He stopped by the corner drugstore and splurged a nickel on the evening post, hoping there might be something in their pages to help him find new work.

As Saturday rolled around, he loaded the family into the car. He drove them down to the ice pond, where they could skate for an hour before visiting the tree lot next door. Finding the right tree took another hour. They all settled on one just taller than Carol Jessica, and no bald spots.

Ben haggled with the owner of the lot for a good ten minutes, dropping the price down a bit. The girls stood around watching with wide eyes as their perfect tree was roped to the roof of the car.

As they pulled up to the house Tati called out that she spied a cat sitting on the porch. The four girls ran up to the porch attempting to pick it up, despite Ben telling them to chase it away. The orange tiger cat wrapped itself between their legs, but skittered away as soon as someone reached for it.

The cat ran off the porch, amid the anguished cries of the girls, as soon as Ben carried the tree to the door. He shouldered his way through the door and set the tree right where they had planned. It fit into the spot between the radio and the desk just right.

"Dot, get the old cookie pan and a wet towel please," Ben said.

Dot turned to run for the kitchen, nearly tripping over the cat sitting in the middle of the room. As she stumbled a bit, the cat took off like a shot up the stairs. Tatiana and Lily ran after it. Dot started after them, but Ben called her back to fetch the pan for the tree.

Kristie helped the girls search for the wayward cat through all the bedrooms. They saw it once as it scrambled back down the stairs. It remained undiscovered as the search moved downstairs. After an hour, they concluded that it must have escaped through the back porch window that was open a few inches until Kristie closed it as well.

Ben tuned the radio into a station playing Christmas songs as Kristie threaded a needle. Everyone helped string popped corn onto the needle, with Lily and Dot pulling the kernels down the thread to the end. They crafted four of the strings to wrap around the tree, and hung crayon-colored ornaments from the branches. Ben topped the tree with the one permanent ornament they owned: a gold painted eight point tin star.

Ben read the girls one of their favorite stories before sending them off to bed. He closed the book just before the monkeys led Mowgli off to the lost city. Ben and Kristie kissed them each good night and pointed them up the stairs.

"I'm getting a bit worried. It's getting to the point that I'll have to drive several miles to find new places to ask about work," Ben said quietly.

"You'll find something. I know you will. If you tried sitting on your hands doing nothing you'd rattle apart before the end of the week," Kristie told him.

In the morning, Kristie went to wake the girls in time for church. She heard a few hushed voices before she knocked on the door, then they went silent. She opened the door to find them all feigning sleep, complete with soft snores.

She pulled back the covers on C.J. and Dot, giving both of them a nudge to get up. They grudgingly sat up, yawning widely as though waking from a long sleep. Kristie reached to pull back Tati's covers and Tati held a finger to her lips.

"Shh, you'll wake Sure Can," Tati told her.

"It's Shere Khan, with a roawr," Dot said.

Kristie pulled the covers back to find the orange cat snuggled up to Tatiana. The cat opened its eyes to squint at Kristie, and purred louder.

"So you named this stray?" their mother asked.

"Papa has to let us keep it now," C.J. said.

The chattering drew the attention of Ben, who peered into the room as he fiddled with the knot on his tie. He finished the knot and folded his collar down before fixing them with his best father glare.

"I suppose you think giving that hairball a name means it stays?" he asked.

"He'll freeze outside. Look, there's more snow already," Dot told him.

"And it isn't a dog like you said we couldn't have," C.J. added.

"Come along," he said. "Time enough for some oatmeal before church. We can discuss the cat's future after that."

"He's Shere Khan, Papa," Lily said.

"Then he better hope we don't have a herd of buffalo run through the house while we're gone."

The girls all giggled when Ben tried to glare at Shere Khan as he stuck his head in Ben's glass to lick the last few drops of milk from the bottom. Ben had to lift the cat off the table and was rewarded with louder purring. Nothing more was even discussed about the new addition to the family when they returned that afternoon.

They had been home only an hour when the phone rang with the series of rings that meant the call was for them. When Ben lifted the handset, he was greeted by the frantic voice of a woman on the other end of the line. It took a few times of her repeating it before he caught her name.

"They come for us!" Mrs. Katomi exclaimed.

"What are you talking about?" Ben asked.

"Police. They arrest Kai. They coming back for me. Hurry."

Ben hung up the phone and kissed Kristie with a quick explanation that he was going to help a friend. He rushed through the afternoon traffic, arriving just in time to watch as Mrs. Katomi was led from the house in handcuffs. Kai was already seated in the rear of one police patrol car.

Ben grabbed the arm of the first officer he could reach, "What's going on? What has he done?"

"He's a Jap. The mayor said to arrest every one of these spying Japs," came the reply.

"What? He spied on boxes of shoes? Or maybe it was the cases of canning jars, complete with vacuum lids. He's a warehouseman, or he was," Ben said.

"Mayor's orders," The officer said. "Take it up with him."

"What about his wife? She's Italian," Ben asked.

"So what. She's Mrs. Japanese."

Ben glanced back at the house as one of the officers tacked a paper to the door. The word impounded was printed at the top in bold lettering.

"What are you doing with his house?"

"Japs can't have property now. Again, Mayor's orders."

Ben leaned in the window of the car, "Kai, where's the deed for the house?"

It took a moment to get his meaning across before Kai finally understood what he wanted. After another moment of thought, he told Ben which drawer to look in. Ben rushed into the house amid calls from the officers that he was breaking the impound order. Two minutes later, he returned with the paper.

"There, now I have the deed. You can't impound my house that way," Ben said as he waved the paper in front of the officer.

"I ought to arrest you for this."

"And explain how you couldn't tell the difference between Japanese and American?"

Several minutes of arguing later, the cars pulled away with the Katomis inside. Only one of the officers even knew where they were headed: Ellis Island. The place that had welcomed so many into the country was now serving as a prison for Japanese businessmen, cooks, tailors, and any number of other professionals.

Ben tore the note from the door and locked the house before returning home. Kristie met him at the door with a worried look on her face. He kissed her before relating what had happened.

"I just purchased a house for five dollars. It's all I had in my wallet," he told her.

"What? How?"

"Everyone has gone to the loony bin, it seems. Kai and his wife were arrested. They think he's a spy or some such nonsense. They were going to take his home away from him."

"So, you bought it for five dollars?"

"Something prompted me to do it. I figure this way it'll be waiting for him when they sort all this mess out and find out he's not really a spy. Oh, and Mrs. Kitomi asked that we water her plants."

CHAPTER NINETEEN

May 7th, 1945 – Winchester, England

Bessie yelled out in excitement as the radio announcer repeated his news. The war was over. Germany had finally surrendered to American and British forces at a town in France, called Reims!

Her shouts brought Rose and the girls running to see if she had fallen or something. Bessie grabbed Rose's hands and danced around the parlor a bit before anybody could get the story of why she had yelled.

"Germany has finally ended the war! No more bombs falling on houses!" Bessie exclaimed.

"That means…, That means we can go home," Abigail said. "We'll find Mother and Father once more."

"Now, wait a minute," Rose said. "You've seen what those bombs did to Southampton. What makes you think Germany will be any better? Remember that plane that got shot down and crashed just two fields over. It leveled the barn and half the house."

"When will the government man take us back? How much should we pack? Will we be able to have more than one case this time?" Abigail asked.

"I'm sure someone will come 'round as soon as accommodations can be made to return you to your parents," Bessie said.

"Then I best gather our belongings for when the man arrives," Abigail replied.

Abigail gathered Aaron and Adalyn in the upstairs bedroom they had occupied for five years. The clothes they wore when they arrived no longer fit. New clothes had been purchased as they needed them.

By the time Rose called them for supper, their beds were piled high with shoes, clothes, books, and an assortment of playthings that children always manage to acquire.

All that remained of the things that had arrived with the children were two books, a hair ribbon for Adalyn, and Aaron's watch. The new things far outnumbered the old things and amounted to more than their little cases could possibly hold.

Bessie's heart was sad. She had become so accustomed to having the children, but it was time to send them back to their parents. They loaded a trunk of their things that they could take with them. Mary decided that she should be the one to take them across to help them find their parents and family again, once they learned that it was up to them to get the three children back to their family. At last, they decided to just take a suitcase each and send for the rest of the items later.

For two days, the children would wake and have breakfast before spending the rest of the day sitting on the bed, with their packed cases, waiting for the government man to return for them. Bessie tried several times to ring through to the office listed on the paper the man had left with her, but her calls were never answered.

For the rest of the week, they would pull clothes out to wear and shove the dirty ones into the cases before spending their day within sight of the house. At the end of the week, Bessie had to empty out their cases to find the laundry that needed washing. As soon as it was dry again, Adalyn took it off the line to repack their cases. Everyone expected that the man would pull up the drive to fetch the children at any minute.

October 11th, 1945 - Winchester, England

The four of them boarded Mary's Joy and settled into the cabin as Captain Fairchild started the motors. Before long, the boat had cleared the harbor and turned eastward. Mary cringed a little as the memory of watching a much larger ship turn eastward with her father standing at the railing. Titanic had sailed smoothly as it made the turn, unlike Mary's namesake that bounced over every grey-green wave, in the early morning sun.

Captain Fairchild kept them within sight of the coast and the children traded waving arms with several other fishing trawlers as they passed. He skirted wide around one boat that flew a string of colourful pennants that he told them meant there were nets in the water.

"No sense fouling the screws and another bloke's catch. Besides, it'd cost us making the coast till afternoon."

"Why don't we put out nets as we go? Then this wouldn't be a wasted trip for you," Mary asked.

"Tis a bit risky dragging nets this close to the harbor, Miss. The Kettlebottom done thought they had a catch worthy of the week and it turned out to be a mine. Whole ship went up in a geyser near a hundred feet high. All that were left of the 'Bottom were bits like matchsticks and only one bloke made it. I'll not risk this boat till the Admiralty says the waters be clear."

The children quieted down and watched the waves roll past for the next while. They all perked up a bit when Mary called out that the shore was in sight. They all craned their neck to watch as spires rose above the low-lying fog.

The first spires they had been watching slowly resolved into rusted steel spikes rising from the water. They passed within reach of the cabin of a ship that had been burned. The spires were all that remained of the mast mounted on the cabin.

"She's got the cut of a coastal freighter," Captain Fairchild remarked. "A few of them were lost when the boys were getting pulled from the beaches. We can't be far from the pier now."

Sure enough, as he said it, a wisp of fog blew clear and they could see the low pier. It lay low to the water, only about three hundred yards ahead. A handful of trawlers and another coastal freighter were tied alongside it.

Captain Fairchild nosed Mary's Joy between a few other trawlers and tossed the rope to a waiting dockworker. The man wrapped the rope around a cleat, pulling it tight as the bow touched.

"Quick, toss over the aft line," the Captain called out.

Mary took the rope from Aaron, who was managing to wrap it around himself more than coil it. As soon as he extricated himself from the tangle, Mary threw the rope to the waiting hands of the dock worker. He tied it to another cleat, bringing the rear of the fishing trawler close against the pier. Fairchild came back and lowered the rope ladder over the side.

Abigail scampered over the side and down the ladder just as soon as the Captain stepped out of the way. She cheered as soon as she set foot on the metal plates. She took a step, wobbled a moment, then sat down with a plop on the pier.

"It moves!" she exclaimed.

"It's a Mullberry," Captain Fairchild said. "After the Germans destroyed the old docks to keep us Britts out, our boys brought in floating docks. They built all this in a couple days."

Mary helped the others climb over and stood with them as the Captain handed their cases to them. Aaron hefted his cases and began marching down the pier as the girls hurried after him. Mary had a single case, so she took one of Adalyn's in her other hand.

The fog cleared a little more, revealing a large grey block sitting by the end of the pier. It sat as large as the house in Winchester, but the only window spouted a large gun barrel poking out of it. Scorch marks around the slit window showed where the inside of the blockhouse had burned. As Aaron got up to it, he traced his finger across dozens of small pockets made by bullets.

The four of them climbed the short rise in the road to make it to the main level of the town. They stopped and gasped at the scene that lay before them. Dozens of buildings sat gutted and little more than solitary walls stood amid piles of rubble. Further into the town were buildings that were only partially damaged. People wandered the street calling out goods for sale, reminding Mary of the market street back in Southampton.

Mary asked a few of the people where they could lodge, quickly discovering that her French was very limited. Abigail did most of the talking when the people didn't understand English enough. Eventually, they found their way into a building with only minor damage. The sign at the front proclaimed it to be the Lily Garden. It looked more like a row house that had been remodeled recently with whatever bits of other homes they found lying about.

"I've always loved lilies," Adalyn remarked quietly. "Mother grew them in the window boxes. Remember that, Aaron?"

Aaron glanced at her and nodded silently. Abigail set her cases down, walking up to the old lady sitting behind a desk. With a bit of bartering, they finally settled upon a price for a single room that was at least twice what a proper room in Southampton would let for.

"Most of my rooms are full up with soldiers waiting to get across the channel and they got decent coin to do it with," she told them. "Tell you what, toss in two more coins and I'll find some more blankets."

Aaron spent the night sleeping on the floor next to Mary, as Adalyn shared the single bed with Abigail. They slept very little, thanks to loud voices coming from the next room. By morning they were hungry and sore, but eager to get on the way as soon as possible. An hour later, they stood on the rail platform where a new ticket booth had been built. A burned shell of a building stood where the proper station ought to have been. Two men worked to tear the damaged boards off that they tossed into a wagon.

Just like the room they had spent the night in, the cost of rail coach tickets seemed far higher than it should have been. They couldn't even get a straight-through to Hamburg, as two bridges were still bombed out.

The mismatched collection of coaches, trailing behind a locomotive that had seen better days, pulled away from the platform and followed the canals heading East. Even out to the outskirts of Calais, the signs of the bombings could still be seen. Adalyn and Abigail gasped when the train pulled past a group of armored vehicles that had fought to the bitter end. One boy stood atop a tank and waved as the train went by. Aaron, for his part, spent the first part of the journey silently fiddling with his father's watch.

Field after field bore the marks of the savagery that had taken place along the countryside. The coach had wobbled along for twenty minutes when Abigail excitedly pointed out the window.

"Look, that house isn't hurt! It even has cows standing by it. Maybe things will get better the closer we get to home."

"The windows of Papa's shop are most likely broke out," Aaron commented. "Even the big one with the watch painted on it."

The train paused at Lille station long enough to take on more water and coal before pulling out northward. Lille looked as though it had suffered as much as Calais, with fully a third of the homes and shops only noticeable as piles of rubble. Only the main road through town seemed to have been kept clear. Nobody said much until they pulled into the station at Ghent. Here, Mary and Abigail haggled with a girl selling sandwiches on the platform, with Mary spending enough for a fine meal, to procure lunch for everyone.

Midafternoon saw the train lumbering to a stop at a severely damaged station called Antwerp. It was the end of the line for their train, as the bridge leading onward had still not been rebuilt. They learned that everyone would need to cross the river to catch the next leg of the train, though it wouldn't depart for another two hours.

Mary reluctantly bid the children farewell, handing the rest of her money over to Abigail. Things had proven to be much costlier than she had anticipated. She held back just enough money to return to Calais. Everything she could spare, she pressed into Abigail's hand.

"I'd intended to see you all the way into the arms of your parents, but that seems folly now. Everything is far more expensive than I had imagined it would be," Mary said. "With this, I feel you should make it there, at least. Bid hello to your parents from all of us. Mum and all of us treasured the time you spent with in our home."

Mary pulled herself free of the tearful goodbyes and hurried back aboard the coach as the whistle screeched the train's departure once more. She stood in the door of the coach waving until the rails turned, blocking them from view. Mary pulled the last of her sandwich from the cloth and nibbled on it, recalling Aaron and Adalyn's wonder on the way northward.

Abigail gathered her siblings as soon as the last of the train wound its way out of sight and hurried them across the wagon bridge. Automobiles bounced their way over the bridge alongside scraggly horse drawn carts. Even the bridge bore scars as the children stepped around holes big enough to see the river below.

The north side of the town looked as bedraggled as the south side and Abigail pulled them along faster. In Calais, the faces had seemed tired, but here in Antwerp, all she saw were haggard faces. Many of them stared at the children with all the compassion of a wolf from their bedtime tales.

As they hurried past a small pile of dirt and bricks that had been a bakery in its past life, she picked up a double handful of dirt to smear all over her siblings. Aaron just stared at her as though he was certain she had lost her mind, but Adalyn cried out indignantly at the damage to her clean dress. Abigail settled it by letting the both of them smear some mud on her face, though she shook it out and glared at Aaron when he squished a handful of the mud into her hair.

Looking more the part of wandering vagabonds, the trio made it to the make-shift station with an hour to spare. The ticket master at first refused to pass them aboard until Abigail pressed another English note into his hand. He grumbled, but let them pass at last. The children hurried and secured themselves a seat on the coach, anxious to see home.

Their short time in Antwerp had rattled Abigail's nerves a little, and she sat quietly holding Aaron and Adalyn close while the train rolled northward. She didn't even look out the window at the stops in Arnhem and Osnabruk, finally glancing up when the conductor strolled through announcing they were closing in on Bremen.

Bremen wasn't home, but she had visited there once with her mother many years ago. It was the signal they were drawing close to the final stop. Her memories of flowered springtime fields battled with the barren churned fields they passed. Many of these fields bore the remains of forgotten armor-clad monsters rusting in the cool autumn sun. Hedgerows, which had stood as neat markers between fields, now lay trampled by the steel machines of ruin. She gave her siblings each a comforting squeeze of the shoulders.

"Hamburg is a big city. Only the outer parts will be crumbled. Papa's shop is fine," she whispered, mostly to herself.

The train rolled to a stop beside a platform sporting a tent surrounded by numerous crates and a few travel cases. Beyond the platform, the area held squares of rubble separated by what passed for roads. Here and there, among the rubble, stood bits of walls that barely reached ten feet high. Lining the nearby roads stood many more tents with cook fires and other oddments. A few motorcars rested along the roadway.

"Why are they all camping in this field of rubble?" Aaron asked nobody in particular. "Why don't they find lodging in the city?"

"Don't you remember?" Abigail replied, the colour draining from her face. "The platform was only a half mile from Papa's shop. That's the road we walked along when we left here."

The children gathered their cases and solemnly trudged down the road. Nothing remained recognizable from how they recalled it. The houses were gone, leveled into lumps of brick and ash. Many of the lots had been cleared of the worst of the rubble, leaving mostly flat squares of brick and tile. Tents stood where houses had once ruled, though there were few tents at that.

They rounded the corner where Henkel's store had stood. Papa had taken them to the market for treats a few times. Now a pair of tents stood, fronted by crates serving as the counters, to display the meager assortment of goods he offered. It brought a little relief to see that a few people remained that they had known. Mr. Henkel had helped them on their way out of the city all those years ago.

Aaron stopped to look at a stack of bricks that had been etched. He reached out to tug Abigail's arm. As she looked back at him, he pointed to the messages scrawled in the bricks. Most of the scratches were names with a brief note. Three more stacks stood along the front of Henkel's makeshift store, all covered in indelible notes scratched on bricks.

The children spread out to read each of the notes. A few times, one of them would call the others over as a name triggered a memory. Most of the notes told of people that had fled the devastated city for someplace to live. An hour passed before Abigail called them to look at a particular brick.

"This one's from Aunt Rachel. We are supposed to find her in the field to the east," she told them.

"Let's find home first," Aaron told her. "I need to see it. So does Adalyn. That's where Momma and Papa are going to look for us. We promised them."

The trio spent a moment to wave to Mr. Henkel before continuing along the road. A block further, they found where the shop had stood. All that remained was a pile of charred bricks behind the brick post that marked the corner of their lot. A few bits of twisted metal stuck up between the bricks. Adalyn idly poked at a brick that was coated in glass.

"That's from the front window," Aaron spoke up. "It melted, I think."

"It makes it pretty," she looked up at him. "I want to stay here till Momma and Papa come home."

"It's far too late in the day to go looking for Aunt Rachel," Abigail told them. "We can find her tomorrow. For now, you both need to help me clear a spot to rest."

"The dungeon stairs were over there, I think," Aaron said.

"It wasn't a dungeon, you dolt. It was the cellar where Momma kept the bottled stuff. But, you're right. Let's find it. It'll be better than a drafty tent."

"We don't have a tent," Aaron muttered.

The children spent the night huddled in the darkness of the cellar, waking several times to the sound of tiny paws scurrying between bits of rubbish and rubble. Adalyn woke with a screech when one of the bolder denizens nibbled at her leg. Abigail and Aaron spent the rest of the night watching as their youngest sibling slept between them.

With the first light of morning, they climbed the steps and sat on the little bit of wall that remained of the three-storied house that had housed their family and their father's clock shop. At Abigail's urging, they only ate half of what remained of the food from travelling, saving the rest for dinner.

Once the sun had risen high enough to light their way, the trio wound along roads leading to the far fields. One road looked much like another until they neared the outskirts of the once great city. The houses along the edge were less damaged and some of them were still inhabited. Here the touch of fire and destruction seemed almost a distant memory.

The field beyond the city had turned into a vast camping area, with people huddled beneath anything that could offer cover. Few of them could be called tents, as most were branches and leaves dragged from the forest beyond. One family huddled under the wing of a downed aeroplane bearing the white star. The remainder of the bomber had returned to ground somewhere else.

Everywhere they looked, they were met with hollow-eyed blank stares from faces atop scarecrow bodies. The people, and everything they wore, resembled the dull brownish grey of the barren fields. Adalyn clung tightly to Abigail's hand as they searched for any face that seemed familiar.

"I could be staring right at our neighbor, Mrs. Ludlow, and I wouldn't know it were her," Aaron muttered. "I'm not sure I want to ask any of them, neither. They're looking at us like you look at cinnamon curls."

"Alright, alright, I'll ask. Just mind stay behind me," Abigail replied.

Some of the people replied merely with stares as though German was an unknown language, while others silently shook their heads and turned away. Abigail had asked for about the thirtieth time before the lady pointed off to the east.

"I heard a name like that from a bi… from a woman over about six spots in that direction. Just don't go asking them for nothing," the woman grumbled.

Abigail led them between more of the makeshift camps, in the direction the woman had pointed. People along the way either held out grubby hands, or shied away from them with tense faces. Most of them pulled children, that were little more than stick figures draped with tattered rags for clothing, close to them. With each one they passed, Adalyn squeezed her sister's arm ever tighter.

As they drew close to the spot, Abigail saw a woman turn their direction. She caught sight of the scar running down the woman's cheek, now highlighted by a smear of mud. The scar seemed to be the only familiar thing about the aunt she had met a decade earlier. Abigail scrutinized the rest of her features, comparing them to a memory already fading.

"What do you want? We can't spare nothing," the woman spat the words at her as though they were rotted cabbage.

"Aunt Rachel?" Abigail started.

The woman stopped poking the ground with the stick she held and focused on the three children before her. Her lip curled up slightly as her gaze followed the children from head to toe, before returning to look straight at Abigail.

"Abe's kids? You're Aaron, Abigail, and… and…"

"Her name's Adalyn," Aaron spoke up.

"Well, how was I to remember that? She weren't more than a bundle of blankets and spit last time I saw you three."

"Where's Momma and Papa?" Abigail asked. "They should have been back by now. Where did they go?"

"Weren't more than a fortnight after you left for the comfort of the countryside that the jackboots came in the night. They dragged them off with little more than the clothes they wore to go work in the brickworks of Neuengamme. I saw them coming and took off for the woods with Noah, Rivka, and Schmuel," Rachel told them.

"But the war's over. Where are they?" Aaron asked.

"I told you, Neuengamme!" Aunt Rachel spat the words.

"But…," Abigail started.

"They dragged every one of the faithful into that brickworks to build their precious buildings. There was only a handful left alive when the Britts marched through them gates. The rest of them, including your precious Papa, went into the same ovens they cooked the bricks in. They're not coming back. Not now, not ever."

"You're lying!" shouted Adalyn.

"Now why would I lie to you? Family is all we got left."

A movement at the edge of the encampment caught Abigail's eye. A boy limped into the camp with an armload of branches. Behind him walked a girl slightly smaller than him. She held a tied kerchief in her hands.

"Is that all you could find?" she asked the boy.

"Who are they?" he asked, disregarding the question.

"Noah?" Abigail asked hesitantly. "What happened? And Rivka? Where's Schmuel?"

The meager brightness of his eyes drained away and he stared at the ground. The girl stopped to simply stare at them, without a word.

"Schmuel didn't make it through that first winter in the woods. Things here were a lot tougher than the balmy English countryside. Noah went looking for food at the general's manor house. I dug the bullet out, but he ain't ever walking straight again."

"How did they flatten the whole city?" Aaron asked. "None of the other places we passed were this bad."

"That were two years ago. They came in the night and dropped fire. Must have been hundreds of them. They dropped fire for two days straight, but those fires went on for weeks. Nobody could put them out. Burned up everything. Houses. Trees. People. Everything turned to ash. All that was left were empty shells where buildings had been. Most been knocked flat by looters trying to find what's left," Rachel told them.

Rivka inched closer to her mother and held out the kerchief to her. Abigail could see a handful of reddish berries held within. Rachel gathered the kerchief in her hand.

"Don't worry, family shares what they can in hard times. You three look as though you haven't missed a meal in years. What have you brought with you from England?" Aunt Rachel asked them.

"I got half a sandwich," Adalyn said softly.

"Maybe Aaron can flit off to the forest and fetch a plump rabbit. I mean, after all, he looks fit enough to run. I mean, Noah ain't got a chance to catch one with his bum leg and all."

After Rachel tore the sandwich in bits to share with her kids, she turned to the trio to hold open empty hands. They only stayed a half hour more before Aaron stood to walk away, pulling Adalyn behind him. Abigail stood and bid goodbye to Aunt Rachel and her cousins before hurrying after him. Nobody spoke another word until they had left all the camps behind them.

"Here, Adalyn. You can have half of mine since you gave yours to them," Aaron told her.

"What do we do now? Momma and Papa aren't coming home," Adalyn said as tears welled in her eyes.

"We're together. We stick together and nothing or nobody can hold us down," Abigail stated.

"Mum Bessie was better family than Aunt Rachel is now. But, if we go back now it means giving up everything our papa had here," Aaron said.

"But what can we do here? There's nothing left," Abigail said.

"I'm going to rebuild the house. We can have the garden spot in the back of it. In fact, we got the whole block to ourselves if we want," Aaron declared.

CHAPTER TWENTY

November 5th, 1945 - Bennett, America

Ben stamped his feet once more, to drive away the cold seeping in through his thin shoes. Years of people waiting at the bus stop had worn a depression in the gravel that often filled with slush when the cold weather hit. Today, at least, the ground lay covered in a thin frost, waiting for the afternoon sun to drive it away.

The grey clouds and chill breeze made everyone bundle tight in their coats as they hurried along the sidewalk. Ben had pulled his hat down over the tips of his ears and peeked around his turned-up collar, whenever someone stepped close. He looked up as the screeching of brakes signaled the arrival of the bus.

A soldier, in his green uniform, hitched his duffle higher on his shoulder and stepped close, anticipating the door opening. As soon as the door swung open, the burly driver hurried down the steps, setting a wooden step on the ground to make debarking easier. The young soldier stiffened to attention, in what seemed to be an instinctive reflex, then stepped back to allow the passengers to exit the bus.

The first ones stepping off the bus were a pair of teen girls, followed by their mother. The driver carried a couple of bags down the steps, setting them at the woman's feet. He tipped his hat and smiled as she thanked him. They all stepped aside to glare as the next man helped his wife down the steps to the ground.

"Our case is brown one with flower," Mr. Kitomi told the driver.

"So? I ain't getting it down," spat the driver, as he turned away.

Ben brushed past them to climb the few rungs to the roof luggage rack. Pulling his flip knife from a pocket, Ben slashed the cords binding it there. The battered case seemed hardly large enough to carry more than a change of clothes for each of them, let alone their entire belongings from years of living.

He swung the case down to his friend before descending the ladder himself. Ben brushed his hands on his shirt and extended it for a handshake. Mr. Kitomi set the case down and bent at the waist in a formal bow, remaining bowed until Ben placed his hand on the man's shoulder.

"I not 'espect see you ever again. You lost work from me," Mr. Kitomi said.

Ben shrugged and gave the man a smile, "Come along. The Olds is parked around the corner. Kristie will have supper ready by the time we get there. I'd show you around town, but not much has changed in the past few years. Any place you'd like to see?"

"You very generous offer. We go hotel to stay until I find new house."

Ben settled them in the rear seat before climbing behind the wheel. Ten minutes later, he pulled to a stop before their old house. He didn't say anything for a minute, until Kai noticed where they were parked and glanced at Ben.

"Just thought you might want to see this place again. I know you loved that funny little garden you made in the back," Ben said with a smile.

"Year ago letter you wrote it had to be sold. I find new house soon, when I earn money."

Ben climbed out of the car and motioned for the Kitomis to follow him. They hurried across the street to stand before the small home with its picket fence. The grass and trees looked a bit brown and bare in the cold weather, but the house looked freshly painted in a light shade of pink with white shutters.

"Why don't you get a closer look at it? I bet it still looks the same as when you left it," Ben said with a smile. "I'm sure the new owner won't mind."

Kai Kitomi and his wife leaned over the low fence and looked closely at the house, before stepping closer. He paused a moment, at the picket gate, glancing at Ben, who nodded. He opened the gate to step through, watching the front of the house carefully.

"I'm sure you can even look inside, if you like," Ben held up the key. "You should have this back now. I told them I sold the house back to you."

Kai stared at him for a few minutes before speaking, "I have no money to pay you for house."

"There's an opening for a rope finisher at Strong Flotation. You can take the five dollars out of your pay, if you like. Jobs were hard to come by, so I started my own company making float rafts for ships. It's a good job. Listen, you'll find a few things in the cupboards that I talked the ward into donating for you, so you have food for about a week. Welcome home, my friend."

Kai and his wife poked through the house for a few minutes, touching photographs and mementos, staring into the rear yard, and sitting for a moment on the padded teak sofa. They looked around the living room, taking in each detail as though memorizing it. Finally, they stood and met Ben by the door.

"I no can believe you did this. All others at camp had everything taken from them. The guards took even the scripture books you sent to me, because could have no books in Japanese. I will replace them to you. My promise."

"It took me six months to find a Bible and Book of Mormon in Japanese. I know you read it better than English. Those were yours to keep. It may take some time to find another set. Now, I'm sure Kristie is anxious to meet you both. Let's hurry while supper is still hot."

Ben held the door open to usher Kai and his wife into the house. Ben's girls bounced excitedly to meet their new guests, and Kristie stood behind them, waiting patiently for the Kitomis to wend their way through the bouncing girls.

Sitting around the table, with Lily and Tatiana perched on overturned buckets, everyone chatted about many different things, though the girls kept asking about where Kai and his wife had been for the past several years. Finally, Mr. Kitomi looked at Dorothy and placed his napkin beside the plate.

"The country I from, grew angry with this country and began fight. Government worried safety because of me and many like me. We moved all like me to a place for safety. Now fighting stop I return."

"Did you have fun there?" Carol Jessica asked. "Was there lots of stuff to do? Daddy read us some of the stuff from letters you wrote."

Mrs. Kitomi spoke up, "I got together with some of the other women to sew blankets for the nearby hospital. We told stories and I even learned needle art, though it was difficult to find thread sometimes. I learned seventeen ways to prepare Spam, when we could get it."

"When warm, I play at two base, the ball game. When cold, I do carving of wood," Mr. Kitomi related. "Was dry there. In desert of Utah. Place called Topaz, but no find any topaz stones."

"What's a topaz?" Dot asked.

"It's a stone, sort of reddish-brown color. Can be pretty when polished up nicely," Ben told her.

With the table cleared after dinner, Ben and Kai settled in the living room to talk while the girls washed the dishes. Mrs. Kitomi insisted upon helping to clean up from the meal.

"I know you've been through a lot. Probably more than I'll ever know about. I'm glad you decided to return here," Ben told him.

"I come because you. You stood for me when job taken away. Most in camp not get letters. You send letters every week. Now you save my home. Others had home and store taken from them."

"What kind of friend wouldn't be there when you needed it? I had a hard enough time getting hired on when they thought I was Irish because of my hair. You owe me nothing."

"I pay back. I sweep floors. Move rubbish. What you need. I do what you need," Kai said.

"I told you there was a spot in the company for a rope crafter. I already have a kid to sweep the floors." Ben pointed to a shelf holding a three-foot-long ship model. "See that ship? That was Titanic. It went down thirty-three years ago. If it had been equipped with proper life boats, my family would not be gone."

"Why no boats?" Kai asked.

"It had boats, just not enough. Sixteen of the rigid bulky kind; those made it off alright. It also had four collapsible boats. Of those four, one went in with the sides still folded down and nigh on sank, and one went in upside down. That made them both useless," Ben said, raising his voice with the excitement of the story.

"You make better boats?" Kai asked.

"Most of the ones I make have been bought up by the Navy, but now the war's over there will be other ships to fit out," Ben told him. "Strong Flotation boats use a carved balsa tube around the outside, with a flexible floor, so it doesn't matter which side is up. It's always right side up and can't sink. You come in with rigging ropes around the outside for swimmers to hold onto."

"Is good work. I happy work with you," Kai said. "Sad for hear you family."

"I know I lost a lot of family when Titanic went down, but I can't shake the feeling that there's still family out there waiting for me," Ben told him.

While Ben and Kai talked, Isabella, Kai's wife, taught the girls how to fold tiny bits of paper into animal shapes. Tatiana loved it the most and folded a dozen tiny cats. With Dot's help, she colored all of them and gave each of the paper cats a name. She handed a little tiger-striped one to Mr. Kitomi.

"Her name is Lulu Belle, but she's a cat not a cow. She likes cow milk, though," Tatiana told him.

"You got to pet her like this," Lily told him.

The next day, Ben had barely begun assigning tasks to his workers when Kai walked in the door. The first one to see him was Farrell Green, who promptly yelled at him to get out. The burly man didn't wait for him to leave on his own and stomped over to block his entrance to the factory.

"You're in the wrong place, Ching. Best get your nippy butt out of here while you can!"

Ben looked over just as Farrell grabbed Kai's shirt, "Green! I hired him. He works with all of you now. Karen, will you get him set up with the ropes?"

"I ain't working with no Nip!" Farrell yelled. "Get rid of him or I'm gone."

"Oh well, get yourself out of here then. Can't have you stinkin' up the place."

"You heard him, ya Nip. Get gone," Farrell yelled.

"I meant you, Green. I've worked with Kitomi before and I know his work. Besides, I doubt Susan and Karen will miss having to dodge your friendliness."

Farrell shoved Kai aside and stormed over to the rack of coats. Watching, as nobody spoke up for him, he grabbed his jacket. He yelled a few more obscenities as he continued his rampage out the door.

"You'll be sorry fer' this!" was the last anyone heard as the warehouse door slammed closed once more.

Ben looked at the faces surrounding him, "Liza, will you show Kitomi where the rope work station is? The rest of you already know what you'll be doing. Susan, I'm going to need you on the tower, since Farrell decided to quit."

Liza turned away sullenly, “I can’t. Get somebody else to show him around. It’s too soon since…”

“I forgot about that. Yorktown. Right,” Ben muttered. ”Kai, I’ll show you around after the inspectors are done. For now, help me on the tower with Susan.”

Kai followed Ben and Susan through the warehouse factory to the lot behind the building. Two men stood waiting with clipboards in hand. Their grey suits seemed somewhat out of place in a neighborhood where dressing up meant putting on clean overalls and rinsing off your boots. One of them stepped forward to meet Ben.

“Looks like you have eight batches ready to go. Here’s the list of the ones we’ll test,” He handed a sheet of paper to Ben.

“Ok, 1709 is right there, so we’ll start on that one,” Ben replied.

Ben and Susan worked to get the hoisting line connected, while Kai watched. A few minutes later, they were hoisting the twenty-man raft up the sixty-foot tower. Susan pulled the release line and the raft plummeted into the pool with a splash.

Susan showed Kai how to move the raft over to the other side of the pool, where the second grey suited man situated himself into a chair with his lunchbox beside him. They marked the side of the raft, right where the water came to, with a grease pencil. One by one, they dropped the other seven rafts listed on the sheet and moved them over to float under the watch of the seated man.

“As good as always,” the man commented. “I don’t suppose any of them will sink in the next twenty-four hours?”

Ben led Kai back inside, to a work area with a raft sitting on stands. He spent the next few hours showing Kai how to string the ropes through the loops around the canvas-covered wood tubes. He had to show him three times how to weave the ropes together to form the double lifeline around the outside of the frame, before Kai finally understood it well enough.

Ben left him working and went off to check the rafts his crew had completed the day before. He could have had any one of the workers checking these floats over, to ensure they were flawless, but he insisted on doing it personally. Once he was satisfied with the raft, he engraved his initials into the wooden plaque attached to the inside of the raft.

With everything in the factory running smoothly for a few minutes, Ben sank into the padded chair behind a desk piled high with paperwork. The overworked basket on the left held the day's mail and Ben grabbed the top envelope. He briefly noted the government seal in the upper corner as he tore the top open.

Blah, blah, blah, with the war ending they were scaling back on ship production. They were cutting back on the next order to only seventy-eight rafts, with no schedule for any rafts after that.

"Well, I saw that coming as soon as they signed the armistice."

The next envelope held a bit more promise to it. Inspectors from the Brooklyn yards were due to arrive the following Wednesday. They would evaluate the rafts for use on the Liberty ships being refitted. The bottom of the letter requested that he have plans ready for a three-day survival box for each raft.

Ben's attention was drawn to the sound of the saws and sanders in the factory shutting down. He had become so accustomed to the constant sound of them, that he never really noticed it, at least until they shut down at the end of the day. However, there was still two hours left to work.

The minute he opened the door, Ben could hear the yelling. He rounded the stack of canvas bolts to find Kai sitting on the floor, holding a bolt of the fabric, while two of the women were yelling at each other from opposite sides of the aisle. Ben stepped between them and promptly received a blow to his head from a wooden mallet. He blinked his eyes back in focus as Liza shook his shoulders and called his name.

"Mr. Strong. Mr. Strong. Oh, polywog! I think I really knocked him for a loop."

"What's all the fuss over?" Ben asked.

"Well, Liza were chasing the Jap and Fanny got in her way. That's when he grabbed a bolt of the twenty-four count to keep her from hitting him," Susan related.

"And that's when Liza smacked me with a mallet?" Ben asked, rubbing the side of his head.

"Sorry boss. I…, uh…, well, I got no excuse. He just came at me with a couple of those sticks and." Liza said.

"I ask her smooth down for chopsticks," Kai said, as he set the bolt of canvas aside. "Is good wood. I make her nice set, yes?"

"Good thought, maybe. You wouldn't know it, but she lost her man when Yorktown went to the bottom," Ben told him.

"How city go somewhere?"

"Yorktown was an aircraft carrier. The Japanese navy sank it."

Kai turned to Liza and bowed, "So sorry for you loss. I know not about any of this. They let us hear nothing about terrible war in camp. Radio play some music. Newspaper all cut. Books taken."

"What's that got to do with you shoving sticks at me?" Liza asked.

Kai excused himself a moment and returned with a pair of dark wood sticks. The lights glinted off the abalone inlay along the side. He held them out to Liza.

"Saw you eat noodle with finger. Wanted make you good set of chopsticks. You have mine. Good teak wood."

Liza stared at him a minute, before turning away, "Keep 'em. Wouldn't know what to do with 'em anyway."

Ben was halfway up the walk to his house when a car pulled to a stop by the gate. A man in his dark navy uniform stepped out and waved to him. He took a few more steps, reaching the door of the house.

"Mr. Strong?" he called.

Ben nodded to him. The navy man pulled a box from the rear seat of his car, setting a small bit of wood on top of it, and turned to catch up to Ben.

"You have a daughter, Dorothy?" the man asked.

Ben again nodded.

"It might be better inside. I won't take too much time. I'm guessing it's time for your dinner."

"Sorry, come in, uh…"

"Flanagan, Lieutenant Donald Flanagan. Thank you. You have a beautiful home."

Ben ushered the man inside, where he was promptly surrounded by Kristie and the girls. Kristie stood brushing the flour off her hands as Tatiana came down the stairs two at a time.

"This is Lieutenant Flanagan, from the United States Navy. Dorothy, get him a chair."

"Actually, this box is for you, Dorothy. You sent a letter to Boiler Mate Grant, asking for leaves."

Lt. Flanagan handed the box to Dorothy and pulled a stained envelope from his pocket. He pulled a ragged paper from it and began reading.

Dear Dorothy;

Thank you so much for telling me about your school class assignment. I have a daughter named Becky that's about your age. I wonder if she has the same task of writing to soldiers. Collecting leaves from all over sounds fun, but unfortunately there aren't any trees aboard the destroyer I'm serving aboard. I can see the trees on the shore and I'll send you a few leaves when I get there.

Signed BM2 Mike Grant.

Lily ran into the kitchen and returned with a knife for Dot to open the box. The top flipped open to show the box stuffed with leaves and yellow flowers. Sitting atop the leaves was a small card bearing the Navy seal on it.

Mike couldn't make it, so we sent you every leaf we could find on Okinawa when we landed.

"Those flowers are from the Bloemb trees. There were so many that we could see them from the ship as we were sailing by. They only bloom in June, I'm told."

"Now I got leaves from Okinawa. Where's that?" she asked.

"That would be the southern end of the Japanese Islands," her father told her. "Not quite the same as Honshu, where Mr. Kitomi came from."

"That means I got leaves from seven countries, plus Kansas, California, and Florida!" Dorothy shouted, as she hopped up and down.

"This is for you, Sir." Lieutenant Flanagan handed the wooden plaque to Ben.

"Raft 491. It's been a while since I made that one," Ben commented.

"When the kamikaze hit, it knocked the raft clear of the ship. Then, when the USS Twiggs went down, there were twenty-nine of us that grabbed onto this raft."

"But it's a twenty-man raft. It's only supposed to hold twenty. Ten in it, and ten hanging on the side." Ben muttered.

"The Zeros made two runs on us and we hung on for dear life. They got Mike, but he used what little breath he had to make us promise to get his letter to Dorothy. There were twenty-three of us left after the Zeros had their try. They put seventeen holes in that raft, including one right through the water can. We floated along for nigh on three days before they picked us up. Everyone that came out of the raft signed the plaque and I pulled the straw to deliver it to you. Thank you from the men who came back. There's one flower from every one of us, plus one from Mike Grant BM2 of the USS Twiggs."

The lieutenant stepped back and snapped a practiced salute at Ben. Ben did his best to salute back.

CHAPTER TWENTY ONE

April 19th, 1953 – Winchester, England

David held the picnic basket in one hand and Eliza's hand in the other. His youngest daughter had asked him and Rose for a picnic, since the weather had cleared enough to dry the dew from the grass. Rose followed along behind them with the picnic quilt folded over her arms.

"You're being a bit cryptic about this," David told her. "Are we finally going to hear about this Thomas?"

"Shh, Love, don't try to spoil her surprise," Rose chided him.

"Thanks, Mum, but no. Well, I mean, it kind of is about Thomas, just probably not what you're thinking."

David came to a stop by the far corner of the yard. The grass in this part hadn't been trimmed in a few weeks, so it gave a bit of cushion under the picnic quilt. Rose spread it out and sat along the one side. David set the basket in the middle, turning to Eliza.

"So, when do we get to meet this Thomas of yours?"

"David!" Rose started.

"Tis alright, Mum," Eliza told her, as she took her father's hand.

Eliza led him over to the small plot of stones. She stood before the first one and waved a hand toward it.

"You've been wanting to meet Thomas. Well, here he is: Thomas Corbridge, born in 1839 and passed away long before I was born."

"I barely remember meeting him, on his death bed, when I was a lad of five or so," David said quietly. "But I thought Thomas was the fellow you had seen a few times."

"You're thinking of Albert. I told him that I wouldn't talk to him again unless he brought me a live dragon, so I could feed him to it."

"What does that have to do with my grandfather?" he asked.

"It's a long story, so sit down and butter up a muffin. I'm going to grab a biscuit."

Eliza settled herself on the picnic quilt and stared at her father for a moment. When it seemed he would remain standing there, staring back at her, she pulled a muffin from the basket to hand him and patted the spot next to her.

"You know how I've been looking into our family history for a bit?" she related. "I was looking through all the stuff in the library upstairs and came across a journal Great-Papa wrote. When he was lots younger, he worked a bit as a glazier. Now, making windows didn't seem like much fun till I thought about Grand-Mama's glass dolls. I was sure I could make something like that. I built a bit of an oven in the barn, right next to Grand-Mama's old truck, that she hasn't driven in nigh on a century, and melted a couple broken windows."

"So, that's why you had me bringing home bits of coal off the coal bunker. You said you were stocking up for Edric's Christmas stocking."

"Anyway, I've been practicing and getting pretty good at it. When I told Albert that I wished I could make glass bowls for the Queen's coronation in June, he said, and I quote him if you can imagine his hoarse voice, 'What good would that do you? That's no kind of work for a woman to be doing. You need to think about making me biscuits and popovers.' So, it's his own fault for saying things like that to me while we were next to a boggy spot."

"You threw mud at him?" Rose asked.

"I bumped him good and he went splat! Waving his arms the whole time. He yelled for me to help him up, but I just left him there. The queen was a mechanic in the war. The Queen! If she can do that, then I can make glass stuff. Look, Elaine has her Rupert. Gag, what a name! Don't tell him I said that, though. And Edric's off on his HMS Royal Pain."

"His ship is the Ark Royal, Dear," David told her.

"Well, it sounded good. He's a pain in the royal bum. Hey, these are the plum filled biscuits. I thought we didn't have any more dried plums."

"I told you I didn't have any more dried plums for you to be pinching the whole sack to your room. How else am I to make plum popovers for your brother and his mates?" Rose asked.

"I just need a load of bricks for a better oven that old man Peabody said I could have for a song. When I asked him what song, he just said that it was one he could fit into a piggy bank. And then, I also need a couple blow pipes. Of course, I'd better clear the straw out of that part of the barn, since I near singed it a few times already. I'll need some borosilicate for the better glass; at least that's what the book calls it."

"I'll tell you what: You get that old truck of your Grand-Mama's running and use it to haul the bricks here. That is, if you can talk Mr. Peabody into trading bricks for a truck. We don't really have the money to part with for whimsical stuff," David told her.

"How am I s'posed to get that truck working? I don't know anything about trucks."

"You're the one that brought up being like the Queen. She was a mechanic when she needed to be. If she can be a mechanic, so can you."

"But, that thing was built in like fifteen-hundred! I bet I find an old crusader sword in the back."

"It's only about forty years old now and she drove it less than five years ago. You'll just need a can of fresh petrol, most likely."

Eliza talked Rupert into bringing his tools over to the big house and showing her how to patch the old Ford truck back together. Mostly, it involved her gossiping with her sister Elaine while Rupert stuck his head under the hood. She rewarded his efforts with a fresh strawberry and rhubarb pie.

After the first few bites of the pie, his mouth puckered so much that he could hardly smile. He laughed it off and talked his wife into giving her sister a lesson in pie making. Eliza succeeded in making a passable pie on her third attempt.

Three weeks after setting her plans in motion, Eliza pulled down the lane in the old truck. Two of her pies set on the seat beside her, while a few bushels of fresh vegetables bounced along in the bed of the truck.

Her mother had let her take the things the family could spare, so that she could try her luck at the farmer's market. Eliza had left the tastiest looking melons still on the vines in the garden and only picked about half of the ripe berries. Sitting on the top of one basket were a few dozen of the first apricots of the season.

By the time she arrived, all the stalls were occupied and a steady stream of shoppers wandered between the booths. Eliza backed the old truck up next to the last stall in the line, and lowered the gate. She tied a parasol to the corner of the bumper to shade two overturned crates: One for her to sit upon, and one to show off the pies.

It didn't take long for people to gather around her. The apricots were the first to go, snapped up by a lady for twice what they would have fetched later in the season. She was followed by a man that nibbled every berry she had. He plopped down coins as fast as he could pop the little berries into his mouth. He even lifted the cucumbers to make sure he hadn't missed a single one.

When two of the other farmers closed up their stalls, her melons began selling. Her pies were looked over a few times, but she refused to give out samples, regardless of how they asked. She finally agreed to trade them for eight bags of cement that would be delivered at her barn the following Tuesday.

Eliza folded up the gate on the truck, and pulled away from the market, slightly past one in the afternoon. She stopped briefly at the post to fold six pounds and a handful of shillings into an envelope to hand over to the Postmaster.

By half-past two, she pulled to a stop in Mr. Peabody's drive. Eliza fairly skipped up to his door, excited to get her bricks. He looked a bit grumpy as he answered the door, beginning to smile as he saw that his visitor was Eliza.

"You said you had bricks I could get from you for a song, but how about a truck? See? I'll get the bricks and you can have Grand-Mama's old truck."

He glanced over her shoulder, to the truck sitting in the drive, "And just how do you plan to get the bricks home if I take your truck?"

"I'll um… I'll bring it back after I get them home and then you can have it," Eliza told him.

"I'll tell you something. Toss in five pounds and you can keep the old rattletrap. That a good enough song fer you?"

"Um, ok. I've got that much left anyway. Now what do I do with a truck?"

"Put a sign on it that reads Eliza's weird and exotic glass creations. That way, when you drive it around, folks will look at you funny and all."

"I've got to get my oven going good, maybe even add a lehr to it. But, first, I need the bricks."

"Right you is, Miss. 'Round the side there you'll find my old tack house, or at least what's left of it. Never got around to cleaning up all them bricks after something fell off one of the planes and smashed it. Help yourself to all the bricks you want."

Eliza walked around to the side where he had pointed and found the pile of bricks and timbers that had once been a sizable shed. She sighed as she realized that the truck was going to be essential in moving all those bricks home.

She carried bricks three or four at a time for several trips before pulling the truck closer. The springs under the truck sagged as the pile in the back grew taller. She was ready to drive the first bit home when she pulled a brick that clanked.

Eliza pulled several more bricks loose as she tried to uncover the bit of metal buried beneath. The flat sheet of metal merged into a rounded shape that reminded her of a jug. The last brick she pulled loose uncovered a word printed on the side of it that looked oddly spelled.

Realization hit her at last that the word was German and she found herself staring at a remnant of the battle that had smashed so much of the country. Most of the bombs had fallen on Southampton, but this one had apparently wound up flattening a shed full of horse gear.

Eliza dropped the brick in her hand and ran. She was halfway to the drive when she remembered the truck. Eliza ran back and furiously cranked the handle until the engine sputtered to life. She pulled the truck down the drive, toward the road, then turned around to park in front of the house.

Mr. Peabody still had a napkin tucked into the neck of his shirt when he answered the door to her pounding. He pulled it loose to wipe his mouth as he swung the screened door open.

"What's got you all in a tussle?" he asked.

"It's one of those… things. Those things they dropped all over Southampton. Bomb, that's what it's called. They dropped a bomb on your shed and it's still sitting there!"

"I ain't got a tele in the house. We'll have to go into town for a proper Bobby."

He lifted his coat and hat from a tree next to the door, then joined her outside. Eliza stood back as he edged close enough to see the metal fins sticking up through the pile of rubble for himself. As soon as he convinced himself that it was like she had told him, he hurried back to her side.

"Now why in blazes did they go and drop that here? You'd think they could tell the difference between a goat house and a big factory."

Eliza drove the truck down to the nearest police station. The sergeant at the desk listened to their story for only a minute before lifting his own hat from the desk. He called two of the patrolmen to join them and Eliza led the way back to Mr. Peabody's farm.

The sergeant pointed his fancy new torch to light up the scene. He whistled when he saw it.

"Well, if that don't beat all! Them Jerries must have been way off course to think this was some vital war effort. What was it? A distillery? A ball bearing plant? Or maybe you had a full tank factory hidden in there."

"My tack shed. I kept the goat here, too."

"I'll get some of the Home Defense lads over in the morning to check it out. 'Probably toss a few sticks of nitro in the hole and stand back."

Eliza chatted with Mr. Peabody for just a bit longer before heading home with her prized bricks. It was near dark and far beyond the time supper would have been on the table, when she pulled to a stop by the house. Grand-Mama Bessie sat rocking in her chair on the porch and greeted her warmly.

Rose had held off serving supper, hoping that Eliza would return in time. She warmed the stew a bit before filling bowls for the three of them. David was off on another night run to London. Eliza related her time at the market between mouthfuls.

"And all these little pipsqueaks stood around whining for a bite of my pies. If I'd done that there wouldn't have been even a bite left to trade for my cement. I even put enough in my pocket for some of that borosilicate."

"Why don't you just call it glass like us normal folks?" Grand-Mama asked her.

"This isn't like the stuff in the windows. This is really neat glass, with more colours than a Notre Dame window."

"Well, you got back so late, I guess you'll be off getting those bricks in the morning," her mother asked.

"I got some of them loaded in the truck. I'll stack those in the barn in the morning. Hopefully, the Home Defense will have cleared the bomb out by then, so I can get the rest of them."

"A bomb? Like the ones the planes dropped?" Rose asked.

"He said they'd be along to pull it out in the morning. One of those German planes must have been rightly lost," Eliza said.

"I hear they're still finding one of those things sitting around every other week in some places," Bessie said.

Eliza stacked the bricks in the barn, right where the old Ford had sat for years. She did a little quick figuring in her head and realized she'd need a few more bags of cement, as well as the rest of the bricks, if she were going to build the lehr for annealing the glass she crafted. Great Grand-Papa's journal talked about how important it was to keep the glass from cracking.

Eliza arrived back at Mr. Peabody's place in time for lunch. She had packed a basket full of sandwiches, hoping that the treat would have the Home Defense boys moving that bomb out of her way faster. Most of them were made from the cucumbers and tomatoes she pulled from the garden, since her mother had used the last of the ham for the stew.

As she pulled into Mr. Peabody's drive, she parked the truck behind a much newer version with government lettering on the side of it. She lifted the big basket of food to hurry around to the side of the house.

Mr. Peabody sat in a chair by the side of his house, far enough back from the excitement that he couldn't even hear them if they shouted. Four of the men stood a good hundred feet from where another man poked at the bomb sticking up from the rubble.

They had already moved many more bricks out of the way to help reach the metal menace. Eliza stood next to the men, watching silently for a minute. Finally, the man poking the bomb stood up and called out.

"I'm thinking this is one of those decoys they liked so much. Drop a bunch of dummies, along with the real boomers, and keep everyone in a right tizzie for weeks wondering if the dummy is going to pop its top."

"How can you be sure?" called the man standing next to Eliza.

The other man picked up one of the bricks and smacked it hard into the side of the bomb. It rang hollow, like a dull church bell, but not a fizzle or a spark.

"Pretty sure, but I'll get my tools to pop open the side and check-see real quick. The bloody nits forgot to even stick the fuse in it."

"Would you…," Eliza coughed, finding her throat dry. "Would you men like to have a sandwich or two? I made enough for ten because I didn't know how many there'd be."

"Thomas, get your tools and be sure about that thing before anybody else gets too close. And mind you now, no showing off like that in front of the lady."

Thomas pulled the side off the bomb, only to find the inside filled with pea gravel. His theory about it being a dummy proved right, though his sergeant grumbled at him a bit more as the men enjoyed Eliza's basket of sandwiches. Thomas ended up next to her as he bit into his meal.

"Just what do you plan to do with all these bricks?" he asked her. "Seems like a lot of work, so it must be something good. My name's Thomas, if you hadn't heard the sergeant nipping at me."

"You'll probably laugh and call me a bloody nit for it, but I want to build an oven for cooking glass. I can make all kinds of glass things that way," she told him. "So, Thomas, What's your last name? I'm Eliza. Eliza Corbridge."

"It's both. Thomas Thomas. My schoolmates always got a good laugh out of it. Got even better in the Corps where we all use our surnames for everything."

Eliza told him about building her oven, thinking he'd turn around and laugh at her the way Albert had done. Instead, he talked the others into getting all of her bricks loaded into the old Ford. They even propped the dud bomb on top of the load, with chalk markings declaring it safe.

"That thing will make a right proper door for your oven to keep the heat in. I'll drop by on Saturday, if you need some help making it. I'm anxious to see your first piece," Thomas told her.

When Saturday morning rolled around, Eliza opened the door to find Thomas and two of his friends sitting in a truck next to the barn. After introducing them, they each lifted a bag of cement from the back of the truck and followed her into the barn. One of the men chuckled at the sight of the oven she had started building.

"I can see your heart was in it Lassie, but let this brickmaster have a crack at it," he said.

"Like I told you, she'll need one hot enough to cook the sun and one for letting things cool down proper for a few days," Thomas said.

Thomas nudged her back and the men set to work. Eliza brought out a basket of sandwiches and biscuits, with a pitcher of butter beer for lunch. They broke off the oven project long enough to eat the sandwiches, but wouldn't let her see the progress they had done. They gathered around the table, under the tree, and chatted about things they had seen while clearing through the rubble the past few years.

"That reminds me a bit, Lassie," Mike told her. "I picked up something right useful for you. Thought about it when Tommy Knockers twisted me arm to come do this today. Got you a wee little vault door, what come out of a silver britches place, when Nob Hill were hit. Thought it would come in handy, but never knew for what, till now. Ought to be just big enough to fit a dowry chest."

The men finished crafting her oven by late afternoon and made a grand showing of it to her. The big oven boasted the vault door, as Mike had told her about, complete with a monogramed T on the door. They finished the presentation with three big boxes from the truck.

"These used to be windows in the East Chapel. This gives you at least half a dozen colours to play with. They haven't gotten 'round to clearing that lot yet, so might be able to get you some more if you run scarce on it," Thomas told her.

CHAPTER TWENTY TWO

September 12th, 1962 – Bennett, America

Ben pulled the daily mail from the box at the curb as he arrived home. The first two letters were invoices from the department stores downtown, but the third envelope caught his eye. It bore several stamps, including a crown from the London post. His heart raced his feet into the house.

He called into the kitchen, where the sound of a spoon banging the side of a pot told him Kristie was hard at work on the dinner.

"Kristie, I'm home. I suppose I shouldn't ask what you charged at Hubbard's. The Sears wish book is here to start shopping for the grandkids."

Ben settled into his well-worn arm chair and reached for the letter opener. He held his breath the whole time it took to tear the top of the envelope open. He pulled two onionskin papers from the envelope, noting how they had typing on both sides.

My good sir;

It seemed highly unfeasible to post you the entirety of the local telephone directory pertaining to the Southampton region. Concerning your interest in the name of Corbridge, I located one such listing within said directory for a Mr. David Corbridge of Winchester, which lies in the region. In looking through the index cards for the paper I found a few more listings for the name. Miss Mary Corbridge married one Edward Hansen in 1922. She had to be someone important enough to be listed in the socialite pages.

The letter continued on with little else other than questions as to why Ben was searching so diligently. The journalist pleaded with Ben for the story of his experience on RMS Titanic.

Ben angrily crumpled the paper in his hands as thoughts of Titanic loomed up. He still found it difficult to separate the mighty ship and the loss of his whole family. All of it still swirled through his thoughts like a black fog. A moment later, his thoughts cleared and he smoothed out the papers in his hand.

"Dinner will be on the table in five minutes, Dear," Kristie called from the kitchen. "Be sure to wash up."

Ben dropped the letter on the side table and walked back to the wash room. Removing his jacket and washing his face and hands cleared most of the smell from him. The new plastics he used in the boats smelled a great deal worse than the wood from a decade previously.

He joined Kristie in the kitchen, just as she placed the butter dish out. The big pot of stew steamed in the pot, holding enough to feed nearly a dozen people. She settled into the chair across from him, stretching out her hands to join his. They bowed their heads as he blessed the meal.

"Even Lily went off to college a year ago," Ben said with a smile. "If you're going to keep making enough dinner to feed an army, we should invite C.J. and the boys over sometimes. They'd liven the dinner up to where I couldn't hear the moths snoring."

"I try not to fix too much. It's just…," she started.

"I know. It's habit from so many years. Lord knows I love you for it," Ben said as he stirred the spoon through his stew.

"You received another letter today, didn't you?" Kristie looked at him. "You say the same sort of things every time a letter shows up. Even if it's been a few years since the last letter came."

"It's…, this came from England. I have a number to call now. It's a family I've sent cables to a few times without ever getting a response. If I call now, it'll be the middle of the night there. I mean, five hours difference. That'd be a great introduction to call them at near midnight."

"So, there's tomorrow. Take the day to do it. Kai can mind the factory for a week, if need be. You've been wondering about this for fifty years. Call them."

The next morning, Ben fixed himself a tall glass of lemonade and stared at the phone for nearly five minutes before lifting the receiver. He first called Mr. Kitomi to let him know that he would be out for the day. His next call wasn't nearly as easy. To reach overseas, he needed the assistance of the operator.

His local operator shifted his call through the New York exchange, where she let him know that reaching England would be a ten dollar charge. Ben agreed to it and she still took another twenty minutes to connect him into London's exchange.

After Ben repeated the number twice, the London operator chided him on his terrible Yankee accent. On the fourth ring, a woman answered the phone and he could hear the operator explaining to her that the call was coming from the colonies. Finally, Ben found himself talking directly to the woman.

"My name is Ben Strong. I'm trying to reach a Mr. David Corbridge."

"My husband is sleeping at the moment, but I will wake him since you are calling from America. Please hold the line for a moment."

Ben waited another ten minutes before hearing the static interrupted by a man's voice.

"Hello? Hello? Are you there?" David asked.

"Yes, I'm here. My name is Ben Strong, though you likely don't know my name this way. This is concerning the Titanic. I understand you were on the ship."

"Listen, my sister may have time for you grave diggers, but I heard all I could stand of it forty years ago. Telephone her if you are that interested. I haven't the time nor liking to regale your interest. Take a swim to the bottom, if you like. That's where your story is."

Even through the static of the connection Ben could hear the phone change hands.

"I'm sorry Sir. There was a bad run in the night. A lorry on the rail and all," Rose told him.

"Wait, he mentioned a sister. He was the only contact I could find. Would you be so kind as to tell me how to reach her?" Ben pleaded.

Rose talked with Ben a few minutes and gave him Mary's number. She apologized once more, for the curt response David had given him, before wishing him better luck with Mary.

Ben listened to the operator tell him that it would be another ten dollar charge, just for the connection, as she dialed him back into the London exchange. The telephone on the other end rang seven times before a woman answered it. After the operator explained that America was calling, Ben finally got a chance to speak.

"Ma'am, my name is Ben Strong. Please don't hang up or yell. I believe you are the person I've been searching for over many years. This is about Titanic. There was a Mary Corbridge on the passenger list."

"I was on the list, though I never set foot on the ship," she told him.

"Did any of your family sail on Titanic?"

"Mr. Strong. That is a very personal question, not to mention touching upon painful memories," Mary said.

"Your brother already disconnected my call when I asked him. I can understand how sensitive the question is. I was aboard the ship also," Ben told her. "Did you have any family that sailed on it?"

Mary's heart skipped a beat as long buried grief and anger surfaced. Memories and feelings that had been shoved down into the deepest corner of her thoughts popped up again, with vibrant clarity. She took a couple of breaths before giving her reply in a voice that cracked with the emotion.

"Half my family was aboard," she told him. "I'm not sure that I'm ready to think about that again."

"Did any of them survive? Do you know?" he asked.

"They were all listed as dead. I'm sorry, Mr. Strong, what is all this about?"

"I think I may know something of the events the night she sunk. It could be very relevant and important if true, but it could prove hurtful if I tell you the full story and it turns out to be incorrect."

"Excuse me, Mr. Strong, have you spoken to anyone else about this?"

"As I said at the first, I talked to David Corbridge. He promptly disconnected my call, but not before his wife gave me your number," Ben said.

"Mr. Strong, how did you locate us?"

"I've been searching for almost my entire life. I've been through the manifest and talked to city offices. I've dug through newspapers in a dozen libraries. I've written to everyone even remotely listed on the ship's manifest: both crew and passengers. Finally, a reporter with the London paper drooled a little at the prospect of a story. Fifty years and all. He gave me the number for David hoping that I'd give him a juicy tale to print."

"I can appreciate your interest in what happened that night, but to us you are merely opening old wounds that have healed long ago. We have no interest in being part of some juicy tale splashed across the papers. Please don't contact my family again."

Ben's voice cracked as he spoke, "Mrs. Hansen, may I please make an appointment to meet with you. I'll fly across and meet you so that I can tell you this in person.

This isn't about a juicy story. It's something very dear to myself, and likely to you as well, should I be correct."

"I shall allow you one chance. I will expect you at ten O'clock on the morning of the nineteenth. If this matter is as vital as you claim, you will not be late. One chance; don't allow me to rue giving you this singular opportunity."

"Thank you Mrs. Hansen," Ben said. "I'd paddle one of my rafts over there if I had to. I will see you next week."

Mary's hand was shaking as she set the receiver back in its cradle. She stood there staring at the telephone, half expecting it to burst into flames or something. Mary slowly released her grip on the receiver and walked into the kitchen to fix herself a cup of tea.

By the time she had reached the bottom of the cup, while staring out the back window, Mary had calmed a bit. She nibbled one of the last biscuits in the jar as she sipped a second cup of tea.

"I need to talk with Edward," she mumbled to herself.

Mary set her cup down a bit more forcefully than she had intended. She picked it back up to inspect it for chips; thankfully there were none. It was part of the set Edward's mother had shipped from the north to celebrate their first anniversary. Mary set the cup back down, gently this time, and smoothed her dress.

She steeled herself to walk up the stairs, trying to keep her hands from shaking once more. She paused outside the door, hesitating with her hand ready to knock. Instead, she twisted the handle and walked into Edward's office. He glanced up from the stack of papers he had been flipping through. Mary watched as the crease between his eyebrows melted into a look of concern.

"What's the matter, Mary? Has someone passed away? Your mother?" Edward asked.

"I'm sorry, Edward. I know you prefer I knock instead of merely barging in unannounced. No one has perished. It's just… I had the strangest telephone call," Mary started.

She couldn't sit down, even as Edward moved a few books off the chair next to his desk. She paced back and forth, nibbling at her fingernails; a habit she had rid herself of before she'd even married.

"Surely you must know who it was."

"Oh, he said his name was Mr. Ben Strong. Short for Benjamin, I'd wager, though I have never heard the name. He telephoned from New York City," Mary said. "He claimed to have information regarding my family on Titanic."

"You've never said much about it, though I know you lost family when it went down. I've left it be. The last thing I'd do is poke at old wounds you felt. I'd lay a stack of shillings on the table that it would be important to hear what the man has to say. A telephone call from New York City is not something a person does lightly," Edward told her.

"That may be true, but I am still nervous to hear what he has to say. I agreed to meet with him in a week. I would like it if you could be there."

"Of course I will be there for you. What shall we pack for New York?"

"I told him to come here. If it is as important as he claims, then it should be no bother to travel here," Mary said.

"If I may suggest, David should be here as well. Perhaps your mother, if she's up for it," Edward offered.

"Not mother. You saw how she was when we married. And that time you gave Edric the sailing boat that was as large as he was. I'll not rattle her nerves over even whispering the name Titanic," Mary said. "Maybe David. No, you're right. I should make him be part of it."

Mary went downstairs once more and picked up the telephone. She didn't have to look as she spun the numbers. The phone barely rang once before her brother answered.

"Mary?"

"Hello, David. Usually it's Rose that answers," Mary quipped.

"I couldn't get back to sleep," David muttered.

"Then you already know what I am telephoning about. I agreed to meet Mr. Strong in a week."

Mary listened to the silence for a minute before continuing, "I think you should be here."

"Are you sure about this? If mother hears anything, it could just send her over the brink once more."

"I sincerely doubt this is some frivolous matter. The man is coming all the way from America at a moment's notice. I need you here for it. After that, we can decide what to tell mother."

"Fine. I'll be there. Just don't be surprised if I toss him into the firebox of number ninety-two," David said.

"Maybe now you can get some rest. Don't you have a run to London in six hours?"

"I'll try. Wouldn't be the first time I made the run without a wink of sleep."

*****

Ben hung up the phone and stretched his arm. He worked his shoulder and wrist a minute, getting the soreness out of them. The call had only lasted a little while, but his arm felt as sore as if he'd just pitched a double game of ball. Ben settled back into his chair and let out a deep sigh.

After a few moments, he stood up and walked upstairs to find Kristie at her sewing machine. She looked up from pinning two bits of flannel together and smiled at him.

"That took a bit longer than I thought it would. How did it go dear?" she asked him.

"It was easier to call Virginia Shipways to tell them I'd gotten that bum batch of poly vinyl and their thirty rafts would take another month to rebuild," Ben said. "I managed to convince her to meet with me. Now all I have to do is fly over there in less than a week."

"We will find a way, Ben. Don't fuss about me. I'll be fine for a week. You just get yourself over there and settle this."

"They might know something about my family. For all I know, they could BE my family," Ben said.

"I think it's wonderful. Just try not to get your hopes up too high though," she told him. "And never forget that you have a family right here that loves you very much."

"I wouldn't trade you and the girls, or even the grandkids, for anything," Ben told her.

CHAPTER TWENTY THREE

September 19th, 1962 - Winchester, England

Mary paced back and forth in the parlor, pausing occasionally to fuss with the flowers in the vase or the curios on the shelf. Another glance at the clock on the mantle told her that Mr. Strong was due to arrive in two hours. Edward poked at the meager fire in the hearth, hiding his nervousness with a poker.

"I can order a new carpet for the parlor, if you're so intent on wearing a hole in this one," He quipped.

"I should have asked for his number. I could have called him to cancel this absurd meeting," Mary muttered.

"If I know your brother, he'll arrive in short order. Perhaps having him here will ease your nerves."

"I'll make some crumpets," Mary said, as she turned toward the kitchen.

"The British answer to everything," Edward laughed. "Enough tea and crumpets will cure anything short of the plague. Don't forget the jam."

Mary slid the first tray into the oven just as the bell for the front door bell jingled. She opened the door to find David standing on the stoop, with Rose beside him. Mary ushered them both inside, glancing down the drive for any sign of other vehicles. She hung up their coats, and waved toward the sofa.

"Thank you for coming, David. Please have a seat. I must check on the crumpets," Mary said.

Edward and David started in on a friendly argument over whose football team was likely to win the national trophy. Rose followed Mary into the kitchen to assist with the crumpets and talk about books she had read recently. Nobody mentioned anything about the impending arrival of Mr. Strong.

Mary carried a plate brimming with crumpets, followed by Rose with a jar of honeysuckle jam and a spoon. They sat, staring at each other in silence, for a few minutes. Mary jumped out of her seat when the door bell jingled again. She stared at the door for several seconds before Edward spoke.

"I expected that you would want to see him first, but I'll greet him."

"Oh…, I'll greet him," Mary said, walking toward the door.

Mary opened the door to find a man standing on the stoop. His familiar face made the colour drain from hers. The mop of red hair drew her gaze up to the top of his six-foot frame. She stepped back to usher him inside.

"Is this the Hansen home? There seems little to mark the streets around here, but the map shows it should be round about here," Ben said.

"Please enter. Mr. Strong," Mary began. "My name is Mary Hansen. My husband, Edward, with the poker. This is David; you spoke to him a week ago. And his wife, Rose."

Ben shifted the tattered book to his left hand and held out a hand in greeting. He startled as David stepped forth to grip his hand and shake it. This close to him, Ben caught the familiar angles to David's face. He'd seen a similar face staring at him in the mirror for several decades.

"Please sit in a seat. I have crumpets, and jam, and… Give me a moment. I forgot the tea," Mary told him in a rushed breath.

"A crumpet sounds delicious with a spot of jam. I'll forego the tea, though. A cup of water would be just fine," Ben told her.

"I'm sorry that we don't have any coffee here. We tend to drink tea often," Edward spoke up.

"Over in America, coffee is the big drink, but coffee and tea are both things I avoid. Water is fine for me," Ben replied.

"Before I make assumptions, I'd like you to tell us what precisely you're hoping to find here," David said.

"Thank you for inviting me into your home, Mr. and Mrs. Hansen. And it's good to meet you too, David Corbridge. It's good to meet all of you," Ben said. "As to what I hope to find here. Perhaps a few answers."

"Please, call me Mary."

"Yes, and call me Ben."

"Very well, Ben, You've come all the way across the pond with some news of the Titanic. That was news fifty years ago. Now, it's mostly forgotten," David said.

"I don't know how else to say this, so I'll just begin. It's a bit of a long story. Since I was about two years old, I grew up in New York. Actually, a little suburb of the big city, called Bennett. I was adopted by a good family. A good mother, at least. She later married a good man. She never hid the fact that I was adopted, though she treated me like her own."

"Where does Titanic come into this?" David asked.

"I'm a survivor of Titanic. She never hid that from me either, though she said she didn't know anything else about me. My parents both passed away many years ago and in the aftermath of that, I found my mom's journal. She wrote a great deal of things that she never told me. For one thing, she never really adopted me. At least not through any legal means. All I had known was that a woman, that I had thought was my mother, had given me to my adopted mother," Ben related.

"That can't be our mum. She's still living," Mary said.

Ben held his breath for a minute, steadying his thoughts to continue.

"As I said, that was the story that I believed was the entire story. It kept me from looking too hard, for many years. But, when I read her journals, there was a great deal more to the story. Jessica, the woman who adopted me, had met the woman who had been with me. In fact, she knew that I had been with two men, the woman, and another child. The night that Titanic sank, Jessica made it to a lifeboat, leaving her husband to do his job with the crew. The woman, she had met days before, handed me over the rail while she tried to put the life vest on the girl with her."

David drew a ragged breath when he heard this part of the story.

"Something happened and several people, including the woman and girl, fell off the ship into the water. She doesn't mention what happened to them after that, but I've read through enough of the testimonies of survivors to paint quite the picture. She protected me and kept me warm when the ship went down. Later, when our boat was picked up, she searched through all the survivors, hoping to find the woman again."

"You're an orphan of Titanic?" David asked.

"I am a definite survivor," Ben told them. "Jessica, the woman who raised me as her son, had lost her own boy about two months before Titanic sailed. Her husband never made it off the ship. Caring for me helped her to hang on and I got a loving mother out of the deal."

"So, how has that brought you to us?" Mary asked. "We were never on the ship."

"Before she died, all I knew was that I had been on Titanic. I searched through all the passenger and crew lists looking for someone that had lost a boy. I ran into dead end after dead end. I built models of the ship, hoping to jog a lost memory. The only memory I had was a vague one about a stuffed monkey, but it made no sense."

Ben pulled out the journal to lay it on the table.

"I found this after she died. It tells about meeting the woman I was with, who wasn't my mother. That put me on the path of looking for a mother that had been left behind. One by one, I crossed off every possible name from the very long list. I came at last to a Mr. and Mrs. George Corbridge. More than fifteen years of letters, to every person I could think of writing, gave me a name that came close. Yours, David Corbridge. I staked all my hopes that you might have some information of Mrs. Corbridge. I searched every ship manifest coming into New York for the last fifty years. She either remarried or never made the trip."

Ben continued to talk about being handed to the woman in the lifeboat and how he hadn't spoken a word for nearly a year afterward. To the questions they asked, Ben simply told them he couldn't remember any of it.

"My mother was very quiet about the adoption, always hushing me if I tried to bring it up. After I found Mom's journal, I had to know. I needed to know if I had some family left. I started by contacting the Cunnard Lines, which bought up White Star Line. Through the transcripts and the ships manifests, I narrowed it down to ten families. I wrote to libraries and then slowly I started to write to each family. One by one, crossing them off the list, I went out to meet a few of them, too. All was a total failure. You are the last family on the list."

As Ben continued talking, David stood up, at last, and stretched his legs. He refilled his cup of tea, sipping half the cup in one go. He set the cup down and began pacing by the window, in almost the same pattern Mary had done before his arrival. Each time he changed directions, his gaze went to Ben. At last, he sat back down and fidgeted with the tea cup.

"Don't you have anything stronger than this, Mary?" David asked.

Mary smiled at him, "You recognize him, don't you?"

"It might as well be his picture hanging in the stairway," David grumbled.

"Go. See if she will come. Just don't say why. Just tell her that I need to have her look at my stitches," Mary told him.

David set his cup down once more, after drinking the rest in a gulp, "I'll see what I can do. I may even get a bottle of the good stuff, as well."

"Paul, I'm sorry. It was rude to talk as though you weren't here. I won't say more until David returns. I'm fairly certain my thoughts on the matter are a bit biased.

It's best if I keep my peace for the moment. Would you care for a tart? There are a few remaining."

"Paul?" Ben asked.

"A slip of my tongue. Please sit. A tart?" Mary asked.

"A tart would be great. I'll just sit down, then," Ben said, taking a spot on the sofa across from where David had sat.

"You picked a right nit of a time to visit us here," Edward spoke up. "Weather bureau says that we're due for a bit of a blow the next few days."

"The plane had to skirt around some mean looking clouds on the way over here. It took us about an hour longer than it should have," Ben told him.

The men talked on, about nothing in particular, while Mary set to work in the kitchen. The clanking of pots sounded like a bit more than Mary fetching a plate of tarts as she had claimed. Edward was in the midst of telling a story about catching a horse when Mary set a stack of plates on the table in the dining room.

"Edward? I believe we'll need both leaves added to the table," Mary called out.

Edward broke off the story to insert two leaves into the table, expanding it to double its normal size. Rose immediately assembled the place settings around the table, making room for six of them. She finished the preparations with a vase of roses in the center of the table.

"I've turned the roast chicken into a Welsh pie and Rose is working on the buns I'd started earlier. I figured that when… Well, when David returns, that we could talk around the table. It's getting nigh on toward supper time. I'm sure… Ben is hungry after flying all the way here," Mary said.

"I actually arrived in London the night before last. Yesterday, I hired a car to bring me out here in time to find the roads. I spent yesterday driving around, so that I wouldn't get lost today. I have a room at a place in Southampton," Ben said.

"He has returned," Edward said.

"Um…, Ben, why don't you sit in this seat right here, facing the door?" Mary said.

Ben settled into the chair, while Edward and Mary stood ready at the door. Edward swung the door open to find David with his knuckles raised. Edward stepped back to wave him in and an elderly woman stood behind him. She stepped in, bracing her steps with a thin cane.

"David said you needed me. Something to do with picking stitchery?" the woman said.

"Not entirely, Mum. Come in and meet our guest," Mary said.

"You brought me here to meet someone? You could have brought them to the house. I'm not so…, George?" Bessie said, catching sight of Ben sitting there.

Suddenly, Bessie's legs shook and she leaned over. David quickly put an arm around her, as Ben leapt forward to take her other side. The two of them helped her into a chair and stood back.

"I'd say that pretty much chased away any doubts I had," David said.

"Who are you? Who is he? He can't be George. He…, Paul?" Bessie said.

"My name is…, that's twice someone called me Paul," Ben said. "I've gone by Ben my whole life."

"Not your entire life. Right up until that ship sank you were Paul Ryan Corbridge, my little brother. This is your mother, Mrs. George Bessie Barlow Corbridge,"

Mary said. “And the goof over there would be your brother, David.”

Ben stumbled back to sit in his own chair once more.

“Fifty years of looking and still not ready when it comes down to it!” Ben said. “Paul, huh?”

“That lady that handed you over the rail was our mum’s sister-in-law, Aunt Elizabeth. The girl was David’s twin, Elizabeth.”

“Handed over the rail?” Bessie said. “I always knew my Paul was alive! Somehow I knew.”

“Come, we can talk around supper,” Mary said. “Rose is just finishing up the buns. The table is even ready.”

"Paul, I mean Ben. What do you want to be called? Are you ok?" Mary asked, as she noticed that tears were streaming down his face.

“It’s so much to take in,” Ben said.

“Just take your seat here and Mum will question you more than she did me that time I stayed out all night with Rose,” David said.

Ben hardly even tasted the dinner, as he spent so much time relating the events listed in Jessica’s journal. Everything he had spent an hour telling to Mary and David, he repeated once more for Bessie. This time, it was even more difficult for him, as the tears kept trailing down his cheeks.

“I don’t know. Every moment that I can remember has been with me being called Ben. She never really adopted me, at least not officially, so I guess I’m still Paul,” he said. “Just Kristie married me as Ben. The girls call me Papa, which sounds the same regardless of Ben or Paul. I’ll try to answer to whichever you call me.”

"You were always Elizabeth's favorite, Paul. I think I spent half my time trying to unspoil you from what my sister-in-law had done. Of course, she liked Lizzie as well. It's hard not to like someone named after you," Bessie said.

David stood and gave his Mum a hug, "I am so happy to see the family together. Well, except for Papa and Lizzie. It's the first time in fifty years we've sat around the table together."

Bessie sighed, "It feels almost good to be able to talk about it now. So many times I…, I won't go into that now. The family's all together again. I want to meet this Kristie of yours!"

"I'm sure she'd love all of you. C.J., I mean Carol Jessica, looks a lot like you, Mary," Ben said.

"Why don't you bring all of them over here, Paul? We have the room upstairs that has been too quiet since Jenny got married. Tomorrow, you can fetch your cases from the hotel in town," Edward told him.

"I remember standing on the pier, watching as the ship pulled away. I waved to the both of you at the railing. Beth was holding you and Lizzie was tugging at her sleeve. When that horn sounded, I was sure the whole pier was going to fall into the sea," Bessie told them. "As soon as the ship turned, we jumped back into the motorcar and raced across England. We missed the ferry to Queenstown by a good six hours. The lot of you were all sleeping in the back when we arrived there and slept most of the way back to Grand-Mama's house."

"I have to say, Paul, that I blamed you for the longest time. We missed getting on the ship because of that ridiculous monkey of yours," David said. "It was the first time I'd been more than five feet from Lizzie and it near to drove me crazy."

"Then, before we could get another ship to follow you, that unsinkable ship did just that. Mum went into melancholia. She hardly ate or slept. Every time the telephone rang, or a knock on the door, she'd expect Papa to walk in with both you and Lizzie tagging along," Mary related.

"Lizzie? Is she coming to the house soon? I've missed her so much! Paul, don't forget Keykey!" Bessie said.

"Lizzie would never have left Paul all alone, unless something terrible happened. I just know it," David said.

"Is Lizzie catching leaves outside?" Bessie asked. "Tell your sister to come inside before she catches a cold."

David glanced at Mary and motioned to their mother. Mary nodded to him, with a sigh. Edward and David moved alongside Bessie, and helped her stand. Bessie slowly walked toward the door, mumbling little things too quiet to hear.

"She's tired, Paul. Tell her good evening so that she can go home and actually rest," Mary told him.

Ben hugged his mother gently, fearful that he might break the woman after searching for her for so long, "Good night, Mother."

"Come home with me, Paul," Bessie said.

David and Rose helped their mother down the front steps and into their car. He waved back at them before climbing into the driver's seat. Ben watched the car pull down the lane, until it was lost to sight around a bend.

Back inside the house, Ben started crying freely. Mary held onto him and joined in, letting the tears flow down her cheeks. Finally, she lifted a serviette from the table, dabbing at her own eyes to dry them.

"Perhaps you should telephone your wife and let her know what you've found," Mary said. "You can both have the room upstairs for as long as you like."

"I just can't believe it. After all these years, to find you," Ben said.

"It's ok, Paul. You're home now. Mum never gave up on you, though she gave up on the world a few times. She always told us that Papa said you would come home someday. I guess you proved her right."

CHAPTER TWENTY FOUR

September 19th, 1962 – Winchester, England

Ben set the receiver back into the telephone cradle. Reaching across the Atlantic Ocean proved to be just as difficult whichever way the telephone call was made. This time, his call had lasted nearly an hour as he tried to tell Kristie all about his visit.

Edward drove with Ben to retrieve his case from the room he'd taken in Southampton. Edward knew the right turns to cut a good ten minutes off the time Ben had taken to drive out. Edward took the time to point out some of the places they drove past. Many of the spots still bore the scars of the bombings the city had endured; all you needed to do was to know where to look.

Edward pulled his car to a stop three doors short of the White Raven Inn, where Ben had his room, and tapped his horn at a young woman just closing up her shop. She turned to glare at him, then broke into a big smile as she rushed over to the car.

"Uncle Edward! What are you doing all the way out here?" she said with a laugh.

"Eliza, I'd like you to meet your other uncle. This is your Uncle Paul, or Ben; whichever he's calling himself now."

"Where did I get another uncle? You didn't decide to divorce Aunt Mary so that she could marry this bloke, did you?"

"Never! Never in an eon of sparrows would I leave Mary! We just sort of added him to the family. He's a tried and true uncle. I'm sure your father will tell you all about it when you get home tonight," Edward told her

"This is David's youngest, Eliza Thomas," Edward said. "She took a liking to glass, after nearly burning down the barn, and now makes everything glass except windows."

Ben gathered his suitcase and settled with the clerk behind the counter. Edward brought him back out to the manor. Ben spent the evening trading stories of his youth with Mary.

"First time I really hit someone with everything I had," Ben said.

"We probably do have a touch of Irish in us, what with that red hair of yours," Mary said. "Little Eliza's the one that's looked into the family tree's roots. She might be able to tell you"

The eastern sky began lightening by the time Mary fell asleep listening to Ben talk about the stray cat his girls had found. He tucked the blanket around her shoulders and went upstairs to the room they had let him use.

Late in the morning, he and Mary drove off in her car, heading for London. Kristie was due to arrive in the early afternoon. She had wasted no time in setting a note for the milkman and closing up the house. Her flight delayed only an hour getting off the ground, waiting for some heavy rain to pass.

Rain began to sprinkle as Ben and Mary stood on the tarmac watching the BOAC aircraft pull to a stop. Kristie descended the stairs behind an elderly couple herding half a dozen gawking children. They stopped twice in the stairway to point at other aircraft parked near the terminal. At last, she stepped off the stairs and ran to her husband. Kristie hugged him for a full two minutes before letting go to look at Mary.

"Kristie, this is my older sister, Mary. I've found them!" Ben said.

"Paul certainly had many things to say about you. All good things, of course," Mary said.

"Paul?"

"Oh piggety poo. Ben. I do apologize, the last time I saw him, he was waving from the railing of the ship. He was Paul, then," Mary said.

"Ben, I married, and Ben he shall be. At least for me. Paul is a good name too, but I spent a lifetime calling him Ben."

"Whichever way it is. We're going to need to be on our way if we plan to arrive before supper is cold," Ben said, with a laugh. "Where is your bag?"

"This is all I brought with me," Kristie said, lifting a small overnight case. "I thought I could pick up whatever I needed while here."

The trio arrived back at the manor house just as Edward pulled his car into the lane. They held another greeting on the porch before walking inside to the smell of dinner cooking. Rose poked her head out of the kitchen door with the sound of their arrival.

"I've plum got everything about ready. Just mind you wash up while I pop the cork on some wine," Rose said. "I telephoned Heathrow and inquired as to when the overseas flight from America would arrive. I guessed that you wouldn't have time for a proper supper unless I wiggled a finger in your kitchen."

"None for me, please," Kristie said.

"It's our beliefs. We skip on a few things that many others take part in. Wine and coffee, to name a few," Ben explained. "Water will be fine for us, but drink what you like."

"David won't be able to make it this evening. He's making a double run of coal to London."

The rest of them sat down around the table, while Mary helped Rose bring in the big plate of fried haddock with a side of chips. Ben and Kristie found themselves the center of numerous questions about life in America, as well as stories of their girls. Everyone did their best to stay away from talking of the sunken ship that had split the family so many years earlier.

September 22nd, 1962 – Winchester, England

The grey sky sent a chill down Ben's back as he looked up to a skyful of clouds that seemed to promise dumping buckets of water on his head. He leaned into the car and helped Kristie step out to join him. They both turned to look up at the big house, admiring the bright green painted shutters against the yellow clapboard siding.

The barn, on the other side of the circle drive, had been painted to match the house. Windows in the upper part boasted curtains, giving the look of a home over the working area. A colourful glass window, in the large door, left no doubt that it held Eliza's shop.

"Mother will be waiting for us inside," Mary said.

Edward rapped his knuckles twice on the door before opening it to usher the others inside. He called out their arrival into the house before helping Mary shrug out of her coat. Ben and Kristie's coats joined hers in being hung on the tree by the door. David came down the stairs to greet them.

"Welcome. Jenny should be arriving shortly, according to the telephone this morning. Elaine and Rupert are stuck somewhere up north, with a motor that conked out, and Edric's still out to sea for another week. It'll be a bit of a close fit, but this is the best welcome home you could hope for," he told Ben.

"David, this is my wife, Kristie."

"Mum's been a bit weak lately. She'll be sticking to the upstairs, but would treasure a bit of time with you both," David said. "Just don't fret too much if she gets a bit confused talking to you. She does that when she tires."

Eliza walked into the parlor, wiping her hands on the apron she wore. She leaned over to kiss a man sitting in the padded chair near the fireplace. He stood to join her and extend his hand.

"You must be the Yank Uncle she's been talking about," he said. "I'm Thomas, Eliza's husband."

"Take the stairs and second door on the right," Eliza told Ben. "And mind you, take a gander at the portrait halfway up. She's been talking about how much… Well, you'll see for yourself."

Ben led Kristie up the stairs and right as they turned the corner, he came face to face with a large portrait. Even if Eliza hadn't said anything, he wouldn't have missed seeing it. A man and woman stood before the very house he was in and three little children gathered before the couple. The woman held a swaddled babe in her arms.

What drew both their attention was the man. He looked just like Ben, complete with an unruly mop of red hair. The style of their clothing seemed to be the only give-away that the scene had been captured decades earlier.

"That can't be you. Who is it?" Kristie asked.

"Mary and David both say that I look just like our father," Ben said. "It was what truly convinced them of who I am."

They stood staring at the portrait for a minute, until distracted by a voice emanating from a room upstairs. It was too indistinct to hear what she was saying, but Ben recognized his mother's voice. He led Kristie the rest of the way to the library, where Eliza had told him she waited.

The door was slightly ajar and her voice stopped as he pushed it the rest of the way open. Bessie sat in a high back chair by the window, with a knitted throw across her lap. She looked toward them as they walked in.

"There you are. I was just talking to you," she said tiredly.

"Mother?" Ben said hesitantly. "Mother, this is Kristie that I told you about."

"Paul?" Bessie asked. "Come closer."

"I'm right here, Mother. I mean Mum."

"You came home, at last," she said in a whisper.

"Mum, this is Kristie. My wife that I told you about," Ben said.

"I'm glad you came home at last. I should go home too. George, can you take me home now?" Bessie said quietly.

Bessie leaned her head over to rest it on the wing of the chair and closed her eyes. Her breathing settled into a gentle pattern, telling Ben that she had fallen asleep. He pulled the throw blanket up to drape it over her shoulder and gently kissed her cheek.

"Come along, Sweetheart. Let's let her rest, for now. We can go mingle with the rest of the family," Ben said. "Every time I turn around there's more of them, too."

"Now you know what it's like to have siblings. You managed to skip out on all the teasing they do, though," Kristie said.

"Is that you, Lizzie? You look so beautiful," Bessie whispered in her sleep.

Ben led Kristie back down the stairs, where he met another young woman just taking off her coat. Beside her a man was hanging his hat on one of the hooks. She flashed him a smile.

"You must be Uncle Paul," she said.

"Forgive me, I can't keep track of anybody," Ben said.

"That's because I haven't met you yet," she responded. "This is my husband, Rupert Mallory, and I'm Elaine. That makes me your niece, eldest of David. He is your brother, right?"

"This is my wife, Kristie."

"Great to meet you both," she said. "I'm just going to pop up to the first floor and tell Nana Hi."

Elaine disappeared up the stairs while Ben and Kristie made their way into the kitchen. The minute he opened the door, Ben could tell that there was little that he or his wife could do that wouldn't be in the way of Mary, Eliza, and Rose. Rupert was busy peeling potatoes. The women bustled around the kitchen in what seemed to be a practiced dance.

"Any minute now, they'll be shuffling us out to the dining parlor. Be ready for a round of cod fresh off the family boats. Eliza will have the chips cut and dunked a'fore you know it," Thomas told them. "Best find a spot you like at the table."

Ben and Kristie pulled in chairs from the parlor proper and sat down halfway along the side. Thomas sat across from them and Elaine joined the gathering right after. While Rose and Eliza brought in the platters of food, Mary walked past with a small plate that she had already served.

"Grand-Mama's a bit out of it," Elaine told her. "She were mumbling to Grand-Papa in her sleep, again. Now she's talking to Lizzie too, but Lizzie's in the kitchen."

"Not that Lizzie, Dearie," Mary said. "Sometimes she talks to your lost aunt. I'll just set it up there for when she feels like eating."

"Would you mind if I offer a blessing over this feast?" Ben asked.

"Go right ahead and suit yourself," David said. "We don't often have anyone say Grace at the table, but it might be nice with all of us here."

Mary stood next to the table while Ben offered a prayer. He thanked the Lord for bringing them all together finally and blessed the food that had been so carefully prepared. As he ended the blessing, he felt a hand gently squeezing his shoulder. He looked up to see Mary walking off toward the stairs.

David wasted no time in serving the fried chips and passing the plate around the table. Rupert ensured that Mary's plate received its fair share of the food circling the table and Ben did his best to keep up with the endless procession of plates. A few of the dishes seemed unusual, but he tried a spoon of each one of them.

Edward saw Mary returning down the stairs and stood to hold her chair while she sat. She still held the filled plate she had taken with her.

"She's gone…," Mary said slowly, with a dazed look.

"She should have pulled the bell cord," David remarked. "I'd have walked her to the loo."

"No, David. She's really gone this time," Mary said. "What do we do now?"

Ben trailed behind David and Mary as they rushed up the stairs. The others followed along as rapidly as they could. They found Bessie still sitting, just how she had fallen asleep after talking to Ben. David felt her wrist and Ben tried to feel for any breath, but both realized there was neither.

Edward worked his way through the others and telephoned the doctor. Ben leaned in and kissed Bessie on the forehead.

"I'm so very happy to have finally come home to you," Ben whispered. "I just wish that I'd have had more time."

September 30th, 1962 – Winchester, England

Ben placed his rose atop the casket, followed by the others. Eliza carefully laid a glass rose she had crafted in the midst of the fresh ones. Ben was the only one of them to have any familiarity with prayer and so they elected him to offer the final words.

Mary went first, with her stories that told how Bessie had held the family together while crossing the ocean from America and then making the mad dash along English back roads in her attempt to catch Titanic.

David spoke next, to tell how she always taught them the best lessons in life. He related how she would warn them of hazards and then console them as things went awry.

Abigail, Aaron, and Adalyn had arrived only the day before, after getting the telegram Mary sent them. They each placed a ribbon next to the flowers and offered a final thank you for opening her home in their desperate time of need.

David laid one final rose on the casket, "For Lizzie."

Ben folded his arms, "When I found Jessica's journal, I had already wished that I could know who my family was. I am so grateful for the home she made for me, but a part of me had been wanting my original family. I know that after reading some of the journal entries, that Mum, that Bessie said that she would probably have done the same thing in Jessica's place. Her words helped settle my heart and forgive Jessica for all the years I had lost with you. I am forever blessed to have had my time with both wonderful mothers: the mother who gave birth to me, and loved me, and the mother that was there to rescue me when you were too far away to do it yourself.

Even though we are separated once more, I feel your love as strong as always. I know that you'll be standing there to greet me when my own time comes. Find your peace in the arms of our Lord and I will see you when my time is due."

David cast the first shovel of dirt after the grave diggers lowered the casket. One by one, the others took their turn to cast a bit of the soil, along with their own personal goodbyes. The three fosterlings waited until the last to stand silently staring into the hole, before turning away.

Ben looked at the stone sitting pulled back from the grave and ran his fingers over the carving of George's name.

"Thank you, Father, for everything you did for us. I've had a good life and can't wait to see you once more."

Ben wiped the tears from his eyes and turned to see David waiting in the light rain that had started to fall. Kristie took his hand. As they approached him, David spoke up.

"What did you mean that you would see her again?" he asked quietly.

Ben took a deep breath, to steady his voice, before replying, "Our faith teaches us that death isn't an end. Our loved ones that have passed beyond the veil of death stand waiting to welcome us in our time."

"She kept calling to Papa," David said, softly.

"When the end is near, the veil can get fairly thin, from what I believe," Ben said.

The

End

Or perhaps, the beginning of eternity

About the author:

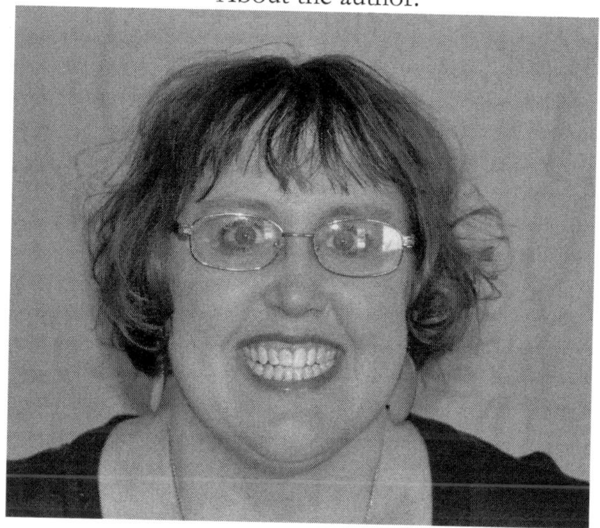

Molly, a native of Utah, graduated from Utah State University with a Bachelor of Science degree. She currently works with adults with disabilities, helping them to enjoy life to the fullest.

Passenger 642 is her debut novel, with several others just waiting to be completed. Mystery and crime stories are her passion.

She met her husband, James Darcey, another accomplished author, at a writing event held at a coffee shop. They currently live in Sunset, Utah with their three spoiled cats.

Made in the USA
Columbia, SC
28 April 2021